T0311995

"Clear and comprehensive, Jacques Berlinerblau's *Secularism: The Basics* is a key contribution to a perennially important topic."

Caroline Mala Corbin, University of Miami School of Law, USA

"Smart, original and provocative, Belinerblau's book is essential reading for anyone who dares to use the word 'secular'."

Lori G. Beaman, University of Ottawa, Canada

"This book is superb. Berlinerblau is careful, fair, and honest in his treatment of secularism and its many manifestations. He has compiled his decades of research on this topic into a short, clear, and very insightful volume. The chapter on leftist critiques of secularism should be mandatory reading for all scholars interested in secularism. Anyone who cares about this topic will need to be familiar with this book. This will be my go-to reference on secularism from now on."

Ryan Cragun, University of Tampa, USA

"What a rare combination of great scholarly expertise and the courage to simplify! This engagingly written book breaks down complex meanings of secularism, discusses its historical manifestations and current controversies and provides a fierce defence of its political relevance in today's world."

Johannes Quack, University of Zurich, Switzerland

"Sharp, informative, insightful, engaging, accessible, authoritative – and beautifully cogent."

Phil Zuckerman, Pitzer College, USA

SECULARISM

THE BASICS

Secularism: The Basics is a concise and engaging introduction to confusing and contradictory public discussions of secularism across the globe.

"Secularism" must be the most confused and convoluted term in the entire global political lexicon. From New York to Paris, to Istanbul, to Addis Ababa, to New Delhi, to Montevideo, there are countless examples of politicians, religious leaders and journalists, invoking the S-word in heated debates about public education, gender, sex, national symbols, and artistic freedom. In this lively and lucid book, Jacques Berlinerblau addresses why secularism is defined in so many ways and why it so ignites people's passions. In so doing, he explores the following important questions: What does secularism mean? Why should we care about this idea? What are the different types of secularism and what are their histories? What are the basic principles of political secularisms? Why are secularism and Atheism often confused? What is the relationship between secularism and LGBTQ rights? What opposition are secularisms up against? What does the future hold for a concept millennia in the making, but only really operationalized in the twentieth century?

With a glossary of key terms, case studies, informative tables, and suggestions for further reading throughout, the book considers key philosophical, religious, anti-religious, post-modern and post-colonial arguments around secularism. This book is an ideal starting point for anyone seeking a readable introduction to the often-conflicting interpretations of one of our era's most complex and controversial ideas.

Jacques Berlinerblau is Professor of Jewish Civilization in the Walsh School of Foreign Service at Georgetown University, USA. He is the author of numerous books and scholarly articles on secularism.

The Basics

THE QUR'AN (SECOND EDITION)
MASSIMO CAMPANINI

RELIGION IN AMERICA
MICHAEL PASQUIER

MORMONISM
DAVID J. HOWLETT AND JOHN-CHARLES DUFFY

RELIGION AND SCIENCE (SECOND EDITION)
PHILIP CLAYTON

THE BIBLE (SECOND EDITION)
JOHN BARTON

QUEER THEOLOGIES
CHRIS GREENOUGH

CHRISTIAN ETHICS
ROBIN GILL

BAHA'I FAITH
CHRISTOPHER BUCK

QUAKERISM
MARGERY POST ABBOTT AND CARL ABBOTT

THOMAS AQUINAS
FRANKLIN T. HARKINS

BIBLE AND FILM
MATTHEW S. RINDGE

RELIGION AND FILM
JEANETTE REEDY SOLANO

SECULARISM
JACQUES BERLINERBLAU

For more information about this series, please visit: https://www.routledge.com/The-Basics/book-series/B

SECULARISM

THE BASICS

Jacques Berlinerblau

LONDON AND NEW YORK

First published 2022
by Routledge
2 Park Square, Milton Park, Abingdon, Oxon OX14 4RN

and by Routledge
605 Third Avenue, New York, NY 10158

Routledge is an imprint of the Taylor & Francis Group, an informa business

© 2022 Jacques Berlinerblau

The right of Jacques Berlinerblau to be identified as author of this work has been asserted in accordance with sections 77 and 78 of the Copyright, Designs and Patents Act 1988.

All rights reserved. No part of this book may be reprinted or reproduced or utilised in any form or by any electronic, mechanical, or other means, now known or hereafter invented, including photocopying and recording, or in any information storage or retrieval system, without permission in writing from the publishers.

Trademark notice: Product or corporate names may be trademarks or registered trademarks, and are used only for identification and explanation without intent to infringe.

British Library Cataloguing in Publication Data
A catalogue record for this book is available from the British Library

Library of Congress Cataloging-in-Publication Data
A catalog record has been requested for this book

ISBN: 978-0-367-69157-8 (hbk)
ISBN: 978-0-367-69158-5 (pbk)
ISBN: 978-1-003-14062-7 (ebk)

DOI: 10.4324/9781003140627

Typeset in Bembo
by Taylor & Francis Books

Cover image: © Getty Images

CONTENTS

List of figures   ix
Acknowledgements   x

1 The S-word: Define your terms!   1

PART I
The ten principles of political secularism   13
2 Who's on top?: The two powers   15
3 "Thought is free": Martin Luther and early Modernity   27
4 "Burning Zeal": John Locke and the Enlightenment   39

PART II
Frameworks of political secularism in global perspective   49
5 American secularism: The (wobbly) separationist
   framework   51
6 French secularism: The *laïcité* framework   64
7 Indian secularism: The accommodationist framework   76

8 Swerves: Secular*ism* and Atheism 88

9 Atheist secularism: The Soviet framework 99

10 Embrace complexity!: Turkey, Ethiopia, China 112

PART III
Anti-secularism, lifestyle secularisms, and a case study 127

11 Anti-secularisms of the right: Conservative religious
anti-secularism 129

12 Anti-secularisms of the left 140

13 Lifestyle secularisms 153

14 LGBTQ rights in Uruguay and Secularstan 166
WITH ALEXANDER LIN AND RIA PRADHAN

15 Love the referee? 178

Glossary 189
Index 201

FIGURES

1.1	Definitional Set 1: secularism = non-belief/anti-religion	3
1.2	Definitional Set 2: secularism = political secularism	3
1.3	Common perceptions of secularism and how they sometimes overlap	4
2.1	Some binary terms used in discussions of secularism	25
3.1	Thinkers and the principles of political secularism	35
3.2	Evolution of the principles of political secularism	37
5.1	The separationist framework (in theory)	61
6.1	The *laïcité* framework (in theory)	73
7.1	The accommodationist framework (in theory)	83
9.1	The Soviet framework (in theory)	109
13.1	Secular identities and their commitment to political secularism	154
14.1	Political secularism: frameworks and corresponding emphasis on principles	166
15.1	Secularisms and African constitutions	184

ACKNOWLEDGEMENTS

I wish to thank my two research assistants, Alexander Lin and Ria Pradhan, for the assistance they provided during the writing of this book. Both were instrumental in researching issues, culling bibliography, brainstorming, and showing me how the student mind processes information. Mr. Lin conceptualized and created all of the tables. He and Ms. Pradhan performed innumerable intellectual tasks. The section on Ethiopia was based on research conducted for another project with Bethania Michael. Her input to Chapter 10 was invaluable (naturally, all opinions expressed on this issue were my own).

I thank my agent Michael Mungiello of Inkwell Agency, and the team at Routledge, especially editor Rebecca Clintworth. Jeffrey Popovich of Georgetown University's Lauinger Library kindly assisted me in tracking down materials for this project. Gratitude to professors Terrence Johnson and Shareen Joshi for reading chapters from this work.

Jacques Berlinerblau

THE S-WORD
DEFINE YOUR TERMS!

According to Google Ngram Viewer, the term "secularism" is now being used more than ever. There has been a three hundred and fifty percent increase in its frequency since 1980, and not just in the English language.

Spend a few minutes on the internet, and you'll notice that the S-word stokes passionate debates from the Global North to the Global South. The good (?) name of secularism appears in the same breath as atheism, colonialism, communism, Fundamentalism, humanism, Islamism, liberal democracy, liberalism, Marxism, multi-culturalism, nationalism, patriarchy, postmodernism, pluralism, racism, socialism, sexism, Stalinism, and every religion there is. Some want to bring secularism "back" or "in." Others want to kick it out. And still others claim it is already dead.

But before we go any further, there is one crucial question we must address: what is (or was) secularism?

The first thing to understand about this term is that *there is no one agreed-upon understanding of the term*! There is little consensus about what this -ism actually is, what it actually does, and whose interests it actually serves. Be that as it may, many people have very strong opinions about secularism, both for and against.

The Dalai Lama appears to be "for it." In 2018 he described secularism as a system that lets "different religions coexist—in the spirit of brotherhood and sisterhood." The atheist intellectual Christopher Hitchens lauded "secular pluralism" as "an urgent and inescapable responsibility: a matter of survival." In 2020 the President of France, Emmanuel Macron, referred to his country's version of secularism

DOI: 10.4324/9781003140627-1

(known as *laïcité*) as follows: "Laïcité is what bonds a united France. We must thus respect laïcité unwaveringly and justly."

As for those who are "against it," they are likely in the majority. Pope Benedict XVI observed that: "There is something deeply alien about the absolute secularism that is developing in the West ... a world without God has no future." "This word 'secularism' is the biggest threat to develop[ing] India's prosperous traditions and giv[ing] it a spot on the global stage," warned the chief minister of the state of Uttar Pradesh, Yogi Adityanath in March 2021. "Secularism is antithetical to Islam," declared the Islamic theologian Yusuf al-Qaradawi, "it has never succeeded in Muslim societies." Archbishop Hilarion Alfeyev speaks of "the consistent, systematic, and well-targeted onslaught of militant secularism on what remains of European Christian civilization, along with the desire to obliterate it once and for all."

A cardinal rule for studying secularism might be described as "*Define your terms!*" Often enough you need to "*Define other people's terms!*" as well. In that spirit, let me note that the speakers above are using the same word to refer to different, though sometimes overlapping, concepts. Secularism for some of these figures was: (1) atheism; and/or (2) the opposite, or nemesis, of religion; and/or (3) a system that wishes to destroy religion. These three understandings comprise our first set of definitions (see Figure 1.1).

We glimpsed a second, very different, definitional set in the comments of the Dalai Lama and Emmanuel Macron. They depicted secularism as (4) a political doctrine for regulating how the state, on the one side, will interact with the church, mosque, synagogue, ashram, what have you, on the other. Some textbooks and dictionaries casually refer to this as "separation of church and state." But for reasons that will be made clear, we think it's much more precise to call it "political secularism." Figure 1.2 describes some of the basic frameworks of political secularism that we will study in this book.

Things get complicated, and interesting, when we consider that at certain points and places in history our two definitions overlapped. The Venn diagram in Figure 1.3 should give you a good sense of the possible relations between our two sets. You will note that Set 1 ("atheism and anti-clericalism") and Set 2 ("political

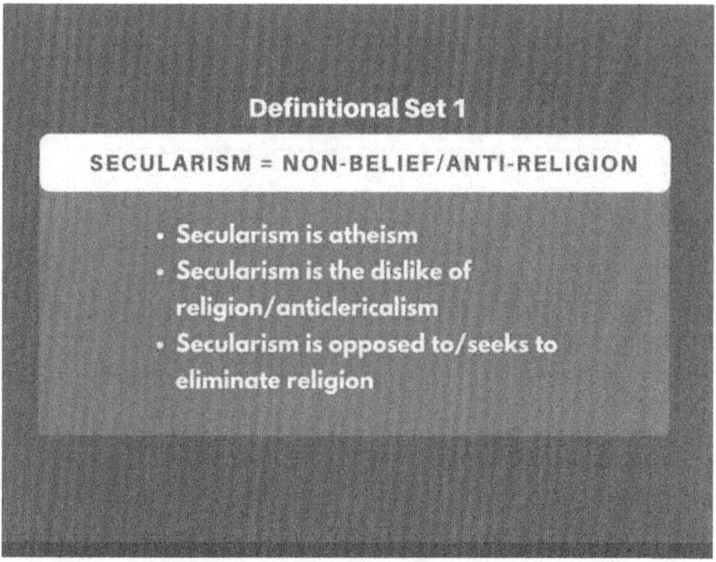

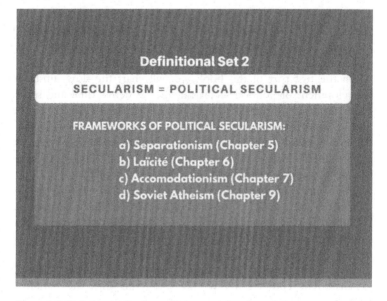

Figure 1.1 Definitional Set 1: secularism = non-belief/anti-religion

Figure 1.2 Definitional Set 2: secularism = political secularism

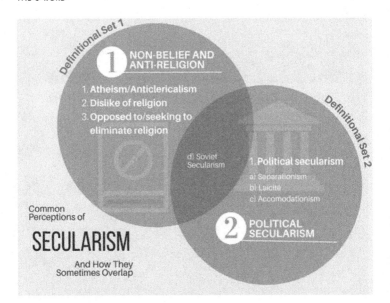

Figure 1.3 Common perceptions of secularism and how they sometimes overlap

secularism") share common ground in an atheist framework of political secularism which we will call "Soviet secularism" (see Chapter 9).

In the first part of this book we will chart the slow, unsteady development of political secularism (Set 2) across time and space. You might be surprised to see that we'll trace its origins to the Bible. From there we will watch how secularism's core principles emerged, in dribs and drabs, during the Christian Middle Ages, the Protestant Reformation, and the Enlightenment. Secularism, some might be surprised to learn, has a religious genealogy.

As I have described it so far, this genealogy might seem awfully "Western" or "Euro." This is true, but we will have occasion to complexify that oft-made claim. Our discussions of India, China, Turkey, and modern Africa will show that, past or present, and for better or for worse, secularism is a truly global concept.

As for atheism (Set 1), it *is* part of our story. A big part. Though it makes its entrance a few thousand years into the narrative.

Atheism and political secularism first synergize in nineteenth-century Victorian England. I will refer to their history-altering union as "the swerve" (Chapter 8).

Then in the twentieth century, after a gestation period of two millennia, political secularisms blossomed and mushroomed in nation-states across the globe. Some secularisms, such as those in the USSR and the People's Republic of China, were atheistic (and hence bring together Sets 1 and 2). Others, in countries like India or the United States, have little to do with nonbelief or dislike of religion (and thus stay strictly within the realm of Set 2 with no overlap). A student must be able to conceptually distinguish one from the other because confusing secularism with atheism is one of the biggest mistakes one can make—and it is a mistake that is made often!

But whether the secularism we are looking at today is atheistic, as it was in Albania's 1976 Constitution, or separationist (and hence non-atheistic), as it is in Chad, Ethiopia, and Gabon, know this: *wherever there is secularism, there is fierce opposition to it as well.* To study the subject of secularism is often to watch as a very *particular* type of religion, which some might call Fundamentalism, goes lunging headfirst and with primordial force into another beast of sorts: the modern nation-state. The purpose of this book is to help readers think calmly, critically, and with nuance, about that collision and the controversies it creates. Let's turn to some of those disputes now.

WHAT WE TALK ABOUT WHEN WE TALK ABOUT SECULARISM

Now that I have defined other people's terms, I will start to define my own. Throughout this book I will argue that the definitional confusion around the term "secularism" is not merely an academic quibble. Rather, it is part of secularism's political weakness and vulnerability. Secularism is perpetually defined by its enemies. Meanwhile, some of its defenders can't accurately and clearly tell you what it is.

So permit me to offer you a very basic definition: *political secularism refers to legally binding actions of the secular state that seek to regulate the relationship between itself and religious citizens, and between religious citizens themselves.* Naturally, we will soon unpack that crucial term "secular state." Too, we will have much to say about political secularisms that do *not* control the state. For now, let's work with this "skinny definition." It will help us understand what is being talked (or screamed) about when people address this theme.

As we saw above, many speak about secularism, erroneously I think, as an adversary of religion. That conception of secularism as "anti-religious," or hostile to people of faith certainly is something we all talk about when we talk about secularism. In addition to that conversation, certain types of issues, or flashpoints, recur in discussions of secularism. Four broad categories leap to mind:

STATE INSTITUTIONS, SPACES, SYMBOLS

When debates about secularism break out, they often concern state institutions, spaces, and symbols. Either the secular state enforces a law which some religious citizens don't like or, in a new twist, a supposedly "secular state" does something that seems to favor one religion (and thus appears to be anti-secular).

One recurring hotspot is public education. Secular and anti-secular columns fight doggedly about how and what students are taught. That's because both know that to control a system of education is to control the future of a country. In secular states like the People's Republic of China and Uruguay, religious instruction in public schools is explicitly prohibited. In India, the situation is more complicated. The ruling Hindu nationalist BJP party recently advocated for history textbooks that demonize periods of Muslim rule while "glorify[ing] ancient and medieval Hindu rulers."

Secularists and their foes have tangled in the United States, where fierce disputes about the teaching of evolution have dragged on for nearly half a century. Mexico in the period 1910–1917 and France in the period 1870–1905 witnessed pitch battles about the place of the Catholic Church in national educational systems. In both cases, the liberal nationalists managed to remove the Church from its once-hegemonic position.

Similar controversies flare about shared public spaces. An ongoing dust-up in Israel (which is not a secular state) concerns gender-segregated seating on public transportation. Ultra-orthodox Jews have requested that female passengers sit separately on trains and buses. They often take matters into their own hands and enforce that preference. Israeli "secular nationalists" (see Chapter 13) urge the state, and its courts, to crack down on such practices.

Then there is public religious symbolism, which is always contentious for secularism. I would draw your attention to the YouTube video entitled "2019 Christmas Decorations at the White House." It featured the first lady, Melania Trump, meandering amidst a forest of towering Christmas Trees in the official residence of the president of the United States of America. Upon viewing this clip one might wonder if there is actual "separation of church and state" in the United States—which, as we shall see, there likely is not!

Another controversy about public symbols broke out in 2013. It started when the European Union commissioned a commemorative coin. This special Euro, designed by a Slovakian artist, featured images of two Byzantine monks, Cyril and Methodius. One grasped a cross, another brandished a bible, and both had halos around their heads. Some EU Members, notably France, objected. They argued that such religious iconography had no place in currency minted by the EU whose founding texts make no mention of Christianity. The coins were eventually circulated.

Let's go back to our skinny definition: *political secularism refers to legally binding actions of the secular state that seek to regulate the relationship between itself and religious citizens, and between religious citizens themselves.* Israel (which is not a secular state) and the EU (which is not a state, but an intergovernmental body) notwithstanding, the cases above, featured a secular state making decisions about how its own schools, spaces, and currencies relate to religion.

Please note that in the case of Melania Trump, the secular state was making an *anti*-secular decision; it appeared to be endorsing Christianity from the White House. The anti-secular spirit was also evident in the BJP's Islamophobic curriculum. The same might be said about the EU "monks in halos" coin. Given that the United States, India and EU are assumed by many to be "secular," this reminds us that political secularisms in the twenty-first century are under siege.

GENDER AND SEXUAL MINORITIES

You might have noticed that all of the speakers cited above who were "for" or "against" secularism were men. In recent years, more and more women have entered the dialogue. Their insights will be shared throughout this work.

But my all-man montage of pro- and anti-secular viewpoints underscores an important truth. Historically speaking, public disputes about secularism have been dominated by one gender. Which is ironic, because these disputes often have huge implications for other genders. Matters are slowly changing, but secularism has traditionally been a dialogue conducted by men whose consequences are felt acutely by women and those who fall outside the traditional binary.

Issues of gender and sexuality are of great interest to those who are opposed to secularism. In Chapter 11 we'll meet conservative religious anti-secular movements (CRAS for short). They are a major part of our narrative and usually advocate positions that restrict the rights of women and sexual minorities. It is impossible to understand political secularism today without understanding these anti-secular groups, be they Christian, Muslim, Jewish or Hindu fundamentalists.

CRAS activism is based on deeply held religious convictions. But there are many different types of religious convictions and *non*-religious convictions within a secular state. If you think of our skinny definition in which the latter must *regulate the relationship … between religious citizens themselves*, you can grasp how challenging it is to run a secular state.

The government has the demanding task of deciding how to regulate, let's say, reproductive freedoms amidst all of this disagreement. Conservative Catholics might oppose contraception; Evangelical Protestants might oppose contraception as well, in support of their newfound political allies; liberal Catholics might wish for contraceptives to be freely available, as might reform Jews, and mainline Protestants, not to mention all sorts of nonbelievers. Should the state craft policies about contraception by listening to the simple majority of its citizens? The counsels of Science? To those people, mostly women, affected by these decisions?

So when we talk about secularism, we are often talking about issues like contraception, abortion, and in-vitro fertilization. Many of those doing the talking, especially on the CRAS side of the divide, are men. This leads secularists to charge that conservative religious men are trying to control women's bodies.

Far less frequently, a secular state might try and exhibit similar control over women's bodies. In 2016, France was rocked by the "burkini" scandal. In Cannes, Nice, and other French towns, law enforcement officials prohibited Muslim women from wearing a modest form of swimwear (i.e., the burkini). Apparently, some French mayors saw the attire as linked to Islamic extremism. Eventually, the ban was suspended by the nation's highest administrative court.

Outside of disputes about gender, questions of sexual freedom are also part of secularism's docket. CRAS groups consistently oppose granting civil rights to members of LGBTQ communities. Uganda, which has no state religion, has garnered international attention for proposed laws criminalizing homosexuality. Some of these laws were vestiges of British colonialism.

Other Ugandan laws, like the so-called "Kill the Gays" bill of 2014 (which was passed but altered the penalty to life imprisonment, and then deemed unconstitutional) were also supported by local conservative faith-based actors; many with backing and financial support from right-wing Christian groups in the West. Transnational movements, as we shall see, are also a big part of the conversation on political secularism.

Disputes about secularism often hinge on the state's control of bodies—bodies that are often not male or heterosexual. There are exceptions to this rule, but in general secular states are inclined to grant those bodies much greater freedom and sovereignty (see Chapter 14). By doing so, they encounter the wrath of their CRAS counterparts.

RELIGIOUS MINORITIES

Other disputes about secularism center around the question of the rights of religious minorities. Here's a rule of thumb: religious minorities in a given country tend to favor secular governments (the same holds for nonbelievers who are almost always in the minority). Here's another: religious majorities in a given country tend to oppose them. Naturally, there are exceptions. But it is remarkable how being in a minority position often makes one a supporter of secular policies, regardless of what one's religion may be.

It's often said that Muslims are anti-secular. It would be more precise to say that Muslims tend to behave like Jews, Catholics,

Hindus, etc. In other words, when they are outnumbered within a national context they usually see the value of secular precepts. In India, the Muslim minority tends to support Indian state secularism whose core theme is the equality of all faiths in the eyes of the government.

In majoritarian Muslim countries, by contrast, there tends to be little enthusiasm for political secularism. Thus the Kingdom of Saudi Arabia, the Islamic Republic of Iran, and the Islamic Republic of Pakistan are not secular states and won't be anytime soon. We'll look at the intriguing case of Muslim-majority Turkey and its "Islamo-secularism" in Chapter 10.

But back to our normative pre-definition. If *political secularism refers to legally binding actions of the secular state that seek to regulate the relationship between itself and religious citizens, and between religious citizens themselves* then its policies have to somehow recognize the diversity of faiths within a given polity. Secular state policies must maintain peace and order. Citizens must believe that the secular state is fair and treats everyone equally.

There's a certain logic, as we shall see, to thinking of the secular state as an umpire or referee. This is a metaphor we will probe in our conclusion.

THE ARTS AND EXPRESSIVE LIBERTIES

One final hotspot in discussions about political secularism takes us into the realm of freedom of expression. Secular states often need to deal with citizens' outrage regarding certain works of art and forms of expression.

In India, the release and production of a 2018 movie *Padmavaat* about a Hindu queen and Muslim ruler led to mass protests. The protestors were affiliated with the Hindu right, a major CRAS movement. The ructions occurred after rumors that the movie included a scene "in which the Muslim king dreams of becoming intimate with the Hindu queen." A BJP regional leader announced a $1.5 million award for anyone who beheaded Sanjay Leela Bhansali, the movie's director, and Deepika Padukone, the leading actress.

The case of the 2015 *Charlie Hebdo* illustrations which resulted in the murder of twelve people in France also comes to mind. So does the Salman Rushdie affair of the late 1980s and 1990s. In that instance, the author had to go into hiding after a fatwa, or religious edict, calling for his death, was issued by Iran's supreme leader, Ayatollah Ruhollah Khomeini. Nobel-prize winner Orhan Pamuk's 2002 novel *Snow*—one of the very few works of fiction that is actually *about* political secularism—made him the target of assassination threats by Turkish ultra-nationalists.

Secular states often claim freedom of expression and freedom of speech as among their core values. As a result, they have to figure out how to deal with the passionate, and occasionally violent, dissent of conservative religious actors who take offense at certain words and images. Of late, groups on the left, especially on social media, have sought to restrict speech deemed hateful to religious and sexual minorities. The governance of a secular state is no simple task!

CONFUSED?

If you're still a little bit confused by what secularism is, then do not worry. Secularism *is* confusing. In addition to being endlessly discussed and argued about, it is also quite fascinating. Although I have spent the better part of two decades teaching, researching, and writing about this subject, it never ceases to confuse and fascinate me and my students.

This book is organized in accordance with what I have learned are "best intellectual/pedagogical practices" for instructing undergraduates and graduates. My goals are to show you:

1   how political secularism came to be;
2   its ten core principles;
3   four basic frameworks of secular governance;
4   how secularism intersects and diverges from atheism;
5   who secularism's opponents and proponents are; and
6   what its relevance is to our world today.

Towards all these ends, we will look at political secularisms in the United States, France, India, Uruguay, Great Britain, the USSR, Turkey, Ethiopia, and China, among other countries. Our final chapter, a case study, will probe the intersection between secularism and LGBTQ rights.

Secularism, as we shall see, is full of surprises and paradoxes. Too, there is a lot about it which is still not understood. The task of this primer is not to drown you in all of the complexity and uncertainty. Rather, I want to render that complexity with clarity. In this manner your own thinking about secularism will be clear to both you and those with whom you discuss this topic.

SUGGESTIONS FOR FURTHER READING

Strangely, there are very few comprehensive overviews of secularism's historical development—a fact that buttresses my claim that there is much about secularism we still don't know. The subject is over polemicized and understudied.

That being said, a relatively recent volume that features a wide variety of diverse opinions from scholarly experts is Phil Zuckerman and John Shook (Eds.), *The Oxford Handbook of Secularism* (New York: Oxford University Press, 2017). The dozens of essays there provide an excellent introduction. Another recent primer is Andrew Copson, *Secularism: A Very Short Introduction* (New York: Oxford, 2019). My own introduction to the subject is *How to be Secular: A Call to Arms for Religious Freedom* (Boston, MA: Houghton Mifflin, 2012).

One handy introduction to political secularism that includes much useful data is Jonathan Fox, *Political Secularism, Religion, and the State: A Time Series of Worldwide Data* (Cambridge: Cambridge University Press, 2015), An excellent comparative analysis is Ahmet Kuru, *Secularism and State Policies Toward Religion: The United States, France, and Turkey* (Cambridge: Cambridge University Press, 2009). A theoretical piece of interest is Cécil Laborde, "Justificatory Secularism," in *Religion in a Liberal State*, edited by Gavin D'Costa et al. (Cambridge: Cambridge University Press, 2013), pp. 164–186.

PART I

THE TEN PRINCIPLES OF POLITICAL SECULARISM

We now come to the main part of this sermon. We have learnt that there must be secular authority on this earth and how a Christian and salutary use may be made of it.

—Martin Luther, "On Secular Authority"

DOI: 10.4324/9781003140627-2

2

WHO'S ON TOP?
THE TWO POWERS

Political secularisms first became fully *operational* (e.g., employed by nation states) in the early twentieth century. Their appearance was a long time coming. How long? My analysis in the next few chapters suggests that political secularisms took *roughly two thousand years to develop*.

It was during those two millennia that ten basic principles, or "building blocks" of secularism, were crafted. By, let's say, 1800, all of the individual key principles had been formulated in their raw essence. Formulated, but not really activated.

For example, the framers of the United States Constitution in the late eighteenth century did articulate a few core secular principles. But it would take another century and a half for these secular principles to be linked together into what we will call a secular "framework" and then applied to actual statecraft. For reasons we shall explain later on, we date the first operational political secularism to 1905.

Still, the individual principles of secularism themselves had been sitting around, unlinked and mostly unused, for centuries, even millennia. These principles were forged independently of one another in the ancient, Medieval, early Modern, and Enlightenment periods. Their far-flung inventors were theologians, philosophers and political figures. Few of them were trying to create something called "secularism." That term, we shall see in Chapter 8, was coined in the mid-nineteenth century.

The point is that secularism came into being inadvertently. True, we'll meet figures like Martin Luther (Chapter 3) and John Locke (Chapter 4) who put their stamp on this political doctrine. But in

DOI: 10.4324/9781003140627-3

reality dozens, if not hundreds, of figures (many of whom are not known to us) are part of the history of political secularism—a history which is long, meandering, non-linear and full of accidents and contingencies.

Before we begin our historical survey of the ten core principles, there is one major misconception about them that we need to immediately dispel and one conception we need to tweak. The misconception is that the individuals who came up with these secular principles were atheists, despisers of religion, and so forth. As we shall see, this is demonstrably false. Political secularism is an idea born of *religious* thinkers contemplating *religious* problems using a *religious* vocabulary to solve them.

The tweak concerns Christianity's role in this story. Standard scholarly accounts portray political secularism as born exclusively of European Christendom. Secularism, so goes the narrative, is a Western export. It thus arrived in the Middle East, Africa, Asia and South America through one of two routes: colonialist invasion of the western powers or the rise of Soviet successor states in the twentieth century.

I myself was partial to this opinion, though in recent years evidence has come to light which cautiously suggests a less Eurocentric reading. Political secularism's alleged exclusive link to Christianity is a thorny question. We will have to treat this issue carefully. This problem will be revisited in Chapters 7, 10, 12, and 15.

For now, I'd like to introduce you to the ten principles of secularism. Each will be situated within the particular historical milieu where it arose. In this chapter we will focus on the ancient and Medieval eras. In the next we will move into early modernity.

PRINCIPLE 1: EQUALITY

In my introduction, I vowed to present the complexity of secularism with clarity. Let's begin with some clarity.

The *equality* principle stipulates that, in the eyes of the secular state, all human beings are equal. In broad terms, this means that a government cannot establish gradations or hierarchies among law-abiding citizens for any reason. Muslim and Hindu citizens in a secular country with a Christian majority must be granted exactly the same rights as Christians and be treated in exactly the same way.

In recent decades, the principle has been expanded to include citizens who *don't* believe in a God or gods. Non-believers too are guaranteed full equality under the law. As are citizens who are considered sexual and gender minorities, regardless of whether they are believers or not. A handy modern synopsis of the equality principle is found in the 1945 Charter of the United Nations and the Statute of the International Court of Justice. Article 1 speaks of "promoting and encouraging respect for human rights and for fundamental freedoms for all without distinction as to race, sex, language, or religion."

The equality principle seems like a pretty straightforward proposition. The complexity sets in when we pose two questions:

1 Who actually lives or lived in accordance with the *equality* principle?
2 Who invented this most noble idea?

The United States Declaration of Independence (1776) affirms that "all men are created equal … endowed by their creator with certain unalienable human rights." Even some of the American founders recognized that this ringing credo rang hollow. After all, this was a Republic that enslaved *hundreds of thousands* of persons of African ancestry. White women, for their part, were completely disenfranchised.

So one question we will always ask about the *equality* principle is: which secular states actually abide by its lofty demands? This reminds us that secularism, like so many other political systems, has a words/deeds problem. Secular states often don't do what they loudly boast about doing.

A second question about the *equality* principle concerns its origins. It is not at all apparent where this building block of secularism was born. I have an unorthodox answer, at least as far as histories of secularism go. I propose that this core impulse can be traced back to the Hebrew Bible, or what Christians call the Old Testament. The crucial verse in question, Genesis 1:27, reads as follows:

> And God created human beings in His image. In the image of God He created them: male and female he created them.

All biblical verses are interpreted in numerous ways. But one popular interpretation of this scripture stresses that since we are all created in God's image (*imago dei*) each of us possesses some undeniable dignity. This is a dignity that exists despite whatever differences we may have from one another.

Dignity, I concede, is not precisely the same thing as equality. Yet I think this verse created the moral platform for later Christian thinkers to innovate admirable (but highly theoretical) formulations about human equality. Such figures included the poet John Milton who wrote "all men naturally were borne free, being the image and resemblance of God himself." In his *Second Treatise on Government*, John Locke spoke of all humans having "natural" rights. And of course, there is the Declaration of Independence's "All men are created equal." Genesis 1:27 can be read to say that because divine matter resides in each and every one of us, we each deserve to be treated the same.

Treated the same by *whom*, you ask? What's interesting is how Genesis 1:27 prompted subsequent generations of Christian rulers to think about governance. If God saw us as all endowed with dignity, then perhaps a ruler must extend the same courtesy to citizens, no?

Truth be told, this principle was rarely ever observed by Christian powers. The history of religious minorities, heretics, and slaves, not to mention to European colonialism, proves that point (notice in my analogy above that the ruler of a polity is placed in parallel with God. This parallel irks many types of citizens as we shall see in Chapter 11).

Yet the concept of *imago dei* would hover in Christian consciousness for centuries. Eventually, it would support a crucial, if often unfulfilled promise, of modern secular democracies. Namely, that all citizens, regardless of their race, religion, beliefs, sexual orientation, must be treated equally by the ruling authorities.

PRINCIPLE 2: TWO POWERS (CHURCH AND STATE)

THE NEW TESTAMENT BINARY

In order to study secularism, you have to think in terms of what is known as a "binary," or something that involves two things.

Most historians trace the appearance of the binary that eventually gave rise to secularism to the New Testament. That religious text, the foundational document of Christianity, sets two concepts alongside one another in a most intriguing way. For millennia thereafter, Christian thinkers wrestled with how these two things should relate to one another.

And what are those two things? Nowadays some refer to them as "church" and "state." In Christian Antiquity, however, the binary was different, if only because nation-states as we know them today did not yet exist. Nor was there an institutional church, the likes of which would develop a few centuries later. In the New Testament, the binary we receive consists of these two levels: (1) the domain of God and (2) the domain of one's (very powerful) earthly rulers.

Various verses in the New Testament try to answer the question of how a follower of Jesus Christ should think through the relation between these two domains. Should Christians obey God, or the authorities? To whom did they owe their primary allegiance?

Jesus himself appears to have pondered this question When he was asked whether it was justified to pay taxes to Roman overlords, his response invoked this binary (Matthew 22:21; Mark 12:17):

> And He [Jesus] said to them, "Render therefore to Caesar the things that are Caesar's, and to God the things that are God's."

Jesus endorses payment of taxes to "Caesar." This is a broader reference to the Roman empire which ruled Palestine at that time. One popular reading of the verse is that Jesus is demanding that his followers behave lawfully as good subjects of their Roman rulers. This reading gains in credibility when Paul says in Romans 13:

> Let every soul be subject to the governing authorities. For there is no authority except from God, and the authorities that exist are appointed by God. Therefore whoever resists the authority resists the ordinance of God, and those who resist will bring judgment on themselves.

Verses like this have led scholars to speak of a "passive," or "quiescent" streak in the New Testament. The good Christian is one who *submits* to his or her ruler. Resistance to this authority is un-Christian and ungodly. This point, striking as it may be to our ears, is made again in 1 Peter 2:13–14:

> Submit yourselves for the Lord's sake to every human authority: whether to the emperor, as the supreme authority, or to governors, who are sent by him to punish those who do wrong and to commend those who do right.

In retrospect, these verses seem awfully naive. Is a Christian always supposed to submit to a ruler? What if that ruler is cruel or insane? The New Testament's curious indifference to tyranny is often explained by the fact that early Christians were confident that the world would soon be coming to an end.

In other words, the writers of the gospels knew that the return of Jesus the Messiah was imminent. If that were the case then obedience to any ruler would simply be a temporary concession and a minor inconvenience. God's kingdom was forthcoming. Under such circumstances one could obey the authorities—if only because the authorities wouldn't be around for that long!

For our purposes, we have identified, in very raw and basic form, *the core binary that exists within every form of political secularism.* There is the domain of God. There is the domain of government. We will call this the *two powers* principle. This might seem like a simple dichotomy. But as we shall see, the attempt to regulate how these two levels interact has given rise to every imaginable form of conflict.

THE AUGUSTINIAN CORRECTION

The messiah, in fact, did not come. But the New Testament binary remained for Christians to ponder. The binary of *two powers* remained even as Christianity's fortunes radically changed. What was once a tiny fringe sect tucked away in the backwoods of the Roman empire soon became an empire in its own right.

The monumental shift occurred in the fourth century AD. The emperor Constantine, who ruled during 306–337, converted to Christianity. A few decades later, emperor Theodosius (347–395), via the Edict of Thessalonica, made the Nicene variant of Christianity the official religion of all Roman lands. Within the span of less than a century the power position of Christianity had completely changed.

This new political landscape demanded a reappraisal of the old biblical binary. After Constantine, most Christians needn't submit to the power any longer. They *were* the power. Most lived in societies almost exclusively populated by Christians.

These Christian populations were ruled by a Christian emperor and/or a Christian king. Their spiritual needs were tended to by Christian clergy, including priests, bishops, and a pope. Initially, this might seem like an ideal situation for Christianity—total Christian control of a nearly all-Christian society! But as we shall see, this arrangement was laden with a structural tension that plagued Christendom for more than a millennium.

An important reframing of the binary was undertaken by the great fifth-century theologian Augustine. In his masterwork, *The City of God*, Augustine readjusts the New Testament's two structural levels. We saw above that one of these levels was the domain of God. In Augustine's writing this domain now has physical representation on earth. This "City of God" functioned like an extension, or "annex," of the heavenly realm. It was inhabited by virtuous and pious souls who comprised the true Christian community.

This outpost of holiness represented all that was godly during a time frame which Augustine called the *Saeculum*. This word is related to our term "secular." The *Saeculum* refers to the period of our collective stay in this fallen, broken world. All of us, saints and sinners, will groan together here in the *Saeculum* until Jesus Christ returns.

This brings us to the second domain posited by Augustine. What the New Testament viewed as the domain of Caesar, or the ruling authorities, Augustine reconfigured as the "City of Man." This abode was filled with sin, vices, contempt for God and self-love.

Yet he acknowledged that this second city had a role to play. Politics and governance occurred in the City of Man. Those activities could *potentially* regulate human lives in a manner befitting God. A truly Christian government, after all, could orient the souls of human beings towards virtue. While we await the Final Judgment, the City of Man and its (Christian) Caesar had a job to perform.

Augustine, then, reframed the New Testament's two domains as *presences* on earth. The domain of God became the City of God as represented by the "true" Christian community. The domain of rulers was located within the City of Man. Ideally, these rulers would govern the people in a Christ-like manner.

Perhaps the reader can anticipate the looming tension in Augustine's dichotomy. The political tasks performed by the City of Man are *necessary* until the arrival of the messiah and the termination of the *saeculum*. But until that event occurs, how precisely are the Christian rulers and the Christian church supposed to interact with one another? Should every Christian submit to the authority of the Christian governing authorities (the "Caesar" of the New Testament)? Or should they submit to the authority of religious figures like bishops and popes (which did not exist in New Testament times)?

Put bluntly, who's on top? While this question may seem crass, it certainly isn't hypothetical. It may be the single most consequential question that secularism asks (and answers).

HIEROCRACY AND THE INTERNAL TENSION

It did not take long for Christian societies to address the question of who was on top. A few decades after Augustine's death Pope Gelasius I, Bishop of Rome from 492–496, made it very clear whose authority he believed was supreme. In a letter to Emperor Anastasius I, the Pope helpfully reminds him that the church is superior to the Crown.

True, the royal and sacred powers (later referred to as the "two swords") should work together. But ultimately, reasoned Pope Gelasius, "the priests carry the greater weight, because they will have to render account in the divine judgment even for the kings of men." This way of structuring a society is referred to as "hierocracy," or rule by priests. In a hierocratic government, supreme power rests with religious officials.

Kings and emperors, as you may imagine, had a different perspective. In many instances they failed to see why, when push came to shove, their authority should be second to that of the clergy. This fundamental tension within Christendom played itself out in various ways across the Middle Ages. Sometimes there was peaceful cooperation. Sometimes tense compromise. Sometimes violent conflict.

We see these hostilities surface in what is known as the "investiture conflict" (1076–1122). The episode signifies the highwater mark of collisions between the Cross (represented by Pope Gregory

VII) and the Crown (represented by Henry IV). The particulars of their operatic feud need not detain us here.

What we should note is that some religious figures of the era soon began to subscribe to a doctrine of the pope's total power, or *plenitudo potestatis*. The two swords, it was argued, were controlled by the church. Naturally, this affirmation of papal supremacy further exacerbated tensions between the Cross and the Crown.

Christian kings were not always at peace with the idea that they were subservient to the church. In Chapter 6 we will read about French secularism. It has been argued that it draws upon a Medieval French tradition of "Gallicanism" whereby the Christian king, in this case Philippe le Bel (1268–1314) made it very clear that he had the power to control the church. Philippe, like many of his monarchal counterparts, thus rejected the idea of *plenitudo potestatis*. When Pope Boniface VIII (who ruled from 1294–1303) claimed "We hold both the swords," one of Philippe's advisers allegedly responded "True, Holy Father, but where your swords are but a theory, ours are a reality."

It's not surprising that kings and emperors pushed back on papal overreach. But in terms of our interests, what is fascinating is that similar resistance emerged *within* the realm of the Cross itself. What is surprising—note this—is that opposition to papal power emerged not only from kings like Philippe, but from *religious thinkers*. Within the churchly domain, theologians expressed misgivings about papal power grabs.

The two names most associated with this internal challenge are Marsilius of Padua (*c.*1275–1342) and William of Ockham (1288–1347). These one-time roommates were ferocious critics of the papacy. Ockham accuses the popes of having "overstepped the ancient bounds and stretched out unholy hands for what belongs to others." Jesus Christ himself, argued Ockham, "assigned certain limits" to the pope's power.

Even more stridently, Marsilius thundered against "the perverted desire for rulership" of Roman bishops. Marsilius believed in a god-ordained division of labor. The pope and the religious classes were to attend to the souls of the population. The ruling and governance of society was to be left to Christian lay rulers.

He then makes a very important, though often unnoticed, argument. Rule by a religious authority, Marsilius insisted, would lead to societal instability and chaos. If you want social order, argues Marsilius, then prohibit religious figures from governing (we will see a great Enlightenment philosopher reason similarly in Chapter 4).

What happened in this pre-modern moment is quite remarkable. Christian thinkers using Christian arguments reasoned that concentrating so much power in the Christian pope's hands was un-Christian. *Plenitudo potestatis*, they warned, was bad for Christianity. The religious authority needed to be subjugated to the political authority (which, of course, was staffed by Christian laypersons). Cross was subordinate to the Crown, City of God was subordinate to City of Man. This is the starting point of political secularism.

CONCLUSION: SECULAR ESSENTIALS

We have now acquainted ourselves with two principles of political secularism. The first, *equality*, may have been born in the Hebrew Bible. It lay dormant for millennia until it was reconfigured as a general principle of governance in liberal democracies. In its modern version, it argues all citizens are equal in the eyes of the state.

The second building block—*two powers*—originated in the New Testament. It was a way of conceptualizing the world by dividing it into two spheres. The continual scrutiny of this binary for thousands of years is likely unique to Christianity's political history. It is hard to think of any other religion that was so preoccupied with working through the theological and practical implications of this dual structure.

The following chart lists various ways that Christian thinkers referred to these two domains across more than a millennia (including some that we will learn about in the coming chapters)

One of the goals of this book is to help you recognize what is and what is not a secular government. The mere act of conceptualizing two powers does not mean that political secularism is present. We saw that in the Middle Ages, religious leaders favored hierocracy. In this scheme, political leaders who were Christians, but not a part of the church, were subordinate to the clergy. Thus there were two levels, but no secularism.

Now, if we reverse this equation we can start to glimpse the essence of all political secularisms. Secularism is present when the opposite happens. Secularism is present when religious leaders are subordinate

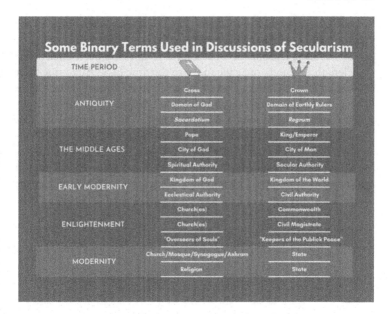

Figure 2.1 Some binary terms used in discussions of secularism

to governing authorities who are not official representatives of the religion (though they may be religious themselves).

Put differently, a prerequisite for political secularism is that the church, or the mosque, or the synagogue is *not* on top. Many societies conceive of the world as being divided between the spiritual and the secular realms. When religious authorities are atop that binary we call it hierocracy or theocracy. When the secular arm is in command we call it political secularism.

SUGGESTIONS FOR FURTHER READING

Strangely, there are no book-length histories of political secularism. This may be because some scholars view secularism as having originated in the modern era (a point challenged by this chapter and the next). The current author tried to piece together a transhistorical sketch in an article entitled "Political Secularism" in *The Oxford*

Handbook of Secularism, edited by Phil Zuckerman and John Shook (New York: Oxford University Press, 2017), pp. 85–102.

The biblical taproots of secular ideas have rarely been discussed at any length. Though, once we move to the time of St. Augustine there is Robert Markus's very good *Christianity and the Secular* (Notre Dame, IN: Notre Dame University Press, 2006). A nice collection of documents about Gallicanism is Charles Wood (Ed.), *Philip the Fair and Boniface VIII: State vs. Papacy* (New York: Holt, Rinehart and Winston, 1967). Ockham and Marsilius are two scintillating and very forward-looking thinkers. For those who want to read original sources (in translation) there is William of Ockham, *On the Power of Emperors and Popes*, translated by Annabel Brett (Bristol: Thoemmes Press, 1998) and Marsilius, *Defensor Pacis*, translated by Alan Gewirth (Toronto: University of Toronto Press, 1980).

3

"THOUGHT IS FREE"
MARTIN LUTHER AND EARLY MODERNITY

The laws that people believe come from God are one thing. The laws of a secular state are another. Oftentimes there is a clash between the former and the latter. For example, certain religious conservatives have interpreted the Bible as saying that homosexuality is a sin, or that the use of contraception is against the will of God. When such groups attempt to act on their beliefs the clash just mentioned is likely to take place.

In 2015, a branch of a pharmacy chain in Washington State (USA) refused to stock emergency contraceptives such as Plan B and ella. The owners of the pharmacy felt that selling these abortifacients violated their religious principles. When the case went to the Ninth Circuit Court of Appeals the state ruled against them. The judges upheld a previous law that all pharmacies must make this federally approved product available to customers.

In Canada in 2002, a school board, responding to the complaints of some parents, tried to remove certain books from a curriculum for first graders. Subsequently, the board passed a resolution that prohibited the materials—materials which were suggested for inclusion in the curriculum by gay and lesbian organizations. The disputed texts had titles like *Asha's Mom* and *One Dad, Two Dads, Brown Dads, Blue Dads*.

The Supreme Court ruled against these parents in *Surrey v. Chamberlain*. The Court's verdict, a few lines of which I cite here, harkens back to the *equality* principle we discussed in the previous chapter:

> A requirement of secularism implies that, although the Board is indeed free to address the religious concerns of parents, it must be

DOI: 10.4324/9781003140627-4

> sure to do so in a manner that gives equal recognition and respect to other members of the community.

These two examples remind us of secularism's *statist* nature. Secularism is a doctrine *of* the *state*. It is based on the premise that the *state* is "on top," that it has the requisite power to enforce its laws over and against the will of religious citizens (and non-religious ones too).

All citizens are subordinate to the state—that is a key and controversial premise of modern political secularisms. It's oftentimes more than a controversial premise. In some cases, the state's exhibition of dominance is downright incendiary, leading to protests, civil unrest, and mass violence. Opponents of a secular state often allege that it is trying to act like God. Secular states, respond, that they are just trying to maintain order.

We will revisit these debates later on. But for now, let's go way back in time to better understand how a new building block of political secularism emerged. In the previous chapter we learned about the "binary," or the tendency in Christendom to think of society as having a spiritual center of authority and a more worldly, civil one. We are about to see how a major religious thinker tilted the balance of power in favor of civil authority.

As with so many aspects of the history of secularism, the development of this principle of *state supremacy* is a bit of an unintended consequence. The theologian who put the idea into motion did so inadvertently. He probably never imagined it would amount to what it did just a few centuries later.

PRINCIPLE 3: STATE SUPREMACY

That man is Martin Luther (1483–1546) and he plays a major role in our story. In the historical narrative of secularism, he is like a central train hub, or relay station. Towards him chugged all sorts of ideas (and rage) from Antiquity and the Middle Ages. He absorbed those ideas during his own turbulent life and hurled them forward. From there, his unique inspirations surged ahead into Renaissance and Enlightenment Europe with astonishing velocity and force. What also surged ahead were some of the beguiling contradictions that characterized Luther's thought.

Perched between Antiquity and Modernity, Luther represents the crucial pivot in the history of secularism. His ideas were later amplified and refined in North America by the Baptist dissenter, Roger Williams (1603–1683). Ironic, is it not, that political secularism, which many today esteem to be anti-religious, was so shaped by men who many in their day considered to be religious fanatics?

But back to Luther, a giant who stood on the shoulders of other theological giants. He started his life as an Augustinian monk and the influence of St. Augustine on his thought is immense. In his 1523 essay "On the Secular Authority," Luther not only replicated Augustine's binary from *The City of God*, he weaponized it as well.

Like his master, the disciple argued that God had created two domains on earth. Luther called these by various names. In one usage he referred to them as "the kingdom of God" and "the kingdom of the world." Elsewhere he spoke of the "spiritual government" and the "secular government." Sometimes he employs another term for secular authority, one which is very on-brand for Martin Luther: "the Sword."

Referring to the government created by God as an instrument of violence and war makes sense given Luther's peculiar theological views. You may recall that Augustine referred to this sinful world we live in as the *Saeculum*. Luther agrees. "The world is God's enemy" says Luther with characteristic flourish. The earth, he believes, is teeming with wicked people. Many of these people pretend to be Christians. But "scarcely one human being in a thousand," Luther declares, "is a true Christian."

Imagine a theology that leads you to see your *own* co-religionists as sinful and depraved!

This dislike and mistrust of the present world and its inhabitants is a huge—and to a modern sensibility, weird—component of Luther's thought. It also partly accounts for why he believes weapons are necessary. Evil is everywhere, even among self-professed followers of Christ. That's why the Sword, wielded exclusively by the secular prince, is needed to maintain order.

All of this might raise a question for the reader: Why didn't a pious man like Luther hand the Sword to the spiritual authority? Why didn't he turn to the spiritual arm to keep the peace? The theological reason was that he thought that humans were incorrigibly sinful and dangerous. So much so that their depravity could not be contained by something as pure and silken as true religion.

But the practical reason is much more relevant. Martin Luther was embroiled in a life-and-death battle with the church and its pope. His hatred of the papacy knew no bounds. He likened the pope to Satan, the anti-Christ and various sorts of prostitutes. This anger towards the church, as you might recall, was anticipated by Marsilius and Ockham, who we met in the last chapter.

Luther's hatred of the church is what led him to entrust princes, as opposed to priests, with maintaining the law. He is not naive. He concedes that princes are vain, arrogant and corrupt. Ultimately, however, he believes that they can potentially do some good.

A proper prince will help "true" Christians who seek "retribution, justice, protection and help for others." He will "catch the wicked ... accuse them ... execute them ... protect, acquit, defend and save the good." In doing so, the prince and his Sword will permit those rare "true Christians" to practice their faith. Further, the secular ruler's leadership might create a space in which some sinners might be brought to see the light.

The upshot of Luther's teaching is as clear as it is controversial: Secular authority can serve the Lord! "Power," he avers, "is the handmaiden of God." And that means that even so-called representatives of God, like those who staff the church, can be straightened out by the Sword.

This faith in the secular arm is also apparent in his 1520 essay "To the Christian Nobility of the German Nation." There Luther writes:

> [S]ince the temporal [i.e., secular] power is ordained of God to punish the wicked and protect the good, it should be left free to perform its office in the whole body of Christendom without restriction and without respect to persons, whether it affects pope, bishops, priests, monks, nuns, or anyone else ...

Writing in the contrails of Marsilius and Ockham, Luther has penned a manifesto for the supremacy of the Christian state over the church. Little did he know that the adjective "Christian" would soon drop out. His teachings eventually gave life to the concept of *state supremacy*, or the idea that when there are *two powers*, the state is on top.

PRINCIPLE 4: INTERNAL CONSTRAINT

Martin Luther is among the most influential thinkers of all time. Not surprisingly, he also comes in for his share of critique. His detractors across the ages have lamented his admiration for the Sword. They view his high praise for the secular prince as a recipe for tyranny.

Remember, Luther justifies obedience to the secular government by citing those verses in the New Testament (Romans 13:1; 1 Peter 2:13–14; see Chapter 2) about submitting to the governing authorities. He sanctifies, as it were, passive citizenship or subjecthood. With so much power given to the prince (and with the counterbalancing force of the religious authorities neutralized), Luther is often judged harshly. He is seen as an unwitting architect of authoritarianism.

I think the criticism is fair. Though there are some crucial nuances in his argument that we need to note. Most importantly, Luther did not give the secular arm total free rein. He imposed restrictions on its activities.

Like Marsilius and Ockham before him, he believed that there was a divinely ordained division of labor between the two powers. The prince had a delimited field of action. Yes, he could control "body, goods and outward, earthly matters." But, no, his power was not absolute. Secular power, he mused, extends "only to taxes, duties, honor, fear, outward things."

This control of "outward things" surely does give the prince a lot of power. But Luther was adamant that the power of the secular prince was not absolute. There are certain places where a Prince is not permitted to go. This ruler, as we are about to see, had no business meddling with "inward" affairs. This is the domain of a human being's soul. Thus, there is a restriction, or *internal constraint*, on what a prince or government can do.

To use a modern phrase, there are "checks and balances" on the prince's authority. These constraints exist in Luther's *theory* and *words*. His abstract objection to princely abuse was sincere. The problem is that he never identified a concrete mechanism that would check and balance a ruler's overreach. Luther's princes seemed to function on the honor system, never an effective deterrent for very powerful people with massive arsenals and treasuries at their disposal. This is why the criticism of Luther as an unwitting engineer of authoritarianism is warranted.

Then again, Luther did try to draw a line which princes could not cross. Later on we will see that this concept of *internal constraint* would be reconstructed by modern political secularisms. A well-functioning secularism should not be an authoritarian regime. It develops mechanisms, like laws, courts, a multi-party system, and free elections, to curtail and monitor its own power. But for now, let's better understand where Luther drew the line and why.

PRINCIPLE 5: FREEDOM OF CONSCIENCE

Martin Luther had a fondness for what today we might call "strongmen." The ideas discussed above were written in a letter he composed to Prince John, Duke of Saxony. Luther wanted to instruct earthly leaders in the delicate art of ruling with an iron fist all the while adhering to Christian values.

For granting so much authority to the mighty, Luther has been justifiably criticized by posterity. As I just noted, however, he did not grant the mighty unconditional power. He insisted that they had to respect certain limits. The particular limit that most concerned him is now known as *freedom of conscience*.

"Thought is free," declares Luther. He believed that no one—not a prince, not a priest, *no one*—can force another to think about God in a certain way. That region of your mind which contemplates the divine is sovereign. This is the "inward" realm we mentioned earlier. It is "folly," he insists, to think that belief can be compelled.

The prince's jurisdiction, as we saw above, is confined solely to the outward realm. This means that no ruler can ever "correct" how a subject thinks about God. In one of those soaring Lutherian rants he exclaims "the soul is not subject to the emperor's power. He can neither teach nor guide it; he cannot kill it or bring it to life; he cannot bind or loose it, judge it or sentence it, hold it or release it."

There are conservative components to Luther's thought and progressive ones. An instance of the latter is his insistence that even heretics are allowed to believe what they want to believe. They cannot be coerced or punished into thinking differently about God by the prince or anyone else.

Wise old Luther added a wrinkle to this argument. He reminded the prince that any coercive attempt to "correct" a "wrong" way of thinking will backfire. It will simply give birth to more errors of thought and anger. "The use of force," Luther concludes, "can never prevent heresy." Come at a heretic with the word of God, not the Sword.

The Sword's blade, then, can never scratch or scuff the soul; to do so is to make matters worse. We could legitimately ask whether Luther and his colleagues observed this principle in their own time (evidence indicates that they did not). But the glorious principle of *freedom of conscience* is what's important here. For anyone familiar with the torture, persecution and murder that heretics endured throughout the Middle Ages, Luther's intervention, theoretical as it may be, is a breath of fresh air.

I think Luther is going much further than just erecting a line that secular rulers cannot cross. He is making a statement about what has come to be known as "inalienable human rights," or "natural law." These would be rights so fundamental to what it means to be human that no person or government can take them away from us. For Luther this psychic freedom is sacred, inviolable. You can think or believe anything you want to think or believe.

As we will see in Chapter 8, the *freedom of conscience* principle will be extended in later centuries to include *freedom of speech*.

PRINCIPLE 6: ORDER

Amid a Europe fracturing between Catholicism and Protestantism (and with Protestantism fracturing among itself into numerous sectaries) all of the ideas above exerted huge influence. To read the seventeenth-century Baptist thinker Roger Williams is to see Luther's imprint everywhere. Given that Williams was an activist of sorts, his interest in Luther's principles was not merely abstract and theoretical. He had the opportunity to put them into practice as he arrived in America.

Like Luther, Williams thought the world was wicked, referring to it as a "dungeon of darkness." Like Luther, Williams embraced the binary and made the spiritual arm subordinate to the secular one. Like Luther, he wanted the spiritual and secular arms to each stay in their lanes; one dealt with souls, the other with governance.

And like Luther, Williams was a passionate proponent of *freedom of conscience*. "It is not lawful," writes Williams in *The Bloudy Tenent of Persecution*, "to persecute any for conscience … for in persecuting such, Christ himself is persecuted in them." To force one's religious opinions on another, Williams averred, is un-Christlike. He even extended this courtesy to Jews—a massive break from existing Christian precedents which often tried to convert them under the threat of punishment or even death: "We must necessarily disclaim our desires and hopes of the Jews' conversion to Christ."

Williams had a fascinating take on religious conformity. He argued that there was no advantage to a society in which all citizens had to practice the same religion. Forcing a uniform faith on all subjects, he shrewdly observed, would cross up the proper duties of the secular and spiritual authorities leading to strife. For the secular rulers would be in a position of legislating that inward realm of the soul—a red flag for Williams (and Luther, and Marsilius and Ockham before him).

Going further, Williams hints that having a variety of faiths in one polity is desirable because it demands the civility embodied by Christianity. Williams, in his own way, sought what we might call "diversity." Differences between individuals were, far from being a drawback, a net positive for a society.

Yet Williams greatest contribution to secular theory, I think, was in the way he balanced his desire for religious pluralism and *freedom of conscience* on the one hand, with pragmatism on the other. Like Luther, Williams granted robust protections for *freedom of conscience*. Never could the authorities interfere with a person's beliefs. In his 1663 Charter of Rhode Island and Providence Plantations, he writes: "our royal will and pleasure is, that no person within the said colony, at any time hereafter, shall be anyway molested, punished, disquieted, or called in question, for any differences in opinion in matters of religion."

Yet Williams adds his own wrinkle, one that had immense consequences for the development of secularism. *Freedom of conscience*, he implies, has limits. Your beliefs, ardently held though they might be, cannot be translated into actions that disturb the civil peace. Notice how Williams juggles religious freedom with good citizenship in this passage from the 1663 Charter:

> all and every person and persons may, from time to time, and at all times hereafter, freely and fully have and enjoy his and their own

judgments and consciences, in matters of religious concernments, throughout the tract of land hereafter mentioned; they behaving themselves peaceably and quietly, and not using this liberty to licentiousness and profaneness, nor to the civil injure or outward disturbance of others; any law, statute, or clause, therein contained,

You can observe your religion as you see fit, *until* you inconvenience others or trample on their rights, or break laws. This is what I refer to as the *order* principle. The secular authority has to perform a complex balancing act: to grant as much *freedom of conscience* as possible, but also to make sure that there is *order*. Easier said than done. This is the dilemma that confronts every secular state.

CONCLUSION

It's a long way from the turbulent sixteenth and seventeenth centuries that Luther and Williams inhabited to the twenty-first

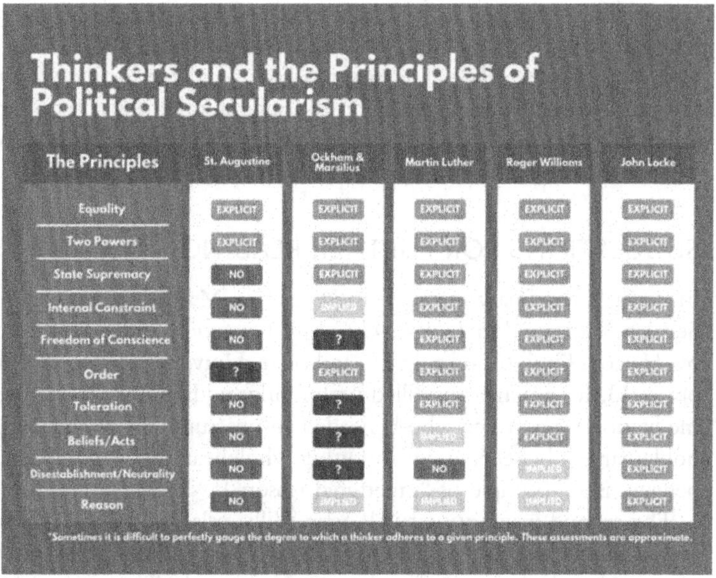

Thinkers and the Principles of Political Secularism

The Principles	St. Augustine	Ockham & Marsilius	Martin Luther	Roger Williams	John Locke
Equality	EXPLICIT	EXPLICIT	EXPLICIT	EXPLICIT	EXPLICIT
Two Powers	EXPLICIT	EXPLICIT	EXPLICIT	EXPLICIT	EXPLICIT
State Supremacy	NO	EXPLICIT	EXPLICIT	EXPLICIT	EXPLICIT
Internal Constraint	NO	IMPLIED	EXPLICIT	EXPLICIT	EXPLICIT
Freedom of Conscience	NO	?	EXPLICIT	EXPLICIT	EXPLICIT
Order	?	EXPLICIT	EXPLICIT	EXPLICIT	EXPLICIT
Toleration	NO	?	EXPLICIT	EXPLICIT	EXPLICIT
Beliefs/Acts	NO	?	IMPLIED	EXPLICIT	EXPLICIT
Disestablishment/Neutrality	NO	?	NO	IMPLIED	EXPLICIT
Reason	NO	IMPLIED	IMPLIED	IMPLIED	EXPLICIT

*Sometimes it is difficult to perfectly gauge the degree to which a thinker adheres to a given principle. These assessments are approximate.

Figure 3.1 Thinkers and the principles of political secularism

century, in which every month brings us a new controversy between a religious group and a secular state. Yet the writings of those hoary old figures put into play some of the ground rules that many liberal democracies abide by today as they try to navigate those controversies.

The parents in Canada who protested children's books about same-sex couples, the pharmacist in the United States who refused to stock contraceptives—they are absolutely free to believe what they wish to believe. No modern secular state denies that. That's an accomplishment whose magnitude is easy to overlook until you consider how some other modern states don't let citizens believe whatever they want to believe.

These religious conservatives in the United States and Canada are also free to use the state's own *internal constraint* (e.g., the courts) as a means of overturning laws they feel violate their religious precepts. In the cases we saw above the secular state prevailed over the pharmacists and the parents' group. Yet it must be mentioned that *internal constraint* doesn't always favor the secular state. Sometimes the courts rule that the secular state has overreached and is reprimanded.

But what the litigants in Washington and Canada learned was a crucial lesson: you can believe anything you want, *but you can't always act on those beliefs*. This too is a core secular principle whose import became abundantly clear to Enlightenment philosophers pondering the faith-based carnage caused by Protestant–Catholic strife. It is to this that we turn now.

SUGGESTIONS FOR FURTHER READING

In terms of primary texts, a must-read is Martin Luther's "On Secular Authority" in *Luther and Calvin: On Secular Authority*, edited by Harro Höpfl (Cambridge: Cambridge University Press, 2008), pp. 3–43. It's a dense text filled with quirky oddities (like its closing meditation on a prince who beheaded an unscrupulous womanizing nobleman—a beheading which Luther wholeheartedly approves and believes is an example of "unfettered reason").

The second primary text is Roger Williams's *The Bloudy Tenent of Persecution for Cause of Conscience Discussed and Mr. Cotton's Letter Examined and Answered* (London: J. Haddon 1848), reissued by Kessinger Publishing. The first 100 pages are especially relevant.

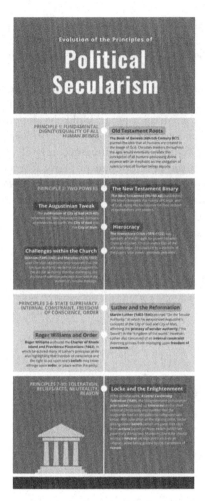

Figure 3.2 Evolution of the principles of political secularism

On Luther's relation to the papacy see Scott Hendrix, *Luther and the Papacy: Stages in a Reformation Conflict* (Philadelphia, PA: Fortress Press, 1981). If you are interested in his two kingdoms approach consult William Wright, *Martin Luther's Understanding of God's Two Kingdoms: A Response to the Challenge of Skepticism*

(Grand Rapids, MI: Baker Academic, 2010), p. 17. Also see Volker Mantey, *Zwei Schwerter—Zwei Reiche: Martin Luthers Zwei-Reiche-Lehre vor ihrem spätmittelalterlichen Hintergrund* (Tübingen: Mohr Siebeck, 2005).

My own analysis of this theory, set in the modern context, is Jacques Berlinerblau, "Donald J. Trump, The White Evangelicals, and Martin Luther: Exploring an Unlikely Hypothesis," *Interpretation: A Journal of Bible and Theology*, 73 (2019), pp. 18–30. Martha Nussbaum has written a definitive account of Roger Williams's contributions to the development of political secularism: *Liberty of Conscience: In Defense of America's Tradition of Religious Equality* (New York: Basic Books, 2008).

4

"BURNING ZEAL"

JOHN LOCKE AND THE ENLIGHTENMENT

Political secularism has an aspiration and a phobia. The aspiration is society-wide peace. The phobia is religiously based violence that leads to complete societal collapse.

The Enlightenment philosopher John Locke (1632–1704) knew all about societal collapse. As with all Europeans of the seventeenth century, he was scarred by decades of endless faith-based strife.

He recalled the intra-Christian bloodletting of the Thirty Years War (1618–1648) in which as many as 8 million people were murdered. He certainly was aware of the doomed insurrection of the Fifth Monarchists, who in the name of "King Jesus" advocated for the overthrow of the monarchy and eventually were massacred themselves upon trying to take possession of London. He recalled the devastation and destabilization that other religious conflicts created across the continent.

These events were the historical backdrop to Locke's *A Letter Concerning Toleration* of 1689. This work is considered a foundational statement of Enlightenment and Liberal principles. It is also the work of a Christian intellectual experiencing a sort of post-traumatic stress syndrome.

What Locke understood was the uniquely negative role that religion played in stoking unfathomable violence. In *A Letter*, Locke referred to the "burning Zeal" that some had for their God, their church, and their own salvation (and that of others). This religious fervor, he felt, was an accelerant to chaos, and a menace to the existence of civilization itself.

DOI: 10.4324/9781003140627-5

One of the aims of this brilliant, but sometimes maddeningly inconsistent text, is to prevent "burning Zeal" from flaming up (again) into an inferno. To achieve this end, Locke expends considerable genius and creativity as he touches upon every core principle of what later became political secularism.

In the process, there is much theological disruption. He upends existing Christian values. He proposes new psychological attitudes towards God and our fellow humans. Leaning heavily on those who came before him, he fashions a blueprint for a functional government (which he refers to as "the secular authority," "the civil authority," or "the magistrate") that can maintain peaceful coexistence among all believers. Locke is well aware many might not like this type of government.

His warning is powerful and compelling (though it is easily forgotten when there is no religious violence and times aren't tough). Without a secular government, there will not be toleration. If there is no toleration there is no peace. And if there is no peace, sighed Locke looking back at a smoldering Europe, no one will get to God.

PRINCIPLE 7: TOLERATION

Locke opens his famous treatise with a statement every bit as worthy of our appreciation as Genesis 1:27 (see Chapter 2). "I esteem," writes the great philosopher, "Toleration to be the chief Characteristical Mark of the True Church."

It is easy to overlook how radical this statement is. The Enlightenment philosopher is offering a completely different way of ordering the values to which a Christian subscribes. For figures like Augustine and Luther, the chief characteristical mark of Christianity might have been obedience to God, or love for God, or fear of God.

That is pointedly *not* what Locke is saying. He is saying that a Christian's foremost duty is to be tolerant of other Christians. Living peacefully among those whom you might disagree with about Christian precepts—that is what it means to be a Christian.

If this is the case, what does it mean to be a properly Christian government? Imagine a ruler who believes, unlike Locke, that the ultimate Christian virtue is disciplined, daily, devotion to the Lord. This government would mandate ritual and prayer night and day.

Domestically, it would punish people who missed, or slept through, church services. Its uniformed "morals police" would prowl the boulevards rounding up sinners, addicts, and reprobates.

Locke scoffs at such a "Christian" government. In fact, he claims that "there is absolutely no such thing ... as a Christian Commonwealth." Any government that proclaims itself to be "Christian" is missing the whole point of the Gospels. Jesus was unconcerned with power, domination, rule of others, worldly things like that. As far as Locke is concerned, it is *un*-Christian for a government to proclaim itself to be "Christian."

This is very confusing. Locke everywhere assumes in *A Letter* that society's ruler *is*, in fact, a Christian. This "magistrate" should have a good Christian heart, be a tolerant saint, etc. All European rulers in the late seventeenth century would have been Christians anyway (although few were tolerant saints). So while Locke denies that there can be a Christian Commonwealth, he seems to be overlooking the obvious: *every society around him is in some way a Christian Commonwealth ruled, and almost exclusively inhabited, by various types of Christians.*

Which raises another inconsistency in his argument. The magistrate, Locke advises, cannot impose his preferred Christian dogma on his subjects. But if that's the case, then why must he abide by and enforce the principle of *toleration*—which is the dogma Locke urged the magistrate to love? After all, Locke told us on page one that *toleration* is the greatest *Christian* virtue of them all. We'll get back to these contradictions in a moment.

For now, we should note that for Locke a state of toleration is best achieved when the functions of religion and governance are kept separate. The magistrate has his sphere of responsibilities. The churches (notice the plural) have theirs. "The Boundaries on both sides," thunders Locke, "are fixed and immovable." If both sides play their parts, stay in their lanes, then *toleration* and ultimately peace will ensue.

And what are those parts? More or less the same roles Martin Luther assigned to the two powers. The secular authority is in charge of what Locke calls "outward things." These include upholding laws, tax collection, maintaining public health, public safety, regulating disputes between citizens, protecting property, and staving off foreign invaders.

As for the churches, they deal with "inward things." They tend to "the Salvation of Men's Souls." They counsel their members on how one worships and contemplates God. Under no circumstances, however, can the churches ever use force. They can't use it against their government. They can't use it against other churches. And they can't even use it against members of their own flock. Religion must lay down its arms. It has no "Compulsive Power."

Force belongs solely to the secular arm, or "the Keeper of the publick Peace." So the secular authority is not only on top, but it is armed and, if needs be, very dangerous. Naturally, Locke abides by the principle of *internal constraint*. There are things the government cannot do. It can never impose "Rites and Ceremonies" on subjects, or forbid such events (as long as they break no laws; see below). Nor can it forbid a religious group's doctrines even if they strike a government as idolatrous.

But the secular authority can interfere in religious affairs for *political* reasons. A Catholic or Muslim subject, Locke reasons, will likely be loyal to the pope or "the mufti of Constantinople." That is seditious. For that political, as opposed to religious, reason a magistrate can trample on their rights.

The Magistrate's task is to govern in a way that makes the (Christian) virtue of toleration possible across society writ large. Locke appears to be saying that mutual toleration—which is akin to a society at peace with itself—is not some natural state of humankind. Rather, this unruly *Saeculum* (see Chapter 2) needs to be carefully managed, regulated, and pacified through the principles of governance expounded in *A Letter Concerning Toleration*.

If we abide by these principles, if we extend *toleration* to others, then there is peace. If there is peace, everyone gets to worship God.

PRINCIPLE 8: BELIEFS/ACTS

John Locke wants all Christians who don't think *toleration* is the chief virtue of Christianity, to behave as if they do think *toleration* is the chief virtue of Christianity. That's quite a significant ask! Put differently, he is asking them to separate what they truly believe from how they act as citizens of the Commonwealth. And not just about the matter of *toleration*.

To this day, political secularisms demand that citizens split themselves into two. There is a private version of you. It has convictions about God, the universe, gender roles, morality, and so forth. Then there is a public version of you, otherwise known as a "citizen." Sometimes the two are at odds.

This demand for a divided self results in what I call the *belief/ acts distinction*. It stipulates that while the state cannot tell you what to believe, *it can tell you how, and how not, to act.* All political secularisms make this request of citizens. Naturally, there are those who refuse to comply. This is where clashes between church/mosque/synagogue and state occur. Consider the following two examples.

Ultra-Orthodox Jews believe that the Sabbath is a day of rest. For these reasons they don't operate their vehicles from sundown on Friday to sundown on Saturday. If they live in cities with large non-Jewish populations, like Brooklyn or Montreal, it is inevitable that other citizens will drive through their neighborhoods on the community's day of rest. The secular state asks Orthodox Jews to not obstruct traffic on Saturdays, even though they believe that this activity contravenes God's will. Being solid citizens, they voluntarily comply.

In Jerusalem, however, some ultra-Orthodox Jews are far less compliant. In the Mea Sharim neighborhood, residents have been known to barricade streets, harass drivers, or even physically attack passing cars during the Sabbath. The drivers who are "violating the sabbath," by the way, are usually Jews who are not Orthodox. The Orthodox, for their part, will not sever beliefs from acts.

I often tell my students that the only truly interesting question about toleration is: what cannot be tolerated? Naturally, Locke could not have entitled his work *A Letter Concerning What Cannot be Tolerated.* Yet he is quite intent on confronting this question and his answer is not complicated. Sure, thought is free and all that. But if the way you think about your religion leads you to act in contravention of laws of the land, then those acts will not be tolerated by the state. Certain acts are off limits even if your religion demands that you perform them.

PRINCIPLE 9: DISESTABLISHMENT/NEUTRALITY (MINORITY RIGHTS)

In one of the most well-known catchphrases from *A Letter*, Locke remarks "every Church is Orthodox to it self." This comment underscores a truth about human beings and their passions: they almost always tend to believe that their religion, their way of practicing their faith, is the right way. All other ways are wrong, or heterodox.

Locke finds that mindset to be both anti-Christian and completely illogical. Anti-Christian because a tolerant individual (that is, a true Christian), will not be so arrogant as to assume she or he is always right. Illogical, because who, after all, knows the ways of God? Where, Locke asks, is that judge who could determine which church's concept of the divine is correct? God is inscrutable, no?

If we humans cannot know the ways of God, then it follows that neither can a government. Churches, Locke concedes, are free to believe that their way of thinking about the divine is one hundred percent correct. That's their prerogative. But the civil authority can never endorse a religious orthodoxy. And with that, Locke takes the insights of his predecessors to their logical ends.

Linking a government to one religion, Locke cautioned, is a sure-fire design for social implosion. He thus doubles down on the old Medieval intuition articulated by Marsilius we saw in Chapter 2: societies ruled and run by popes and priests are structurally unstable. In *A Letter* we also hear echoes of Luther who warned us against enforcing an orthodoxy, preferring to give heretics space to believe what they wanted. One also feels the presence of Roger Williams's insight that religious diversity is desirable for a society.

This demand that the government divest itself of any religious orthodoxy, or any loyalty to one faith over another, constitutes the *disestablishment/neutrality principle*. This is an absolutely crucial concept for understanding political secularism. Every secular government claims it abides by this principle. And every secular government is accused of not abiding by this principle.

In our next chapters we will see how *disestablishment/neutrality* gave birth to the nineteenth-century framework of "separation of church and state." For now, we should observe that this principle demands that the civil authority remains "above the fray." The government has no established or "official" religion. It is to remain agnostic, so to speak, on the truth claims made by faith-based groups. In order for there to be *toleration*, your rulers must be religiously unaligned at least when they are "on the job" as rulers.

As we shall see, no secular principle creates more controversy than this one. Again and again, critics charge that where there is supposed to be disestablishment there is *non*-neutrality as well. The United States favors Protestants. Quebec and France favor Catholics. Turkey favors a certain type of Sunni Islam. In each case it is alleged that the secular state practices *false* neutrality.

A recurring dilemma confronting secularism, I repeat, lies with states that profess to be following *disestablishment/neutrality* when, in actual practice, they are not. Sometimes the state has no formal established religion, yet it clearly favors one religion, and/or discriminates against after another. We might call this disestablishment/*non*-neutrality.

Locke himself veered into the disestablishment/*non*-neutrality domain. In *A Letter* he famously argued that Catholics and atheists could not be tolerated by the magistrate. The former because they swore allegiance to the pope. The latter because they could not be trusted to take oaths in God's name. The logic here has always struck commentators as sketchy.

One crucial thing to recall when thinking about the *disestablishment/neutrality* principle is that, when properly applied, religious minorities tend to favor it very much. Muslims in India, and Jews in the United States are a good example. They generally appreciate the idea that the religions of the majority in those nations (Hinduism and Christianity respectively) are not officially endorsed by the government. This provides them with significant legal protections against discrimination.

Here's what's ironic though. Many Muslims in Pakistan, a Muslim-majority country, prefer that it remain an Islamic Republic. Many Jews in Israel are at peace with it being "the Jewish State." Unlike their co-religionists in India or the United States, these Pakistani Muslims and Israeli Jews have no need for the *disestablishment/neutrality* principle.

Often, your love or hatred for secularism is not ethical and unchanging, it's situational and context-dependent. It's all about where you are standing!

PRINCIPLE 10: REASON

Another of Locke's arguments in favor of a secular government is very apt for an Enlightenment philosopher. He is confident that the idea of toleration is not only "agreeable to the Gospel of Jesus Christ," but in harmony with "the genuine Reason of Mankind." *Toleration* as the foundation of society, Locke surmises, is what Jesus himself would have wanted. He is also certain that it is a perfectly rational form of governance.

Locke thus slipped into secular discourse the claim that religion accords with reason. The raw intuition was picked up a hundred years later by Thomas Jefferson and James Madison (see Chapter 5). "Reason and free enquiry," declared Jefferson in 1781, "are the only effectual agents against error. Give a loose to them, they will support the true religion."

We don't have the space here to discuss nineteenth-century Christian movements (such as liberal Protestant evolutionary theorists or geologists dating the age of the earth), and twentieth-century Islamic moments (like the Nechari school during British rule of India) which argued that a given faith was in perfect harmony with science. We'll just say that with each passing decade it became more and more difficult to maintain that there was no contradiction between the words of scripture and scientific findings.

For modern political secularisms, scripture and revelation are irrelevant. A good government runs on reason, not on passion. It bases its decisions on logic, not prayerful emotion. Science and data are the drivers of public policy, not biblical verses or suras from the Quran.

THE OVERRIDE CLAUSE

In many ways, *A Letter Concerning Toleration* simply tightened and sharpened the insights of Ockham, Marsilius, Luther, and Williams. But Locke's hints about the principle of *disestablishment/neutrality* are something new. He discouraged the magistrate from bringing his own beliefs to bear on the work of the Civil Authority. The latter was to have no religious preference when governing. Too, his government was to be impartial in mediating disputes *between* religious groups. This line of reasoning would be expanded and made more explicit in the coming centuries.

Disestablishment/neutrality has become one of the defining features of political secularism. As we saw above, "Disestablishment/ *non*-neutrality!" has become the rallying cry of secularism's many detractors. Critics nowadays complain that secular states, despite their lofty constitutional rhetoric, are not religiously neutral.

Anti-seculars also bristle at the overwhelming power of the secular state. That too is a problem in Locke's thought (and Luther's as well). In one passage, he wondered aloud about a rogue magistrate who ignored the teachings of *A Letter*. Let's say that an unscrupulous leader forced his subjects to believe something, or act in opposition to their religious conscience. What to do in this instance of what Roger Williams once called "Soule Rape"? As with Luther before him, Locke disappoints on this issue. He counsels the trampled upon subjects to suffer in silence—God will sort it out in the Hereafter.

Let's close by pointing to another aspect of Locke's theory that is relevant to contemporary debates. In a passage that has been virtually unnoticed by commentators, Locke makes a controversial— and given what we just read, contradictory—point. He is trying to show that no one should ever be forced to believe in something against their will.

He writes: "It appears not that God has ever given any such Authority to one Man over another, as to compell anyone to his Religion." So far, so good. But after this protest against "Soule Rape," Locke says something unexpected: "Nor can any such Power be vested in the Magistrate by the *consent of the people*."

Permit me to offer a reading of this obscure verse. If the majority of voters in a society *want* their magistrate to impose a religion on others (i.e., "*the consent of the people*"), then that majority must be ignored. Let's reflect upon that for a moment. Locke is saying that *the principles of secularism override the democratic, but intolerant, will of the people.* We shall refer to this forthwith as "the override clause."

This means that the legitimacy of a secular political order comes from… … where exactly does it come from? Who gets to decide that belief can or cannot be compelled, if not the people themselves? The answer here can only be: John Locke decides. John Locke decides on the basis of his intimate acquaintance with "the genuine Reason of Mankind" and his interpretation of the gospels of Christ, Jesus.

Why does Locke disenfranchise citizens like this? My hunch is that he concluded, grimly, that tolerant individuals (like Luther's "true Christians") are rarely the majority in a given society. That's why he made the secular principle of *disestablishment/neutrality* "off limits," beyond the reach of popular consent and some sort of recall. The people cannot override the secular government, but the secular government can override the people.

What the (intolerant) majority wants must be disregarded; because if it gets what it wants then the secular state's aspiration of peace and *order* will never be achieved. Secularism is haunted not only by the phobia of mass violence, but by a dread of the masses themselves and their religious passions gone wild.

SUGGESTIONS FOR FURTHER READING

The 1994 French film *La Reine Margot* (based on the novel by Alexandre Dumas), which dramatizes the 1572 St. Bartholomew's Day massacre, offers a visual foretaste of the staggering religious violence of the seventeenth century.

For more advanced students of secularism, John Locke's 1689 *A Letter Concerning Toleration* (Indianapolis, IN: Hackett Publishing Company, 1983) has to be read in its dense entirety.

A discussion of Locke's similarities to the philosopher John Rawls can be found in John Perry, "Anglo-American Secular Government," in *The Oxford Handbook of Secularism*, edited by Phil Zuckerman and John Shook (New York: Oxford University Press, 2017), pp. 125–141. Also interesting in this regard are two articles from the very good volume *State and Secularism: Perspectives from Asia*, edited by Michael Heng Siam-Heng and Ten Chin Liew (Singapore: World Scientific Publishing Company, 2009). They are Ten Chin Liew's "Secularism and its Limits" (pp. 7–22) and Saranindranath Tagore's "Rawlsian Liberalism, Secularism, and the Call for Cosmopolitanism" (pp. 37–60). In the same volume, a discussion of the Nechari school, mentioned above, can be found in Ishtiaq Ahmed's "The Pakistan Islamic State Project: A Secular Critique" (pp. 185–212).

PART II

FRAMEWORKS OF POLITICAL SECULARISM IN GLOBAL PERSPECTIVE

—May I ask you another question, sir?

—Please. Go right ahead.

—My question is this, sir. Does the word secular mean godless?

—No.

—In that case, how can you explain why the state is banning so many girls from the classroom in the name of secularism, when all they are doing is obeying the laws of their religion?

—Honestly, my son. Arguing about such things will get you nowhere. They argue about it day and night on Istanbul television, and where does it get us? The girls are still refusing to take off their head scarves and the state is still barring them from the classroom.

—Orhan Pamuk, *Snow*

DOI: 10.4324/9781003140627-6

AMERICAN SECULARISM
THE (WOBBLY) SEPARATIONIST FRAMEWORK

Whereas John Locke wrote *A Letter Concerning Toleration* in 1689, the first durable secular constitutional moment in history occurred in 1789, in the United States. It was, indeed, a "moment." The newly formed American government, as we are now going to find out, did not really abide by secular principles in any consistent and meaningful way *until the mid-twentieth century*. The first comprehensive, binding, and long-lasting application of secular rule anywhere on earth, as we shall soon see, occurs in France in 1905.

This raises an intriguing question, one that has almost never been asked: if Locke published *A Letter* in 1689 why did it take more than two centuries for political secularism to become a coherent feature of governance in the United States and Europe? The best explanation I can muster is that certain types of Christians resisted secularisms rather ferociously.

Which is intriguing because John Locke, of course, was a Christian himself. His *Letter* was steeped in a lengthy Christian conversation that stretched back to St. Augustine. All the participants in that transhistorical dialogue were Christian intellectuals. They were reflecting upon the proper relationship between the Christian church and Christian rulers of Christian territories. Locke pondered these Christian theological dilemmas and emerged with a theoretical sketch of political secularism. A very *Christian* sketch, some critics would say (see Chapter 12).

But Locke's lofty religious standard of Christ-like tolerance and humble self-doubt, while embraced by many, never achieved majority status among the followers of Jesus. Few religious figures

DOI: 10.4324/9781003140627-7

were eager to submit to the secular authority. They didn't generally warm to the idea that the magistrate was "on top"—even though the magistrate, or (eventually) the president, or the prime minister was always a Christian!

For Catholic or Protestant leaders to accept this hierarchy in the eighteenth, nineteenth, or even twentieth centuries, was to cede immense power and privilege. Better for their churches to co-opt, or work with, the royal families and their networks as a means of maintaining their standing. That union of Cross and Crown is known as *l'ancien régime*. It is the exact opposite of a secular state, and had little tolerance for the profound insights of Enlightenment political philosophers like John Locke.

In the following chapters we will encounter *l'ancien régime* many times as we learn about powerful churches enmeshed with ruling classes in pre-revolutionary France, pre-revolutionary Russia, and pre-revolutionary Ethiopia. In a sign that this arrangement is not unique to Christendom, an anti-liberal *ancien régime* will be spotted in the Ottoman empire as well.

The resistance to secular governing principles was especially fierce in Catholic countries. The nineteenth century witnessed a continent-wide backlash among conservative Catholics to the Enlightenment and its associated modernizing innovations. This came in the form of "ultramontanism," a movement which foreshadows the rise of the twentieth-century conservative religious anti-secular (CRAS) formations to be studied in Chapter 11.

Ultramontanism was named to describe the faithful who looked beyond the mountains (i.e., the Alps), towards Rome. There they would find a powerful, infallible pope who was ready to combat the scourge of Liberalism.

What emerged was a full blown "culture war." Liberal, modern, and secular ideas were strenuously contested by Catholics in France, Italy, Spain, Prussia, Belgium, Austria, the Netherlands—wherever there were large numbers of Catholics. Mexico provides an interesting example. Its 1857 constitution actually proclaimed "separation of church and state." Pope Pius IX responded by claiming it had no validity. From 1858 to 1861 a bloody civil war ensued. The liberalizing nationalists won, but would have to wait until 1917 to fully render their country secular.

In 1864, the same Pius IX, issued the *Syllabus of Errors*—a document whose objective seemed to be to cancel the Enlightenment. It considered the following statement to be an error: "The Church ought to be separated from the State, and the State from the Church." It would take the Vatican many more decades to come to peace with the secular principle of *state supremacy*. Even Protestant nations, like Locke's native England, had little tolerance for grand secular scruples. Meanwhile in the United States a group called the National Reform Association fought hard to add an amendment to the Constitution which acknowledged "the Lord Jesus Christ as the Ruler among nations."

So to answer our question: If the practice of political secularism (which came to fruition in the twentieth century) trailed its theory (whose essential components were in place by the eighteenth century), then blame it on the relentless pushback of powerful Christian churches and their monarchical partners. Ruling authorities generally had little interest in divesting their governance structures of Christianity and conservative Christian leaders had little interest in relinquishing power. As a result, the implementation of political secularism was slow, uneven, and riddled with setbacks.

But this doesn't mean that there weren't significant developments in the 18th and 19th centuries. The latter century, in particular, is decisive in the history of political secularism. It was in the "fateful nineteenth," as I call it, that various figures in various countries started pondering the ten secular principles we identified and fighting to apply them to actual statecraft. What slowly emerged, in the face of intense resistance, were what I call secular "frameworks."

A secular framework mixes and matches, emphasizes and de-emphasizes, our 10 principles in its own unique way. It then tries to apply its package of principles to its work regulating relations (1) between itself and religious groups, and (2) between religious groups. In the coming chapters, we are going to look at four broad frameworks and the countries where they were first conceived or implemented. We'll start with the *separationist* framework, born in the United States.

THE RELIGION CLAUSES

Two of the American Founding Fathers, James Madison (1751–1836) and Thomas Jefferson (1743–1826), were avid readers of

John Locke ("Where he stopped short we may go on," exclaimed Jefferson). These politicians and intellectuals tried to turn Locke's abstract theory into laws, constitutional amendments, and actual statecraft. Their effort to merge Lockean principles into an operational governing framework didn't entirely succeed in the nineteenth century. It did, however, set the stage for the rise of separationist secularism in the United States a hundred and fifty years later.

To get our bearings, let's start with the First Amendment of the Constitution. Written in 1789 and ratified in 1791, it says very little about the proper relation between religion and government. In fact, it devotes exactly 16 words to the subject. Those are in addition to the 20 words in Article VI prohibiting a "religious test." That makes for a paltry 36 words in all! The sixteen words of the First Amendment are:

> Congress shall make no law respecting an establishment of religion, or prohibiting the free exercise thereof.

The brevity of the religion clauses of the First Amendment is, in some ways, an advantage. Their sparsity created space for subsequent generations to interpret and think through these issues in changing circumstances.

In other ways, all that emptiness creates problems. Countless concerns involving religion and government are left completely unaddressed by this short and cryptic sentence. All of which raises the question of *who* gets to address them and tell us what they mean and how they should be enforced.

That task was ultimately delegated to the judicial branch of the United States government. Secularism in America has been constructed and reconstructed and deconstructed through state and federal courts trying to figure out what the religion clauses meant. The ideological tilt of the courts in the United States changes over time—often within short periods of time. As a result American secularism evolves and devolves. It moves in one direction, and then lurches in another.

Sometimes the American government endorses a framework called "separationism" (see below). At other times, it moves toward "accommodationism" (see Chapter 7). On occasion, an anti-secular ruling ethos emerges as was seen during the administration of Donald J. Trump (2017–2021). That lack of stability can be blamed on the brevity of the religion clauses.

The religion clauses were written by James Madison as an amendment to the Constitution in something known as The Bill of Rights. Legal scholars sometimes praise the brilliant concision of those 16 words. Others, by contrast, have accused Madison of sloppy and distracted draftsmanship. The future president originally composed an earlier draft of the First Amendment religion clauses which reads as follows:

> The civil rights of none shall be abridged on account of religious belief or worship, nor shall any national religion be established, nor shall the full and equal rights of conscience be in any manner, or in any pretext, infringed.

Before we proceed, we should note what the religion clauses, be they the drafts or the final version, do not say. They never speak of "secularism." This makes perfect sense because that word with the "-ism" attached would not be coined for another half century (see Chapter 8). More importantly, the Constitution never uses the phrase "separation of church and state." We'll see why that is so important below.

FORGETTING PRINCIPLES

The religion clauses are usually divided into two parts. The first (i.e., *Congress shall make no law respecting an establishment of religion*) is called the *establishment clause*. An "establishment" is a "legal union of government and religion." The Constitution thus stipulates that the *Congress* of the United States federal government cannot make laws that would recognize one faith as the nation's official religion (*states*, however, are free to have an establishment, as Massachusetts did until 1833). Put differently, the United States government can never proclaim Lutheranism, or Catholicism, or Sikhism, what have you, as its national religion.

The roots of this provision lie in what we called the *disestablishment/neutrality* principle, which we viewed in John Locke's thought. When it comes to religion, says the establishment clause,

Congress (i.e., the United States government's legislative body) takes no sides. That seems clear, as far as it goes.

But countless scenarios would arise where matters are less clear. Can a state government—which is not, after all, the United States federal government—like South Carolina, have an establishment of religion in its own constitution? Can a priest, rabbi, or imam open a congressional session with a prayer? Can the military hire chaplains of different religions and denominations to cater to the nation's soldiers? The establishment clause, on its own, doesn't answer these questions; throughout American history the courts have had to intervene and figure out how it is applied.

Then comes the *free exercise clause* (i.e., *or prohibiting the free exercise thereof*). It tells us that Congress cannot prohibit a citizen from practicing her religion. This is one of those places where the charge of sloppy draftsmanship rings true. For the First Amendment fails to consider what the *restrictions* on free exercise of religion might be.

The law neglects to do what states and even American colonies had been doing for centuries. Namely, reminding citizens of the *limits* of religious acts based on religious beliefs. The early colonial constitutions stressed that free exercise had *a limit*. The Charter of Carolina (1663) guarantees free exercise as long as persons "do not in any wise disturb the peace …" The Constitution of Georgia (1777) permits free exercise "provided it be not repugnant to the peace and safety of the State." North Carolina (1776) grants free exercise under the condition "That nothing herein contained shall be construed to exempt preachers of treasonable or seditious discourses, from legal trial and punishment." New York (1777) for its part sought to prevent "acts of licentiousness, or justify practices inconsistent with the peace or safety of this State." The colonies dreamt Locke's nightmares as well!

You might remember the *belief/acts* and *order* principles we discussed in previous chapters. Both imply that you cannot always follow your religious scruples. As early as 1630, Roger Williams posited a red line: worship the Almighty but don't disturb the peace! Locke made the same stipulation. As did the American colonies in their constitutions. As did Thomas Jefferson in "Notes on the State of Virginia." The point is the Anglo-American world fully understood that there was no such thing as unbounded free exercise. The First Amendment of the Constitution did not.

Its 16 words ignore other secular principles as well. Jefferson was a huge proponent of *reason* and *freedom of conscience*. Madison had serious ideas about *toleration*. Yet one would not know that from the skimpy text of the First Amendment. As for *equality*, how much of that could there have been when white women were disenfranchised and persons of African ancestry were enslaved?

The brevity of the First Amendment is a real dilemma. It left us with an abundance of interpretive space. Mr. Jefferson, as we are about to see, was eager to explore that space.

SECULAR FRAMEWORK 1: SEPARATIONISM

Some Americans believe that their Constitution guarantees a "wall of separation between church and state." Critics respond that none of those words appear in the Constitution. The critics are correct.

Still, the "wall" image has roots in America's founding. It was none other than President Thomas Jefferson who invoked that famous metaphor (which had been in play at least since the time of Roger Williams). One problem was that he did so in a private correspondence, not an official document of state.

The letter was written on January 1, 1802, to a group of Baptists. Interestingly, until recent decades most American Baptists have always been among those Christians who wanted the secular and spiritual authorities to be kept far apart. In that letter to the Danbury Baptists, President Jefferson wrote the following:

> I contemplate with sovereign reverence that act of the whole American people which declared that their legislature would "make no law respecting an establishment of religion, or prohibiting the free exercise thereof," thus building a wall of separation between church and state.

This is a fine example of how the sparseness of the religion clauses created room for differing interpretations. President Jefferson used that room to draw a one-to-one equation between the Establishment clause and the idea of separation even though the Constitution says no such thing.

Disestablishment and separation are often mistakenly assumed to be identical. Disestablishment is what we have called a "secular principle." Separation is a "framework." *Every* secular state claims that it has no established religion. But not every secular state is separationist. As we shall see, some adopt different frameworks in which a government aggressively tries to control and regulate religion (thereby nullifying any authentic separation).

Separation conjures up a wall—an impregnable barrier that divides what is on one side from what is on the other. It makes us visualize partitions—an image that has mired this framework in all sorts of confusion. Disestablishment, by contrast, does not presume this type of rigid division between religion and government.

This distinction between disestablishment and separation might seem minute. But as the following example illustrates the distinction completely changes how Congress (the subject of the religion clauses) should act. Imagine that a certain religious group runs a soup kitchen for unhoused persons. The food is healthy, the meals are rendered professionally, in accordance with all nutritional standards, etc. The providers deliver their services to the needy regardless of the religious identity of the recipients. They never attempt to convert their clients or discuss religious matters with them. They simply want to feed the hungry.

Now let's imagine that a department of the Federal government has a budget for the alleviation of food insecurity. Can those funds be allocated to the religious group? What does the Constitution say about that? The answer depends on whether one follows the principle of *disestablishment/neutrality* or the framework of separation.

A Congress that abides by disestablishment can plausibly delegate monies to the faith-based charity in question. After all, Congress is not establishing any given religion by using taxpayer dollars to help the unhoused through the intermediary of a religious charity.

The separationist framework has a harder time supporting the good works of the soup kitchen. The wall should prevent any sort of flow between the government and religious groups—including the flow of tax monies collected from citizens. The argument could be made—and it's a reasonable argument—that the onus for helping unhoused citizens lies *solely* on the shoulders of the government, not churches. In a true separationist framework, the religious provider is free to continue its good works, but it cannot count on receiving allocations from Congress. Disestablishment and separation might seem identical, but they are not.

Both disestablishment and separation are "religion-neutral." They are neither for nor against religion. Yet separationism, perhaps because of its tight association with the controversial Mr. Jefferson, has always had a whiff of the anti-religious about it. In truth, both Mr. Madison and Mr. Jefferson were suspicious of religious overreach, or "the danger of encroachment by Ecclesiastical Bodies." Then again, compared to, let's say, their French contemporaries (see Chapter 6) their attitudes toward religion were generally supportive.

SEPARATIONISM AS BAD METAPHOR

Separationism as a framework is popular because it all seems so simple. You build a physical barrier between the government and religion. What could be easier than that? Yet it is almost impossible to partition one from the other. The boundary between government and religion is always porous. This truism is what anti-seculars have seized upon in the United States, with great success.

First and foremost, if the majority of your citizenry is religious—as is the case in the United States—it is unworkable to "wall off" religion from the state. The government, for its part, has to serve religious citizens. As a Supreme Court judge once observed, if a church is burning, strict separation would demand that the fire department not respond to the emergency.

Further, people of faith will work for the government, as everything from mail carriers to the president of the republic. If you prevent them from being employed in the name of separation, only nonbelievers, whose numbers are quite small, could run the country. How can there be true separation?

Interestingly, Jefferson's separationist reading of secularism was ignored by the courts until the 1870s. That's partly because, as we saw above, it was enshrined in a personal correspondence (i.e., the Danbury Letter), not an official government document (i.e., the Constitution). Further, the idea was resisted by the Protestant majority. Catholics and Mormons, however, found a judicial refuge in separationism since they were minorities who were often the targets of religious discrimination (as noted in Chapter 4, one's support for secularism is situational).

After some cases in the 1870s (involving Mormons) it was another seventy years before separation and the wall metaphor became relevant again. It is warranted to say that separationism as a binding principle only became operative in the 1940s when Justice Hugo Black invoked Jefferson's Danbury Letter in the *Everson v. Board of Education* (1947) case.

"The First Amendment," thundered Justice Black, "has erected a wall between church and state. That wall must be kept high and impregnable. We could not approve the slightest breach." As with Jefferson a century and a half before him, Justice Black interpreted the silences of the First Amendment in a separationist direction.

In 1960, John F. Kennedy, soon to be president, proclaimed "I believe in an America where the separation of church and state is absolute." With dizzying speed, separationist secularism had become the official federal policy. Non-denominational prayer in public schools was deemed unconstitutional (*Engel v. Vitale*, 1962) as was Bible-reading (*Abington School District v. Schempp*, 1963). The *Lemon v. Kurtzman* ruling (1971) stipulated that government action must have "a secular legislative purpose" and forbade "excessive government entanglement" with religion. In 1973 abortion was legalized in *Roe v. Wade*.

But then came the backlash from conservative religious groups that we will read about in Chapter 11. By the mid-1980s, via the *Wallace v. Jaffree* case (1985), the courts began to abandon separationism. In that case, Associate Justice William Rehnquist did some thundering of his own:

> It is impossible to build sound constitutional doctrine upon a mistaken understanding of constitutional history, but unfortunately the Establishment Clause has been expressly freighted with Jefferson's misleading metaphor for nearly 40 years ... The "wall of separation between church and State" is a metaphor based on bad history, a metaphor which has proved useless as a guide to judging. It should be frankly and explicitly abandoned.

For all intents and purposes, separationism as a judicial doctrine in the United States is dead. As we shall see later, the government has moved to a model closer to what is called accommodationism.

In terms of our ten secular principles, the separation framework leans on the *disestablishment/neutrality* principle. In fact it is almost identical. The hitch is that it tries to achieve that neutrality by demanding a stark division—a division that I and others believe is impossible to achieve.

WOBBLY SEPARATION

American secularism has always been unstable, wobbly. Hopefully our discussion above helps you better understand why that is.

To begin with, the project was nearly stillborn; there was tremendous religious resistance to Mr. Madison and Mr. Jefferson's "burning Zeal" for the ideas of Locke, Williams, and Luther. Just as the two American Founding Fathers were trying to install their own secular vision, the Second Great Awakening, a decades-long religious revival of tremendous intensity, was kicking into high gear across the new nation. That too stalled the advance of the *disestablishment* principle and the separationist framework.

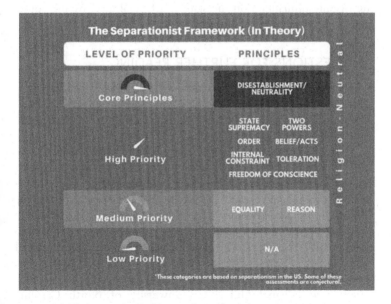

Figure 5.1 The separationist framework (in theory)

It certainly did not help that Jefferson was a polarizing figure; he was accused by his many enemies of being an atheist and a despiser of religion (he usually identified as a Unitarian, though once wrote that he was "a sect unto myself"). Yet the biggest problem about the religion clauses are the clauses themselves. Simply put, Madison's verses are too short and too ambiguous to provide a blueprint for an entire country, let alone one that would grow to be so large and religiously diverse.

That brevity and ambiguity gave rise to Mr. Jefferson's separationist reading. Yet his Wall metaphor has confused American secularism; the First Amendment is based on the deeper Lockean principle of state *disestablishment/neutrality*, but Mr. Jefferson thrust it into a separationist direction.

Amidst all this ambiguity and confusion, the job of interpreting those 16 words has been left to the judiciary. In the United States the courts are often pressured by partisan and political interests. The result has been that American separationist secularism is weak tea. It has lurched from irrelevance in the nineteenth century, to dominance in the mid-twentieth century. Now it is being systematically dismantled on the state and federal level by the courts and the advocacy of the Christian right (see Chapter 11).

SUGGESTIONS FOR FURTHER READING

The idea that American secularism is far less stable and coherent (and understood by scholars) than is typically assumed has been explored by me in "Let the Study of American Secularisms Begin!" *Critical Research on Religion*, 1, no. 2 (2013), pp. 225–232.

There are many excellent discussions of the American founding and the manner in which the religion clauses came into being. An fine primary source text is Forrester F. Church (Ed.), *The Separation of Church and State: Writings on a Fundamental Freedom by America's Founders* (Boston, MA: Beacon Press, 2004). A classic study of the period has been offered by John Witte Jr, "Essential Rights and Liberties of Religion in the American Constitutional Experiment." *Notre Dame Law Review*, 71 (1995), p. 371. Also see Leonard Levy, *The Establishment Clause: Religion and the First Amendment* (Chapel Hill, NC: University of North Carolina Press, 1994).

For more readings on Mr. Madison's state of mind and views about religion, see Phillip Vincent Munoz, "The Original Meaning of the Establishment Clause and the Impossibility of Its Incorporation." *University of Pennsylvania Journal of Constitutional Law*, 8 (2006), p. 585. It appears that Madison, unlike Jefferson, was not a staunch separationist, and perhaps not a separationist at all (interestingly, he spoke of "lines" of separation, not a "wall"). Historians looking deeper into his writings notice that Madison's true preference was to stipulate that the government should not take note of religion—an untested secular framework, called "non-cognizance" (see Glossary).

For the draftsmanship of Madison, also see Donald L. Drakeman, *Church-state Constitutional Issues: Making Sense of The Establishment Clause* (Westport, CT: Greenwood Press, 1991). For some recent studies of the establishment clause see the legal scholarship of Caroline Mala Corbin, "Opportunistic Originalism and the Establishment Clause," *Wake Forest Law Review*, 54 (2019), p. 617.

"Separation of church and state" is sometimes used as a definition or synonym of secularism. Hopefully, this chapter demonstrates why that is incorrect. For general studies of the nineteenth century and separationism, one should consult Philip Hamburger, *Separation of Church and State* (Cambridge, MA: Harvard University Press, 2009). Hamburger offers a much more critical reading of separationism, arguing that its exponents were often nativists and bigots.

Two important overview studies of American secularism are Noah Feldman, *Divided by God: America's Church-State Problem— and What We Should Do about it* (New York: Farrar, Straus and Giroux, 2005) and Martha Nussbaum, *Liberty of Conscience: In Defense of America's Tradition of Religious Equality* (New York: Basic Books, 2008).

On the "culture wars" see Christopher Clark and Wolfram Kaiser (Eds.), *Culture Wars: Secular-Catholic Conflicts in Nineteenth-Century Europe* (Cambridge: Cambridge University Press, 2003).

FRENCH SECULARISM
THE *LAÏCITÉ* FRAMEWORK

After separation, our second secular framework is known as *laïcité*.
To get ourselves situated, let's recall our skinny definition: *political
secularism refers to legally binding actions of the secular state that seek to
regulate the relationship between itself and religious citizens, and between
religious citizens themselves.* French *laïcité* is often criticized internationally for the overbearing manner in which it *regulates* the lives
of its religious citizens. The government, some complain, leans too
heavily on the secular principle of *state supremacy* and its license to
subordinate religion in the name of *order*.

In France, there is little ambiguity about "who's on top." *Laïcité*
demonstrates its supremacy by permitting itself to "exclude religion
from the public sphere and push it to the private domain."

In 2004, President Jacques Chirac signed into law a provision that
prohibited the wearing of conspicuous religious symbols or clothes
in primary and secondary schools. These included Muslim headscarves (including hijabs), Christian crosses, Jewish skullcaps, and
Sikh turbans. A similar law was recently forwarded that prohibits
those under eighteen years of age from wearing such symbols. In
2011 France's National Assembly and Senate banned Muslim
women from wearing the niqab (i.e., full face veil) in public.

Actions such as these would be unthinkable in the United States.
There, the state's subordination of religion is kept to a minimum.
In fact, the government tends to get out of religion's way, unless
provoked into some sort of confrontation. Even when provoked,
the American government often backs off. During the COVID-19
pandemic in 2020–2021, the Supreme Court repeatedly defended
the right of religious groups to worship communally in spite of

DOI: 10.4324/9781003140627-8

public health concerns about the spread of the virus. Let's recall that the American First Amendment actually *restricts* the government's power—it stipulates what Congress *cannot* do. Free exercise of religion in the United States is often given free rein.

France is a different story altogether. In this chapter we will briefly familiarize ourselves with the *laïcité* framework and its dramatic history. From there, we will consider some of the controversies that surround what is likely the most influential secular framework in existence.

FRANCE IS DIFFERENT

The best way to explain *laïcité* to puzzled Anglophone audiences is getting them to understand the seemingly obvious fact that France is not the United States. Its religious history, and culture are radically different. In the Great Chain of Secular Being, *laïcité* seems to have evolved "autochthonously," on French soil, in response to unique French dilemmas and through the mediation of French intellectuals. This accounts for why the *laïcité* framework is so unlike the American Separation framework.

The American model, as we learned in Chapter 2, descends from German Protestantism and British political philosophy. Some of separationism's intellectual ancestors are Martin Luther, Roger Williams and John Locke. Their thought deeply influenced those American Founders like Jefferson and Madison who were advocates for Enlightenment ideas.

French *laïcité*, however, developed independently of those Anglo-American traditions. Moreover, its "conversational partner" across the centuries was not Protestantism, but Catholicism (which had a far more antagonistic relationship with secular principles than Protestantism ever did). In Chapter 2 we noted Philippe le Bel's rather forceful insistence that a French monarch need not bend to the will of a pope. He thus set a precedent of "Gallicanism," a willingness on the part of some French rulers to challenge the supremacy of the church.

The intellectual influences are also starkly different. If British John Locke was a proponent of Enlightenment, then Gallic philosophers in the eighteenth century were proponents of *radical* Enlightenment. This school of thought was far more extreme, especially in its attitude towards religion. True, Locke cautioned us about the dangers of religion's union with the state. Yet as with so many Protestants before and after him, he feared that this union was also bad for *religion*. Political power, he believed, corrupted what was sacred and sublime about religious faith.

It's not that the French philosophers were soft on state power. They weren't. Yet they were also quite often hostile to organized religion in and of itself. They were particularly fixated on the French Church, the so-called "eldest daughter" of Catholicism. These eighteenth-century intellectuals, sometimes known as *les philosophes* (e.g., Voltaire, Diderot, Rousseau, d'Holbach) were usually culturally Catholic themselves. Yet their mistrust and dislike of their native faith had few parallels among Protestants thinkers in America.

Les philosophes had two obsessions, anticlericalism and materialism, which lent a particular edge to their critique. Anti-clericalism refers to skepticism of religion and its dogmas. Naturally, this skepticism extends to the personnel of organized religion, such as clergy and religious leaders. Many religious leaders in France had found ways to align themselves with the power of the monarchy, thus creating the most infamous, and doomed, *ancien régime* in all of history.

Another feature of the French radical Enlightenment thought was its commitment to materialism. This word can be defined in many ways. For our purposes, we should see it as an intellectual approach that rejects supernatural explanations of natural, social, and political processes. The materialist perspective eliminates gods, or ghosts, or spirits as variables which account for how our world functions. It seeks rational answers to life's mysteries.

Being materialist and/or anticlerical is not precisely the same as being an atheist. Most French radical Enlightenment figures believed in God. Some toggled between Deism (a form of belief that acknowledges a Supreme Being who does not meddle in human affairs), worship of the Goddess Reason, and so forth. Others may have been atheists but disguised their nonbelief for their own safety. As philosophers, they railed not against God per se, but types of inquiry that relied on metaphysical explanations. They also railed against institutions that claimed to represent God.

Anti-clericalism and materialism, as we shall see in later chapters, would travel more easily across the channel, than the ocean. British intellectuals in the nineteenth century were hugely influenced by anti-clericalism and materialism. American intellectuals, Jefferson and his colleagues notwithstanding, far less so.

THE TWO FRANCES

The often scathing materialist and anticlerical critique of these French intellectuals set the tone for what was to come. The first key period stretches across thirty years. It begins with the overthrow of *l'ancien régime* in 1789, to the bloody 1790s. After the French Revolution came Napoleon Bonaparte's rise as First Consul (1799), to his self-appointment as emperor in (1804), to his *two* exiles (1814 and 1815), and his death in 1821.

These three turbulent decades were littered with carnage, senseless domestic violence, and endless foreign wars. Throughout it all, many sorts of experiments and innovations in secular statecraft were put into play. In terms of the entire history of secularism, these decades must be seen as among the most intellectually consequential. Between 1789–1821, Mr. Jefferson and Mr. Madison's modest secular ideas were being mostly ignored in the United States. Meanwhile, French revolutionaries of different affiliations were spewing forth radical secular initiatives through what might be described as a network of heavily armed think tanks.

As they did so, they leaned on many of our secular principles, all the while adding unique flourishes. Let's begin with Article X of the Declaration of the Rights of Man and Citizen (1789) which states: "No one may be disturbed for his opinions, even religious ones, provided that their manifestation does not trouble the public order established by the law." Notice that the principle of *freedom of conscience* is recognized; religious opinions may not be "disturbed"— presumably by the authorities.

Also notice the inclusion of the *order* principle. Article X is so different from the Free Exercise clause of the United States (Chapter 5). The French version acknowledges one can manifest their beliefs in acts. Yet those acts cannot imperil public order.

The Civil Constitution of the Clergy of 1790 is full of innovations. Most astonishingly, it made the Church subservient to the government. The salaries of priests were to be paid by the state which now regulated their activities. Priests now had to take an oath of loyalty to the state. Those who didn't, the so-called "refractory priests," were either murdered (as between two-three thousand were), or exiled (as occurred to roughly 32,000). The boundaries of French dioceses were redrawn in a manner that stripped many Bishops of their coveted positions. The state was unambiguously supreme.

The revolutionary period is also known for a variety of "de-Christianizing" initiatives, the likes of which had never been seen before. These were not attempts to remove Christianity altogether. Rather, their intent was to loosen the vice-like grip that the Catholic Church had on all aspects of politics, culture, daily life, the economy, and so forth.

For example, the National Convention tried *to reorganize and rename time itself* (thus, they divided the year into ten day weeks, or *décades*, the last day of which was called *décadi* and served as a day of rest). The Christian calendar was annulled and traditional worship days abolished. There was also a short-lived effort to nationalize Church properties and sell them off to private interests.

Then came Napoleon Bonaparte who overturned some of these initiatives, while retaining others. In an agreement known as the Concordat (1801), Napoleon and Pope Pius VII hammered out a compromise between State and Church. Catholicism was now restored and described as "the religion of the great majority of the French people."

Napoleon did indeed help the Catholic Church claw back many of the privileges it lost during the revolution. Then again, he was not about to create a potent rival to his own authority. The old Gallican impulse resurfaced. He thus continued and even expanded existing policies in which the state was in control of all religions.

Priests and religious personnel remained *salaried* employees of France and had to swear an oath of allegiance. His government devised a system which made religious groups designate representative bodies that reported to, and were held accountable by, the state. Such agreements were signed with Protestant groups (1802) and the Jewish community (1806). Napoleon thus shared the revolutionaries' insistence that the state was explicitly on top.

Napoleon's form of governance was certainly not secular. By recognizing Catholicism as the majority religion there was a quasi "establishment" of religion. This would violate the *disestablishment/ neutrality* principle. But by doubling down on the idea of *state supremacy* and *order,* he made the subordination of all religions,

majority or minority, explicit. He thus followed the revolutionaries' impulse to get religion *explicitly under state control*. For many
scholars that is the true essence of *laïcité*.

The period from 1789 to Napoleon's death in 1821 was, overall,
a setback for the French Catholicism. One historian suggested the
church went from "half mistress of the realm" before the 1789
revolution, to "a pensioner of state" by the time of Napoleon's
death. In doing so, he planted the seeds of secularism that would
germinate later in the nineteenth century.

He also, inadvertently, built a platform for the "ultramontanism"
we discussed in the previous chapter. With the national Catholic
churches of Europe being laid low by liberal movements, the papacy
in Rome re-emerged as a potent counterbalance to emerging political
secularisms.

FROM THE CONCORDAT TO *LAÏCITÉ*

French history between the 1789 revolution and the end of World
War II can be seen as a long, bruising battle between "the two
Frances." One France, we can call *la vielle France* (the old France).
It was royalist, conservative, and traditionally Catholic.

The other, *la France republicaine* (the Republican France) was also
mostly Catholic, though within its ranks one found liberal Catholics, socialists, radical democrats, anarchists, Protestant minorities,
Freemasons and eventually Jews. The Republican France, culturally Catholic though it might be, was deeply suspicious of the
Church and committed to the ideals of the French revolution.

A similar dynamic, with similar players, developed during the
nineteenth century in other Catholic countries such as Spain and
Italy. Scholars sometimes use the term "adversarial nationalisms" to
describe a state in which the population was split between religious
conservatives and religious liberals, each with a very different
understanding of what their nation "stood for." Nowadays, a parallel division is seen in the United States and Israel. Though, there
the ranks of the religious liberals are increasingly swelled by the
"religiously unaffiliated" (see Chapter 13).

As we saw in Chapter 5, wherever and whenever secular initiatives sprang up in the nineteenth century, they encountered fierce
resistance. France is no exception. After Napoleon's removal,

Catholic France often conveniently aligned with monarchical, conservative, and even reactionary French rulers. Their coalition stymied the ideals of the revolutionaries.

It was in the turbulent period between 1879 and 1905 that Republican France, slowly and with many setbacks, began to gain the upper hand. The disputes were bitter and passionate. They occurred after episodes like the carnage of the Paris Commune of 1871 and during the tumult of Dreyfus Affairs in 1894–1906.

The battles between the two Frances centered on a variety of issues, the most important of which was education. The conflict was about what would be taught (i.e., a secular or a Catholic curriculum), and who would teach it (i.e., clergy or non-clergy). This reminds us that many secular controversies center on schools; whoever is on top gets to dictate how future generations will understand the world. This reminds us that *freedom of conscience* has its own contradictions. After all, if the state provides a non-Catholic education to Catholics isn't it shaping the conscience of the nation's youth?

In addition, the two Frances were drawn into disagreements about divorce. Divorce was legalized in 1792, abolished in 1816, and rendered legal again in 1884, much to the Church's chagrin. The pendulum swung back and forth, as it did across Europe experiencing a "culture war" in what we called the "fateful nineteenth."

The breakthrough for Republican France came with the "December 9 Law Concerning the Separation of the Churches from the State" ("Loi du 9 décembre 1905 concernant la séparation des Églises et de l'État"). Many assume it is some sort of Gallic reboot of Mr. Jefferson's Wall philosophy of the previous century. Yet anyone who reads its six chapters and forty-four articles will immediately understand that the French government is not committing itself to merely separating from the Church. Instead, it is articulating the ground rules of a new church-state relationship in which religious groups are explicitly subordinate to the latter (My guess is that the reference to "*séparation*" had more to do with cutting links between state and church made lawful by Napoleon's Concordat than separation in the Jeffersonian sense).

To read this detailed document is, once again, to see how the French state controls and regulates religion. Article 1 stresses *freedom of conscience*. It also grants Free Exercise, but with the provision that there must be *order*. Secular principles are being linked, and they are being operationalized.

Article 2 insists that "The Republic does not recognize, pay, or subsidize any religious sect." What's ironic is that this stipulation is followed by a bevy of exceptions which mandate when and how the state will subsidize religious sects. For instance, military chaplains will be paid by the state. In addition, since existing houses of worship and religious properties are now (in 1905) property of the state, then the future upkeep of these structures will be funded by the French government. This means that to this day, the state subsidizes Catholic churches that are grandfathered in through the 1905 law.

Article 28 points to a unique French obsession: prohibiting religious symbols in public spaces. This law extends way back to revolutionary days and it might be said that the French are very particular in believing shared public space belongs to the state. No one should be surprised by Article 27 which regulated when and how Church bells are to be rung. Once again, in the French system, the state controls religion.

Anti-secular forces staged a bit of a comeback during the period of Vichy France (1940–1944). The fact that remnants of *l'ancien régime* aligned with Nazism should indicate how bankrupt this reaction was. After World War II, Republican France had prevailed and the Church made its peace with secularism.

With the traditionalist column now vanquished, France could now explicitly claim its secular identity. The Constitution of the Fourth Republic (1946) and the Constitution of the Fifth Republic (1958) feature the exact same line: "La France est une République indivisible, laïque, démocratique et sociale." The translation is: "France is an indivisible, secular, democratic and social Republic." Unfortunately, the Constitution nowhere explains what is meant by the term *laïque*!

THE FRAMEWORK AND THE FUSS

Unlike its American counterpart, *laïcité* is *not* weak tea. It was forged in the tumult of a bloody revolution, followed by a century of bitter national conflict. What resulted was the 1905 Law: political secularism's first binding and comprehensive governmental application. In terms of the two-millennia history we have been tracing, the 1905 Law is political secularism's greatest accomplishment. We'll learn about its outsized influence on the rest of the world in subsequent chapters.

French *laïcité* is a much more robust and built-out secular framework than American Separationism. That's not only because of France's unique history and its influential and prickly intellectuals. The reason is much more mundane. The 1905 law is much longer than sixteen words! It thus works through secular principles in a much more comprehensive manner.

Laïcité, as we have seen, places a premium on *state supremacy* (or control of religion) in the name of *order*. It is essential to recognize, however, that *laïcité* is not some brute operation of force and coercion. There absolutely is a place for religion in France. It has no particular dislike of citizens of faith. This distinguishes it sharply from the Soviet Secularism we will soon study.

A true secular framework *balances* the different principles. *Laïcité* leverages its fondness for *state supremacy* against explicit commitments to *equality, internal constraint, freedom of conscience, the beliefs/acts distinction, and reason*. As for *disestablishment/neutrality,* in principle the state has no preference for any religion. Whether France complies with the neutrality principle is something we shall discuss in a moment.

Laïcité always has a religion that it argues with, an adversary. From 1789 to the end of World War II, the nemesis was the Catholic church. After that, *laïcité* scrummed with small religious groups like Scientologists and Jehovah's Witnesses. In the past few decades the collision has been with political Islam and radical militant Islamism.

We mentioned above the 2004 and 2020 laws prohibiting the wearing of religious attire in public. The law did not come out of nowhere. France's suspicion about public displays of religion stretches back to the 1790s. But many believe that these contemporary laws target Muslims and serve as a vehicle of Islamophobia. It's a fair point. We should never discount the likelihood of anti-Muslim discrimination in France. It is, after all, one of the few countries where secular policies are supported by the far right.

Another fair point, however, concerns France's legitimate fear of extreme transnational Islamist movements. Their role in everything

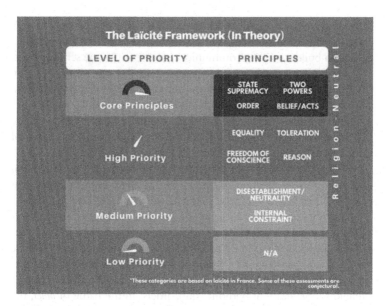

Figure 6.1 The *laïcité* framework (in theory)

from pushing strict veiling practices, to radicalizing imams, to supporting direct acts of violence cannot be denied. I mention this because much of the critique of *laïcité* is framed around the narrative of a state bullying a small minority (French Muslims are roughly 9% of the population). Yet today's secular states are confronted by formidable international actors who routinely meddle in national affairs. In so doing, they have created considerable threats to public safety.

These issues are complex. There is undeniable truth to the claim that the French state has underperformed in extending *equality* and *disestablishment/neutrality* to Muslim citizens and Islam respectively. The 1905 law provides an excellent example of how these principles have been violated, albeit unintentionally. As we saw above, the Law delegated government resources for the upkeep of existing religious buildings, most of which were Catholic properties. There were few Muslims in France at the time.

The 1905 law is still in effect. This means that while 90% of Catholic church buildings are subsidized by the government, mosques are not "grandfathered in." The rapidly growing French Muslim community has little recourse other than to seek foreign assistance to build mosques, community centers etc. As one scholar put it, the state is "governing a religious community that was not party to the [1905] settlement." This points to a serious failure of France to observe the *disestablishment/neutrality* and *equality* principles.

Yet, I repeat, that the issues are complex. For the past three decades France has endured horrific acts of violence at the hands of militant Islamists. In the aftermath of the beheading of a schoolteacher, Samuel Paty, in 2020, the extent of foreign radicalization became, once again, manifest. The government, in turn, has amplified its reliance on the *state supremacy* and *order* principles.

The response of the Macron administration was to issue a raft of "anti-separatism" measures. These laws demand that citizens sign "declarations of allegiance," prohibit home schooling, monitor online hate speech, etc. Moreover, President Macron proposed legislation that would allow the government to close down houses of worship and religious organizations without court orders. In the name of *order*, the state is ratcheting up its level of control—an escalation that inadvertently meshes with existing anti-Muslim sentiment on the far right.

While *laïcité* strikes critics as too aggressive in its treatment of religion, a few qualifiers are necessary. The first is that this aggression has been historically directed not just towards Muslims, but to *other* religions (notably Catholicism). It is thus crucial to tease out what is Islamophobic in French secular policy and what is simply France doing what it has been doing to religion since 1789. Both impulses are present in France today, and this recommends great analytical caution.

The second point to be stressed is that there *is* considerable religious freedom in France. People are all free to worship as they see fit, but within rules of *order* that strike outsiders, but not the French, as too severe. This brings us to our last and crucial point. The overwhelming majority of the French population supports *laïcité*. In poll after poll the population views it as a core national attribute. To use Locke's term, it has "the consent of the people."

SUGGESTIONS FOR FURTHER READING

There is no lack of quality studies about *laïcité*. I would suggest Henri Pena-Ruiz, *Qu'est-ce que la laïcité?* (Paris: Gallimard, 2003);

Jean Bauberot, *Histoire de la laïcité en France*. (France: Presses universitaires de France, 2003); and Jon Bowen, *Why the French Don't Like Headscarves: Islam, the State, and Public Space*. (Princeton, NJ: Princeton University Press, 2010). On the 1905 law see David Saunders, "France on the Knife-edge of Religion: Commemorating the Law of 9 December 1905 on the Separation of Church and State," in *Secularism, Religion and Multicultural Citizenship*, edited by Geoffrey Brahm Levey and Tariq Modood (Cambridge: Cambridge University Press, 2009), pp. 56–81; and James McMillan, "'Priest Hits Girl': On the Front Line in the 'War of the Two Frances,'" in *Culture Wars: Secular-Catholic Conflicts in Nineteenth-Century Europe*, edited by Christopher Clark and Wolfram Kaiser (Cambridge: Cambridge University Press, 2003), pp. 77–101.

On the resistance to secular ideas in nineteenth-century Italy see Francesco Margiotta Broglio, "La laïcité en Italie, pays concordataire," in *La laïcité à l'épreuve: Religions et libertés dans le monde*, edited by Jean Baubérot (Paris: Universalis, 2004), p. 77–94. On Spain and "adversarial nationalisms" see Joseba Louzao Villar, "Catholicism versus Laicism: Culture Wars and the Making of Catholic National Identity in Spain, 1898–1931," *European Historical Quarterly*, 43 (2013), pp. 657–680.

INDIAN SECULARISM
THE ACCOMMODATIONIST FRAMEWORK

To this point, we have learned about two secular frameworks. The United States gave us separation which emphasizes the *disestablishment/neutrality* principle. In our study of France we surveyed, *laïcité*. This framework doubles down on *state supremacy*.

Our third framework comes to us by way of the Republic of India. There, secularism is regarded as a basic and integral part of the Constitution that was adopted after independence in 1947. In 1976 an amendment was added to the document's preamble that made this status explicit. It declared India to be a "sovereign, socialist, secular, democratic republic." Just as with the French Constitution, which nowhere defines the term *laïcité* (see Chapter 6), the Indian Constitution never tells us what "secular" means.

I will use the term accommodationism to describe India's particular secular framework. What undergirds accommodationism is the idea that religion, in and of itself, is something that the state has an interest in promoting. The core belief is that supporting religion is good for the people and hence good for the state.

India thus provides us with a "religion-positive" secular framework. This type of secularism seeks to accommodate all religious faiths equally (in order to strengthen the state). It emphasizes the *equality, toleration, freedom of conscience,* and *disestablishment/neutrality* principles all at once.

How different this all is from *laïcité*! The anti-clerical suspicion of *all* religions seen in France is nearly absent in India. Many Indians view their civilization as deeply spiritual, unthinkable without its various faiths. Accordingly, there are few restrictions on public

DOI: 10.4324/9781003140627-9

displays of religion. That French conceit strikes most Indians as unnecessary, a killjoy, and even bizarre.

In India, a premium is thus placed not on controlling, but *assisting* religion, especially religious minorities. Some examples of this support include government funding and administration of religious schools, Hindu temples, the Islamic Central Waqf Council, Buddhist monasteries, and Christian institutions. Most controversially, the government permits Muslims to abide by Sharia law and maintain their own courts and legal infrastructure.

In this chapter we will introduce you to India's accommodationist framework. In order to do that we will first need to consider the effects of Britain's rapacious colonial rule from 1612 to 1947. From there, we will familiarize ourselves with the manner in which a newly independent India melded British "pseudo-secularism" with its own innovations.

BRITISH COLONIAL SECULARISM

Great Britain, the birthplace of John Locke, was not, and is not, a secular state. Since 1534, and until this very day, England has had an establishment of religion in the form of the Church of England. Likewise, the Church of Scotland has been the national Church of Scotland since the sixteenth century. (The Welsh Church is Anglican in orientation.)

There was no nineteenth-century British equivalent of powerful secular-minded leaders like Jefferson and Madison (there were power*less* secular-minded intellectuals who we'll meet in the next chapter). Had there been such parallel figures in Britain, they likely would have been stymied by the same religious opposition that confronted political secularism across Europe during "the fateful nineteenth."

Yet in a sinister twist, the British did impose secular principles of statecraft—not on their own land, but on their colonial holdings in the South Asian subcontinent. Secularism, as far as the British were concerned, was good for "them," but not for "us." And with that, we can begin to understand some of the animus we see today towards secularism; it is viewed by many as the lieutenant of Western colonialism.

To grasp what the program of British colonial secularism entailed, let's glance at an edict of 1858. This was one year after the Sepoy Mutiny commenced. During this episode Indian soldiers, Muslim and Hindu alike, rebelled against the British East India Company. Their uprising, which spread far and wide, was partly triggered by the religious insensitivity of the colonizers. What ensued was a chain of events that led to massive fatalities, perhaps numbering in the hundreds of thousands, or even more.

In response, the British Crown formally took charge of ruling British India. Through the Government of India Act of 1858 it flooded the land with edicts. Eventually this addendum was proclaimed by Lord Canning on behalf of Queen Victoria:

> Firmly relying Ourselves on the truth of Christianity, and acknowledging with gratitude the solace of Religion, We disclaim alike the Right and the Desire to impose our Convictions on any of Our Subjects. We declare it to be Our Royal Will and Pleasure that none be in any wise favored, none molested or disquieted by reason of their Religious Faith or Observances; but that all shall alike enjoy the equal and impartial protection of the Law: and We do strictly charge and enjoin all those who may be in authority under Us, that they abstain from all interference with the Religious Belief or Worship of any of Our Subjects, on pain of Our highest Displeasure.

The proclamation *sounds* secular. In a way it is. The Queen invokes the *disestablishment/neutrality* principle (e.g., "We declare it to be Our Royal Will and Pleasure that none be in any wise favored"). She voices the *equality* principle ("all shall alike enjoy the equal and impartial protection of the Law"). The *toleration* principle, *order* principle, and *belief/acts* distinction are also identifiable ("that none be in any wise favored, none molested or disquieted by reason of their Religious Faith or Observances"/"that they abstain from all interference with the Religious Belief or Worship of any of Our Subjects").

As regards other principles, there is no *state supremacy* per se, because there is no state. Rather, there is a colonial overlord. The British Raj's mechanisms of *internal constraint* are rather flimsy since the empire is not greatly interested in governing the people or heeding their will. Britain is in India as a colonizer; the people are "subjects," not citizens. Secular rule, instead of being an end in and of itself within a broader platform of democratic governance, is simply a means of dominating "unruly" religious charges.

That domination facilitated Britain's continued economic exploitation of India's people and natural resources. The lofty secular aspirations of Locke, originally aimed at maintaining peace between hostile Christian sects, were retooled. Now they served as a mechanism to protect Britain's quest for raw materials, cotton, spices, textiles, and agricultural rents.

Yet even as a means of maintaining *order* and placating "unruly" religious subjects, British colonial secularism failed. India had known religious conflict prior to the arrival of the British. Studies show, however, that after the British arrived there was *more* religious conflict.

The pseudo-secularism of the British Raj invites us to confront the darker potential of secular rule. John Locke's desire for *order*, after all, was a desire for order within his *own* society. What the British in India used their half-baked variant of political secularism for was something entirely different. Namely, it functioned as a command–and–control operation atop a civilization that was not their own.

THE HYBRID?

American secularism is very "Anglo" and influenced by Protestantism. French secularism is very Gallic and influenced (negatively) by Catholicism. Trying to pinpoint the identity of Indian secularism is more complicated.

Like the French, but unlike Americans, Indians nowadays have a tradition of discussing, debating, and analyzing political secularism quite thoroughly and intelligently. It is a topic of national interest that has attracted great scrutiny from leading scholars, jurists, journalists, religious leaders, and so forth. Not surprisingly, these experts disagree on the identity of Indian secularism.

For some, Indian secularism is nothing but a hollow vestige of British colonial rule. As such, these critics advise the nation to cast it off immediately. Only in this manner will this ancient civilization rediscover its own pre-colonial governing arrangements. This argument is shared by conservative religious figures *and* leftist intellectuals (see Chapters 12 and 13). Needless to say, those are two groups that rarely agree on anything else.

Other authorities, however, contend that accommodationism has deep roots in India's rich past. For these writers, core secular principles are an organic part of south Asian culture. They refer to the Buddhist emperor Ashoka in 250 BC who anticipated the *toleration* principle when he averred: "There should not be honour of one's own (religious) sect and condemnation of others without any grounds."

Many point to the sixteenth-century Mughal emperor Akbar (1542–1605) as a proto-secular ruler. A Muslim by birth, Akbar showed an interest in learning about other spiritual traditions, arbitrated disputes between religions, and seemed more than willing to override Sharia law. Influenced by Sufism, he believed in the equality of all religions, and accommodated others, as when he built a Hindu temple in Kashmir.

Some have called attention to philosophers who advocated skepticism and maybe even atheism. Thus while the French had *les philosophes*, India had the ancient Charvaka school of materialism. In a civilization as old and intellectually rich as this one, it is not surprising that so many ideas anticipated those that later developed in western Europe.

Aside from a past that may have featured "proto-secular" impulses, the Indian present created distinct problems to be solved. Consider the demographics. France with its tiny percentage of Protestant and Jewish minorities was a virtual Catholic monoculture. Britain and the United States were dominated by different Protestant sects.

India, by contrast, was multicultural to the core—a vast multi-ethnic, multi-linguistic, and multi-religious land. The presence of large religious minority groups, we shall see, raised very particular governing challenges. India had to solve those during independence and continues to wrestle with them today.

Our preference, then, is to cautiously suggest that Indian secularism is a hybrid. It employs some Western principles and concepts. At the same it customizes them with its own sensitivies, solutions and innovations. The result is something totally new and quite dynamic.

NEUTRALITY VERSUS EQUALITY

When the British finally did withdraw in 1947, India's legislators set out to chart the country's future. Unlike America's religion clauses, India's constitutional pronouncements on these issues were the result of intensive deliberation.

The pro-secular triumvirate of Mahatma Gandhi (1869–1948), Prime Minister Jawaharlal Nehru (1889–1964), and B. R. Ambedkar (1891–1956) were among the many who deliberated upon the Indian Constitution between 1947–1949. Each man was in favor of secular arrangements, though each had a different conception of secularism in mind.

True to its hybrid nature, Indian secularism incorporates many edicts that can be sourced to British colonial rule. In 1937, the British enacted the Muslim Personal Law (Shariat) Application Act which permitted Muslim subjects to live by Sharia law. The 1950 Constitution did nothing to change the status quo (though it suggests via the non-binding Directive Principles of State Policy that in the future the nation should move towards a "Uniform Civil Code"). So the legality of Muslims living by Sharia law moved from the colonial period, to Independent India, and exists to this day—albeit precariously since the present government wants a Uniform Civil Code.

The significance of this should not be underestimated. It means that Muslim citizens in India can abide by *two* parallel codes of law: civil law and Sharia law. From a secular perspective, even an accommodationist one, this creates massive complications. Women's rights, for example, tend to suffer when they are subject to two legal systems, especially when each is dominated by men and steeped in patriarchal assumptions.

Why didn't the Indian Constitution, with its three secular architects, try to annul sharia law?

One reason is that Gandhi, at least, made much of equality and toleration. He spoke of *sarva dharma samabhava*, "equal respect for all religions." This entailed letting Muslims follow their laws to the greatest extent possible. Such is a good example of how unique cultural sensitivities pervade Indian secularism.

Another likely reason is that the framers were legislating against the backdrop of a full-blown ethnic/religious war in the Punjab. When the partition occurred on August 14–15, 1947, British India became two states, Pakistan and India. Violence intensified between the fledgling nations. Nine million Muslims were displaced to Pakistan.

Yet 35 million Muslims remained within the borders of India. With Pakistan veering towards becoming an Islamic republic, gestures of good will toward India's Muslim minority were deemed necessary (though it's often forgotten that at its formation in 1947, the founder of Pakistan, Mohammad Ali Jinnah, advocated a vision for his nation that was for all intents and purposes a form of political secularism. It was soon thereafter scotched). It would not have been prudent for the Hindu majority to aggravate their compatriots by eliminating Sharia law and mandating only Uniform Civil Code.

Secularisms, we are learning, can be very messy. India is no exception. Three core secular principles were being championed in the Indian Constitution: *equality* of all believers, and *toleration* for minority rights via the *disestablishment/neutrality* principle. The problem was that they were being championed in a way that made them collide into one another.

Gandhi and his colleagues thought it essential for the massive Muslim minority to feel that they were equal Indian citizens within a Hindu majoritarian state. To do that, they carved out exceptions, such as the non-annulment of the Muslim Personal Law (Shariat) Application Act of 1937. These exceptions, paradoxically, appeared to give Muslims *greater* rights than others, thereby undermining the *equality* principle. By the same token, these accommodations tend to take rights away from Muslim women and sexual minorities who may be subject to discriminatory interpretations of sharia.

As for other issues, the 1950 Constitution is deeply committed to secular principles. Its preamble guarantees *freedom of conscience*. Articles 15 and 16 intimate the *equality* and *disestablishment/neutrality* principles. They prohibit discrimination by the state on the basis of religion and in the field of employment. Article 28 declares no religion will be taught in schools entirely funded by the state.

The *order* and *belief/acts* principles are defended by Article 25 which stipulates: "persons are equally entitled to freedom of conscience and the right freely to profess, practise and propagate religion" as long as they do not threaten "public order, morality, and health." As noted above, Indian secularism rarely pushes religion into the private realm; propagation is legal (another striking difference with France).

Article 30 permits minorities to establish their own schools. It then mentions, somewhat cryptically, that when the state grants aid to these schools it will not "discriminate against any educational institution on the ground that it is under the management of a minority, whether based on religion or language." The implication is that the government will in fact partially fund the schools of a religious minority.

The result is, once again, that minorities may have educational options not available to the majority. "Minority appeasement" is a term used by today's Hindu nationalist critics of Indian secularism. To them, the Muslim minority would seem to be the beneficiary of greater privileges. They further allege that liberal political parties like Congress harvest huge Muslim voting blocs by supporting this "communalism" in the name of "secularism." To others, these privileges granted to the minority were a form of just compensation for the discrimination and second-class status that they faced.

Nowadays, there are 200 million Muslims in India, making it one of the two largest Muslim-populated countries in the world. In Chapter 11 we will meet the current ruling "anti-secular" BJP party of India—it insists that secularism does not treat all faiths equally. Instead, the BJP claims, it favors, or over-accommodates, the Muslim minority.

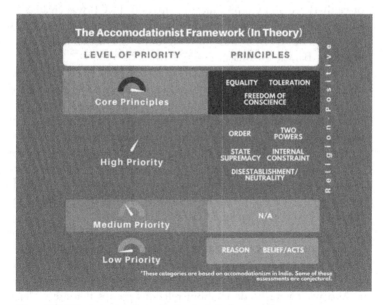

Figure 7.1 The accommodationist framework (in theory)

LEEWAY

The religion-friendly accommodationist framework has many positive attributes. I speak not only of its willingness to materially support all religions. In Gandhi's thought there is another assumption that is likely very attractive to many. In his perspective, the secular state should give religious groups the maximal benefit of the doubt and as much leeway in conducting their affairs as possible.

Accommodationism blunts a lot of political secularism's sharp statist edges. It maintains that the state should intervene in a religious group's life only as a last resort and due to potential risks to the public. This "leeway" idea is the polar opposite of what one encounters in *laïcité*.

For these reasons, accommodationism may have a promising future as an export. It has already made inroads in the United States. In Chapter 5 we noted that separationism in that country has been abandoned. In its place, recent American presidents have created government bureaus whose task was to partner with faith-based organizations. The highly controversial White House Office of Faith-Based and Community Initiatives (OFBCI) was created by George W. Bush in 2001 (his first Executive Act). To everyone's surprise, The OFBCI was super-sized by the *liberal* Democratic president Barack Obama in 2009.

The OFBCI distributes funds to charitable faith-based groups. Its many predictable failures have incensed American secularists. But it does mark a shift in the United States from the separationist framework to an accommodationist one. It also testifies to the vitality and potential adaptability of India's ongoing experiment in secular governance.

That said, there are a few kinks to be worked out in the accommodationist framework. Let's imagine that a secular government sets aside a billion dollars to accommodate religious groups that need funds for the upkeep of their houses of worship. How exactly is that pot divided?

In India, for example, should Hindus receive four times more because they are roughly four times the size of the Muslim population? Conversely, should the government pay attention to need and thus support the poorest religious groups more generously?

Also what is to be done about religious groups that are violent, or seditious, or highly critical of the state and other faiths? Is the government required to accommodate them as well? In the United States, should a soup kitchen run by, let's say, an explicitly racist and anti-Semitic religious group (such groups do exist) be eligible for financial support from the OFBCI? If not, what is the legal rationale for that exclusion?

The single biggest looming drawback of accommodation, however, concerns non-religiously affiliated people. As we shall see in Chapter 13, their ranks are growing rapidly. If the state views religion as a social good, then doesn't this implicitly devalue citizens who are religiously unaffiliated? It would seem that this positive attitude towards religion is a breach of the *disestablishment/neutrality* and the *equality* principles. The religious are valued more by the state than the non-religious.

CONFUSION IS NOT HELPFUL

When in 2015, the Indian Parliament member and former BJP president Rajnath Singh referred to "secular" as the "most misused word in the country," he spoke to this book's central obsession. For now we'll forgo an attempt to get into some very complicated questions regarding Hindi translations of the term "secularism." Instead, we simply repeat: confusion about secularism's meaning is never a good thing for secularism.

Consider the massive confusions created by this analysis from a BJP party website (that would be Rajnath Singh's BJP):

> The western vision of looking at a man is divided. Its individualism is the enemy of socialism and socialism is the enemy of individualism. They want the victory of man over nature; here nature versus man is their equation. By adopting secularism, they have snapped spiritualism from the public life. Therefore, dialectical equations of materialism versus spiritualism, state versus church and religion versus science have emerged.

The quote is remarkable in how much it diverges from what we've just learned. In this reading secularism is Western, individualist, materialist, anti-spiritual, anti-environment and deeply alienating. The quote we just read is a caricature—not of Indian secularism, but of *laïcité*!

The politics of Prime Minister Narendra Modi and his BJP party are decidedly anti-secular. Every month brings a fresh round of micro- and macro-aggressions directed from the *government* towards the Muslim minority. A recent example being laws to prevent the so-called "love jihad," or instances of Muslim men marrying Hindu (or Sikh) women. Reports of nationalist gangs working extra-legally with law enforcement officials to enforce endogamy have alarmed many in India. In the words of one commentator, secularism's future in India seems "gloomy." Indian secularism, like American secularism, is being dismantled from within.

Conservative political actors have risen to power through free and fair elections. Old allies (like the Congress party in India, and the Democratic party in the United States) are downplaying or walking away from their previous commitments to secularism. In both countries, the rights of minorities, be they religious, gender or sexual, hang in the balance.

SUGGESTIONS FOR FURTHER READING

India's secularism, as noted above, is perhaps the most intensely and intelligently studied national secularism in the world. There is an embarrassment of riches pertaining to nearly every aspect of this subject. Above, I referred to Indian secularism as an example of "accommodationism," though sometimes other writers use different nomenclature.

For general studies, I would suggest, Abhinav Chandrachud, *Republic of Religion: The Rise and Fall of Colonial Secularism in India* (India: Viking, 2020); Shabnum Tejani, *Indian Secularism: A Social and Intellectual History, 1890–1950* (Bloomington, IN: Indiana University Press, 2008); Amartya Sen, *The Argumentative Indian: Writings on Indian History, Culture, and Identity* (New York: Farrar, Straus and Giroux, 2005); Shefali Jha, "Secularism in the Constituent Assembly debates, 1946–1950," *Economic and Political Weekly* 37, no. 30 (2002), pp. 3175–3180; and Ganesh Prased and Anand Kumar, "The Concepts, Constraints and Prospects of Secularism in India," *The Indian Journal of Political Sciences* 67 (2006), pp. 793–808.

On the indigenous secular tradition in India, see Iqtidar Alam Khan, "Medieval Indian Notions of Secular Statecraft in Retrospect," *Social Scientist* (New Delhi), 14, no. 1 (1986), pp. 3–15.

For information on the current state of "love jihad," see "Hindu Vigilantes Work with Police to Enforce 'Love Jihad' Law in North India," available at https://theintercept.com/2021/07/03/love-jiha d-law-india.

On women in secular countries subjected to dual legal codes see Pascale Fournier and Jacques Berlinerblau, "Reframing Secularist Premises: Divorce among Traditionalist Muslim and Jewish Women within the Secular State," *Secularism and Nonreligion*, 7 (2018). An attempt to correlate secularism with economic policy in India is made in Jacques Berlinerblau and Shareen Joshi, "Modi's India: Optical Neoliberalism In! Secularism Out!" *Culturico* (March 17, 2021), available at https://culturico.com/2021/03/17/modi s-india-optical-neoliberalism-in-secularism-out.

SWERVES
SECULAR*ISM* AND ATHEISM

Now our story takes a fascinating swerve. Three swerves actually—a swerve in one new direction and then, immediately after that, a swerve in another. Then a few decades later, yet another swerve. That last swerve changed history.

To this point our narrative has routed us through ancient Palestine, India, and Europe. We have moved from biblical times, through Medieval Christendom, into the Reformation, and then into the Enlightenment. In each case, secularism was understood to be a political program regulating a state's relationship with religious groups and the relationships of the groups themselves.

Then, in the nineteenth century, came two swerves. The first occurred when the Englishman George Jacob Holyoake (1817–1906) started writing about and promoting something called Secular*ism* (I add the italics from here on in to refer to Holyoake's specific usage of the word even though he did not use italics). As with a few anglophone writers in the decades before him, he added the fashionable -ism suffix to the ancient stem, "secular."

Secular*ism*, as defined by this British freethinker, had very little to do with politics, subordinate religious groups, or the *order* principle. Rather, Holyoake depicted it as a philosophy and a system of personal ethics. One could—one must—he insisted, lead a secular *life*. That life would be led in accordance with the precepts of Secular*ism* that he was describing.

That's a far cry from the way figures like Luther, or Williams, or Locke, or Jefferson, or Madison, thought about the word "secular." They never used the precise term Secular*ism* (because it didn't

DOI: 10.4324/9781003140627-10

exist until Holyoake's generation put it into play). Instead, they used variants of the term "secular," without the -ism. To them it wasn't a philosophical or ethical system. It wasn't a lifestyle choice. To them, it was merely an adjective. It modified words like "government" or "authority," or "leaders."

This brings us to the second swerve. Holyoake was ferociously criticized by one of his fellow British freethinkers. This critic was a colleague, a one-time friend, a fierce professional rival and "the foremost nineteenth-century unbeliever in the British empire." Charles Bradlaugh was his name and this charismatic, hot-headed man insisted that Holyoake was wrong. Secular*ism*, he declared, was *atheism*, not some abstract philosophy.

I have spoken of the confusions that surround the S-word. The most common contemporary misperception is that secularism and atheism mean the same thing. We are about to learn when that error likely set in: the 1870s, around the time of a debate between Holyoake and Bradlaugh that we shall scrutinize below.

Once we understand this episode from the Victorian era, it will position us to study our third swerve, the one that changed history. This would be the rise of Soviet (atheist) secularism in 1917, which we will explore in the following chapter.

FREE SPEECH

Holyoake and Bradlaugh lived during a time when the British Raj was imposing colonial secularism on South Asian subjects abroad (see Chapter 7). While doing that, the British government was imposing *anti*-secularism on its citizens at home. Among those anti-secular measures, aside from an establishment of religion, were hard restrictions on free speech. And if the speech in question concerned the Christian religion, the "blasphemer" was about to encounter trouble.

Freedom of conscience, we have seen, has been a major tenet of secularism since the time of Luther. Its derivative, *freedom of speech*, is also a principle of secularism, albeit one that entered the discussion a bit later. It is not entirely clear to me at what point in history it became bundled in with discussions about secularism. It certainly sits close to the religion clauses in the First Amendment (i.e., "Congress shall make no law … abridging the freedom of speech, or of the press.").

But to the best of my knowledge, the tight, explicit connection between free speech and secularism first occurs in Victorian England (1837–1901). Interest in free speech can be traced to John Milton's 1644 *Areopagitica*, and England's 1689 Bill of Rights. John Stuart Mill in *On Liberty* famously argued that freedom of thought and freedom of expression were "practically inseparable." Chalk this up as yet another contribution to secularism by Britain, a country that *still* has an establishment of religion!

Freedom of conscience and *freedom of speech* are not identical. All the political secularisms we have seen so far agree that "thought is free." All concur that you can think or believe anything you want. Yet they all limit your ability to act on those thoughts via the *belief/acts* distinction. If your religious convictions threaten order, then you are liable to be penalized for acting upon them.

Freedom of speech is distinct from *freedom of conscience*. The latter is a private mental act that can become a physical act. The former involves not a physical act, but a communicative one— be it spoken, screamed, written, sculpted, and/or performed in an artistic context. It's easier to police speech than it is to police conscience.

Every secular nation places limits on what you can communicate. For instance in the United States you can't engage in speech that incites or produces "imminent lawless action" (*Brandenburg v. Ohio*). In France, Holocaust denial is illegal (the Gayssot Act). India banned the import of Salman Rushdie's *The Satanic Verses* in 1988 for being insulting to Islam. This last incident reminds us that the arts are often an arena in which freedom of speech controversies play out.

In nineteenth-century England, you could run afoul of the law for a speech act critical of Christianity (in fact, blasphemy laws were only repealed there in 2008). If we think of George Jacob Holyoake as the father of Secular*ism,* then he was propelled to that position because of a crackdown on his expressive liberty which we turn to now.

BLASPHEMY

In 1843, Holyoake, a freethinker, recounted the story of a lecture he gave in Cheltenham—a lecture which, apparently, went very wrong. After the address, an audience member (a "religionist") grilled Holyoake about God, his fellow man, etc. One thing led to another, the conversation got heated. Holyoake's response to the gentleman was "garnished with a simile." Next thing he knew, Holyoake was "apprehended *without a warrant*," and sentenced "to six months imprisonment in Gloucester County Gaol, for this liberty … taken with Christian doctrine." While he was imprisoned his young daughter who was ill, passed away.

Holyoake's incarceration did little to shut him up or down—a truth which teaches us that when authorities try to suppress speech, they may create even more problems for themselves. He described his ordeal in a cheeky piece published in 1843 called *A Short and Easy Method with the Saints*. The "liberated blasphemer," as his fellow Victorian infidels called him, was now a hero. Suddenly, he had a national platform to express his thoughts.

And upon that platform, the young Holyoake relentlessly lambasted the national faith. "The boasted leniency" of Christianity, he complained, "extends only to those who wear the mask of orthodoxy." In a theme that coincides with the *reason* principle and the *freedom of speech* concept we just discussed, he charged that Christian censorship retards the growth of the "arts and sciences to which we owe our rise as a nation." "The genius and tendency of Christianity," sighed Holyoake, "is intolerant persecution."

There is a clear link in Holyoake's thought to the French radical enlightenment philosophers we read about in Chapter 6. The anticlerical rage is clearly present. The themes of the corruption, close-mindedness, and hypocrisy of religion are prominent. So too, as we shall see, is the emphasis on materialism, or the idea that little can be explained by spiritual or metaphysical causes.

There are intellectual common denominators between eighteenth-century France and Victorian England. Voltaire was read widely on both sides of the Channel. As was Thomas Paine's very popular work *The Age of Reason*. Paine agitated in France and England, and spent time in the prisons of both countries for his efforts!

Though there are a few crucial differences between the Victorians and the French philosophers. For starters, Holyoake and his fellow infidels were focused on Protestantism, not Catholicism. Further, the French of the eighteenth century were a tiny group of brilliant, idiosyncratic individuals with unusual training, skills and talent.

The population of British freethinkers was much larger. It may have been small in proportion to the rest of the country. But whereas the French anti-clerical writers numbered in the dozens or hundreds in the eighteenth century, the Victorian infidels numbered in the thousands and perhaps tens of thousands at their peak. They were a movement—the first "secular" movement in history.

Last, there was a class dimension which distinguished England from France. Holyoake and his cohort were not elites like the French *philosophes*, but mostly working-class men and artisans. They floated in sometimes overlapping socialist, communist, unionist, utopian and millenarian circles. Amidst the dislocation of Britain's rapid, and dizzying, industrialization, a space was cracked open in the nineteenth century for skilled and common laborers to visit anti-clerical and materialist ideas.

THE PRINCIPLES OF SECULARISM

Although the dating is a bit in doubt it would appear that Holyoake first made use of the term Secular*ism* in 1851. Over the next few decades his popularity waxed and waned as he drifted in and out of the vibrant, fractured freethought moment. As he aged he mellowed considerably.

Through it all he lectured widely on the subject and wrote numerous pamphlets and books. In those texts he addressed the question we've been breathlessly asking and answering throughout this study: What is secularism?

If that question, to this very day, is hard to answer, then some of the blame rests with the wise and humane George Jacob Holyoake. His ideas on Secular*ism* are not only inconsistent with how the term "secular" was used in the centuries before him (see below). They are also *internally* inconsistent. By which I mean that within his own work he defines Secular*ism* in numerous and contradictory ways.

In his 1871 *Principles of Secularism* Holyoake equated it with (1) "making the service of others a duty of life," (2) positivism, (3) materialism, (4) utilitarianism, (5) naturalism, (6) free thought, (7) sincerity, (8) humanism, and (9) rationalism, among other connotations. Not all of these concepts, obviously, are the same thing.

Still, reading through Holyoake one can sense that some of these themes receive greater emphasis than others. He opens *The*

Principles with this aside: "Secularism is the study of promoting human welfare by material means." The emphasis on materialism directly links Holyoake to the French philosophers before him.

Central to his thought is the idea that Secular*ism* is this-worldly, geared to the here and now. "Secularism," writes Holyoake, "concerns itself with the work of to-day." Holyoake overlaps just a bit with Augustine's notion of the *Saeculum* discussed in Chapter 2. But whereas the *Saeculum,* where mortals toiled, was a degraded, sinful, place for Augustine, for Holyoake the current moment is full of hope and wonder and charitable tasks.

What Holyoake wants secularists to do is improve the world by committing themselves to public service. "Secularism teaches," he avers, "that the good of the present life is the immediate concern of man." In a later work, *English Secularism*, Holyoake affirmed that "it is good to do good."

The mechanism for doing all of that good is science. In perhaps the most memorable line In *The Principles*, he writes: "Science is the available providence of life." This meshes with Holyoake's lifelong interest in rationalism. In *Rationalism: A Treatise for the Times* (1845), he opined that "Rationalism advises what is useful to society without asking whether it is religious or not … and declares that from the cradle to the grave many should be guided by reason and regulated by science."

It is here where *freedom of speech* enters the conversation about Secular*ism*. For science and rationalism to flourish there must be robust protections of expressive liberty. In order to create knowledge that is helpful to humankind, Holyoake identifies three freedoms. The first is the "Free search of truth." That is followed by "the Free utterance of the result." Last, comes "the Free Criticism of the Alleged truth." Secular states, as we saw above, all arrogate to themselves the right to *limit* free speech. Holyoake never explored what those limits might be.

A few other dimensions of Holyoake's thought need to be stressed here. One is his interest in issues pertaining to women. This too may be considered a swerve; it seems like the whole of political secular thought up until 1851 had not one word to say about women. One of the major contributions of the Victorian infidels was to place this issue forevermore on the secular agenda.

As regards women, it is estimated that they comprised roughly 12 percent of the official membership of the free-thought movement. The interests of the Victorian infidels centered around the right to vote, the right to divorce, "free union," and the use of contraceptives, among other initiatives. Most were highly critical of existing gender roles. They blamed the existence of such roles on the stranglehold which the Bible possessed on British culture.

Holyoake wrote reverently, and perhaps cloyingly, about women. The following passage is characteristic: "Any one woman in her own individuality and experience is unlike all others. A man possessing the love of an honourable and intelligent woman, has a priceless treasure worthy of constant preservation in the casket of his affections." Kind as these sentiments may be, many of his free-thinking brethren found him to be too stuffy and conservative on women's issues. This, as we are about to learn, isn't the only instance where his colleagues found fault with him.

SWERVES 1 AND 2

We are now positioned to understand the first and second swerves or radical changes in the historical trajectory of secularism. For reasons that I cannot explain, Holyoake did not connect his thinking on Secular*ism* to the eighteen centuries of thought on political secularism that preceded him.

Here and there, he alludes to issues related to what *we* have been calling political secularism. Thus in *English Secularism* he comments: "The State should forbid no religion, impose no religion, teach no religion, pay no religion." This pithy remark appears to make Holyoake a Separationist Secularist who emphasizes the *disestablishment/ neutrality* principle. Yet Holyoake, who clearly read Luther and Locke, etc., never saw fit to delve deeply into the political workings of a secular state. This baffling disconnect with the past constitutes the first swerve.

There is, however, one definition of Secular*ism* that Holyoake explicitly and categorically rejected: atheism. He was adamant that Secular*ism* was not atheism. It was a distinction that he was eager to make at every turn. Given that Holyoake was legendary in freethought circles, his denial of any link between Secular*ism* and non-belief was equivalent to taunting his own crowd. This precipitated the second swerve.

Holyoake had a penchant for making cryptic statements, as when he called Secular*ism*: "a religiousness to which the idea of God is not essential, nor the denial of the idea necessary." The confusion increased when he set Secular*ism* above theism and atheism, though welcomed *both* believers and atheists into his new movement's ranks.

Holyoake's Victorian audience was a marginalized and eclectic group of individuals. Many of them had negative views about, and experiences with, religion. Some were veering into atheism. In doing so, they risked widespread ridicule and reprimand. To many of Holyoake's followers, his conception of Secular*ism* was utterly perplexing, even infuriating. As was his increasingly respectful and indulgent attitude towards people of faith. What ever happened to the young atheist firebrand?

Maybe a new, younger atheist firebrand should lead the movement?

ATHEISM AND SECULARISM

Charles Bradlaugh was that firebrand. Brilliant, arrogant, bellicose and larger than life, he played the role of the angry atheist to perfection. When Bradlaugh ran for, and was elected to parliament in 1880, he wore his nonbelief and dislike of Christianity on his sleeve. Formal admission to the House of Commons required swearing a religious oath. Bradlaugh's reputation as an atheist led many of his colleagues to doubt that any oath he would utter was sincere.

They used this as a pretext to not seat him. This created a lengthy national scandal. Bradlaugh kept trying to take his rightful seat. He was once dragged out of parliament and imprisoned. Only in 1886 did he win his six-year battle to perform his duties as a member of Parliament.

His colleague was Annie Besant, a freethinker of considerable stature. In 1877, Besant re-published a pro-contraceptive tractate by Charles Knowlton entitled *The Fruits of Philosophy, Or the Private Companion of Young Married People*. Its endorsement of what we would now call "family planning" created an uproar. So much so that more conservative freethinkers left the National Secular Society and formed a rival organization, the British Secular Union.

Prior to all of this Bradlaugh and Holyoake had a two-night debate about Secular*ism* in 1870. Their contretemps foreshadows the tensions that will divide atheist movements in the West for the next century and a half. Holyoake urged moderation and suggested building coalitions with like-minded believers. He doesn't want to waste time arguing about theology. Bradlaugh, sounding a bit like a New Atheist (see Chapter Thirteen), wanted to fight the Christian powers that be and prove theology to be illogical and dangerous.

Holyoake argued that atheism and theism are speculative, they deal with things that are unknowable. Therefore neither can ever "be made the basis of a Secular philosophy of life, which is limited by time and regulated by human experience." Lest the point be missed, he stressed: "Secularism is not Atheism, although many Secularists are Atheists." Holyoake showed that he was thinking of Secular*ism* as a big tent. It would welcome "liberal theists" and "liberal believers."

Bradlaugh, for his part, would have none of it "I hold," he roared, "that the logical consequence of Secularism is the denial, the absolute denial of a Providence." "In my opinion," he continued, "the logical consequence of the acceptance of Secularism must be that the man gets to Atheism; if he has brains enough to comprehend." Elsewhere, the future MP peppered his comments with asides about destroying the priesthood and "war against religion."

Neither speaker seemed particularly interested in discussing political secularism. In one short comment, Bradlaugh would show himself to be a proponent of disestablishment and making religion and "speculative opinion" equal before the law. By this Bradlaugh meant that freethinkers would have the same rights as Christians— a provocative claim for the time, but not one he elaborated upon.

The debate foreshadowed the coming fractures of the movement. Holyoake would become the respectable grand old man, Bradlaugh the polarizing figurehead. Yet because of internal tensions, poor leadership, and the conservatism of the Victorian era, freethought would never generate mass appeal.

Bradlaugh's atheist secularism would remain a radical and embattled minority position in Britain. Yet it certainly paved the way for titans of anticlericalism such as Bertrand Russell (1872–1970) and Richard

Dawkins (1941–). Bradlaugh may also be recalled for having engi-neered a hostile takeover of the term "Secularism" on behalf of atheism.

As for Holyoake's Secular*ism*, it lived on almost entirely as an encyclopedia entry, without spawning an actual movement. To this day, lazy writers who need a quick definition of secularism consult their reference books. They read about Holyoake and then write of Secularism as if it were Secular*ism*—an ethical system that seeks to make the world a better place through science, rationality, and kindness to one's fellows.

CONCLUSION

Holyoake's Secular*ism* burst upon the scene in the mid-nineteenth century (swerve 1). It was soon challenged and interrupted by Bradlaugh's atheist intervention (swerve 2). The Victorian era, then, marks the moment where Secularism and atheism first became entangled with one another.

The irony is that both Holyoake's Secular*ism* and Bradlaugh's secularism-as-atheism stood at a remove from—swerved away from—any serious engagement with all the thinking on political secularism which came before them. As we shall now see, a different triangula-tion occurred in the Soviet Union. Holyoake's Secular*ism* faded into obscurity. This left atheism and political secularism to find one another, become fused, and radically alter the future (swerve 3).

SUGGESTIONS FOR FURTHER READING

Figuring out when and who first used the term "secularism" is a bit difficult. The best treatment is that of Phil Zuckerman and John Shook, "Introduction: The Study of Secularism" in *The Oxford Handbook of Secularism*, edited by Phil Zuckerman and John Shook (New York: Oxford University Press, 2017) pp. 1–17. The period itself is captured through a variety of books such as Michael Rectenwald, *Nineteenth-Century British Secularism: Science, Reli-gion, and Literature* (New York: Palgrave Macmillan, 2016); and Edwin Royle, *Victorian Infidels: The Origins of the British Secularist Movement, 1791–1866* (Manchester: Manchester University Press, 1974).

Many of George Jacob Holyoake's original writings quoted above are freely available online. They include: *Rationalism: A Treatise for the Times* (London: J. Watson, 1845); *The Principles of Secularism Illustrated* (London: Austin & Co., 1871); and *English Secularism: A Confession of Belief* (Chicago, IL: The Open Court Publishing Company, 1896).

The debate described in this chapter is enshrined in George Jacob Holyoake and Charles Bradlaugh, *Secularism, Scepticism, and Atheism* (London Austin & Co., 1870).

An interesting study of Holyoake is Lee Grugel, *George Jacob Holyoake: A Study in the Evolution of a Victorian Radical* (Philadelphia, PA: Porcupine Press, 1976).

A key work on gender in this period is Laura Schwartz, *Infidel Feminism: Secularism, Religion and Women's Emancipation, England 1830–1914* (Manchester: University of Manchester Press, 1917).

ATHEIST SECULARISM
THE SOVIET FRAMEWORK

The two Victorian swerves we just studied are, in the grand global sweep of history, relatively minor occurrences. Holyoake and Bradlaugh are largely unknown to anyone but students of secularism. The third swerve, however, is anything but minor.

Our final framework will be referred to as Soviet (atheist) secularism. It came into being soon after the October 1917 revolution in Russia. It was then that the Bolsheviks, led by the philosopher and militant, V.I. Lenin ousted the Provisional Government which just a few months prior had overthrown the Romanov dynasty and the Imperial Russian Empire (1721–1917).

Lenin and his victorious Bolsheviks quickly set about erecting their new society. This project included executing their enemies, among whom were many members of the Russian Orthodox Church. The revolutionaries built up their state in accordance with their reading of Karl Marx's (1818–1883) writings on historical materialism. As part of achieving Marx's vision of a communist, religionless society, they established a new framework of secularism. It served as an integral part of governance from the formation of the Union of Soviet Socialist Republics (USSR) in 1922, to its expiration in 1991.

In many ways, Soviet (atheist) secularism is the most consequential development in the history of secularism. Consequential because it spread to "successor states," like Cuba, Cambodia, North Korea, Vietnam, and most importantly China, among others. That many consider Soviet secularism (and its afterlives) to be a disastrous development, might account for why some try to disavow that it was ever a form of political secularism to begin with.

DOI: 10.4324/9781003140627-11

This is not an entirely unreasonable disavowal. Soviet secularism *does* diverge significantly from other secular frameworks. Then again, it checks the boxes and displays some undeniable genetic resemblances to secularisms we have studied in our previous chapters. At the very least, a study of how the Soviet framework bundles together secular principles, and creates a new one, (i.e., *freedom from religion*, see below) can help us understand why so many are skeptical of the secular project itself.

LINKS AND CHAINS

Throughout this book we've tried to gain a better grasp of the poorly understood links among global secularisms, or what I have called the *great secular chain of being*. The political secularism that developed in the USSR was placed in the service of a rigid Leninist reading of Marxism. For that reason, it had many, shall we say, "unique" features. Let's figure out how Soviet (atheist) secularism was similar to, and different from, other political secularisms. Our question being: which previous secular developments influenced the model that emerged in Russia?

George Jacob Hoyoake's ethical Secular*ism* was not on the minds of the Soviets. His credo (e.g., "it is good to do good") does not seem to have left much of a mark on V. I. Lenin and Joseph Stalin. It is possible, however, that those autocrats may have been familiar with the thought of the more radical atheist thinker, Charles Bradlaugh.

The conduit between England and Russia would be Karl Marx whose writings the Bolsheviks revered like sacred scripture. During his London days, Marx knew of Bradlaugh. He disliked him and reportedly tarred the freethinker as the "pope of atheism." Bradlaugh, for his part, was a high-profile opponent of Marxism.

In any case, the Russian revolutionaries—hardscrabble militants with all sorts of historical scores to settle—had good reason to reject the Victorian infidels as role models. After all, the British freethinkers were a minority party. They were wracked by infighting and lack of discipline. They had no experience of governing, or connection to state power. If there is one thing the Bolsheviks had after the October 1917 revolution, it was access to state power.

So did the French Jacobins in the 1790s. With that we come to Soviet secularism's closest influence and relation: French *laïcité*.

THE FRENCH CONNECTION

Any discussion of similarities between Soviet secularism and *laïcité* must be conducted carefully. There is a tendency among critics to argue that the failures of the USSR are representative of every secular state, past, present, and future. Anti-seculars (who we will meet in Chapter 11 and 12) often point to the mass murder and human rights abuses that characterized the Soviet Union as evidence of the bankruptcy of *all* political secularisms. For these reasons, we must be precise in how we describe these links.

It is undeniable that the Russian revolutionaries looked to France for instruction and inspiration. They admired the French Revolution, the Leftist agitations of 1848, and the ill-fated Paris Commune of 1871. They often performed the French national anthem, "La Marseillaise," as a means of paying their respects. Lenin was often reproached by his own comrades as "the Russian Robespierre."

Soviet secularism does display historical and structural similarities to French *laïcité*. Both came into being as a result of an epic conflict with *l'ancien régime*. The Jacobins revolted against the union of the Bourbon monarchy and the Catholic Church. The Bolsheviks harbored equal hatred for the union of Czars and the Russian Orthodox Church.

Like the French in the 1790s, the Russian anti-religious program was extreme. They tried to cancel Christian holidays, override Christmas, and so forth. As with France, the opening act of the Russian revolution was gory. In Paris, Louis XVI and Marie Antoinette were guillotined. In Yekaterinburg, the entire Romanov family was executed in cold blood. In France there was "the Reign of Terror." In Russia, there was the Red Terror. Both resulted in massive carnage.

The histories of *laïcité* and Soviet secularism begin to significantly diverge in terms of what happened after the first act of the revolution. Jacobin rule and French Directory of the 1790s, as we saw in Chapter 6, gave way to Napoleon in 1799. As far as state-sponsored dislike of religion goes, his ascension ushered in a "cooling off" period which lasted a century.

Napoleon's Concordat partially re-centered the Catholic Church in France's political, cultural and social existence. It resulted in

"Two Frances," adversaries that kept each other in check until one prevailed in 1905 (Chapter 6). The murderous anti-clerical impulses that surfaced in the 1790s were extinguished.

While France endured a momentary spasm of anticlerical violence between 1790 and 1799, Soviet aggression against religious citizens ran rampant for a quarter century. After the 1917 revolution, millions of people were murdered by the state because of their religious beliefs. If Lenin could be compared to Robespierre, Joseph Stalin did not play the Napoleon role and unlink anticlericalism from massive state power—at least until 1941.

With World War II raging, Stalin suddenly reversed his anti-religious policies and relaxed decades of persecution that nearly decimated the Russian Orthodox Church. For reasons pragmatic, not sentimental, he rebranded the old enemy as "patriotic." With that gesture, he somehow secured their support in fending off the German onslaught. Stalin's reversal, obviously, came way too late for the untold millions he murdered. In any case, after his death in 1953 hostilities towards all religious groups soon resumed.

THE UNIQUE FEATURES

What made Soviet secularism distinct from other political secularisms, especially *laïcité*? My own view is that the difference lies in how it synergized two popular tenets of Communist thought. Each tenet existed in previous secularisms, but was never amplified to this extent, never read through a Marxist lens, never twinned with one another, and never yoked to the type of unchecked governmental power brandished by the Soviets. The first tenet would be an extreme anticlerical orientation. The second was a desire for a society in which all citizens subscribed to the tenets of "scientific atheism."

We first took sight of anticlericalism in the French radical Enlightenment and, later, Victorian Britain (Chapters 6 and 8). Among the Soviets, however, anticlerical ideology was taken to a completely different level. The Bolsheviks didn't merely construe religion as a menace to society. Instead, they viewed it as *something that should be eliminated*. The conceit can be traced back to a particular Soviet reading of Karl Marx.

In a famous essay entitled "On the Jewish Question" the young Marx called for the abolishment of religion. Interestingly, that appeal was never a major theme in either his or his co-author Friedrich Engels's work. They wrote a great deal about capitalism. They pondered its inner workings and how its demise would come about. Their observations on religion, by contrast, were far less plentiful. What few observations they did make were quite ambiguous; a great deal of space was left open for later generations of communists to explore.

Most Marxists agree that the mere existence of religious belief is the sign of an underlying problem or "contradiction" within a society's economic base. In Marxist parlance, religious belief was "superstructural." This means that religion was the symptom, not the cause of a society's illness. That's why Marx and Engels devoted so little attention to this issue. After all, who tries to treat a sneeze, when the source of the sneeze is the flu?

In orthodox Marxist theory, one analyzes the means of production and the relations of production. One rails against the existence of private property and tries to undo the material conditions that make it possible. One attempts to bring about revolution to liberate the working class from ruthless bourgeois exploitation. But what does one do about religion?

History, argued Marx, is naturally progressing from capitalism, to socialism, to communism. As for religion, it's just a symptom, a sneeze; it should disappear by the time we transition to socialism. And as far as Marx was concerned, the transition to socialism is inevitable because that is where history is going.

From the Bolshevik perspective, the dilemma was that religion in their country was aligned with the interests of Russian nobility and the bourgeoisie. The Russian Orthodox Church, in the mind of the revolutionaries, was a dangerous foe—a foe that didn't appear eager to obey Marx's law and simply wither away. What was to be done with a foe which Marx told us was just an effect, not a cause?

Many Soviet communists resolved this ambiguity in the most frightful way imaginable. Marx prophesied that the disappearance of religion was bound to eventually occur anyhow. The revolutionaries set out to *accelerate* the process. Whether this was a correct application of Marxist theory is not for us to determine. We simply observe that this was Lenin's, and then Stalin's, reading, and it was animated by their boundless rage towards the Russian Orthodox Church.

In the period 1917–1941, the Soviet state used not only coercive tools of violence, but consensual ones to pursue its goal. Through the law, through education, through culture, through media, through every possible organ, the state endeavored to abolish religion. This emphasis on mechanisms of "consent" or convincing people as opposed to brutalizing them, by the way, is the hallmark of the philosophy of the great Italian Marxist political philosopher Antonio Gramsci (1891–1937). Still, the Soviets used far more coercion than Gramsci would have found acceptable.

This is where the aforementioned "synergy" between anticlericalism and atheism occurred. For the Bolsheviks didn't only want to abolish organized religion. In addition, they wanted to replace it with something called "scientific atheism."

Nothing like this is seen in France in the 1790s. Full-blown atheism was a minority position among the Jacobins (in fact, there were very few atheists anywhere on earth during this period). Many were deists, or worshipped the Goddess Reason. Some wanted to strip Catholicism back down to its essentials, simplify the church, and start clean from there, under God.

The Russian revolutionaries, by contrast, were all atheists as per party rules which prohibited religious believers in its ranks. They assumed power with a determination to eliminate religion *and* put nonbelief in its place. To achieve this the Soviet authorities tried to make the population abandon its faith through a program of "scientific atheism."

They established bodies like the League of Militant Atheists (1925) as a means of moving the population to a materialistic worldview. The de-Christianization initiatives included everything from lecture programs, to the creation of atheist museums (often built on seized church properties), to denying Party membership to religious believers. The task of converting people to "scientific atheism" was a virtual state industry in the USSR, employing tens of thousands of people, until the program was abruptly cancelled during World War II.

Predictably, these ventures failed again and again (the Soviets never really mastered the Gramscian art of achieving consent). Some Soviet citizens did abandon their religion. But most kept their faith in secret or quietly embraced other religions that the clumsy, inefficient Soviet bureaucracy was incapable of properly monitoring. The failures would be comic if it weren't for the cat-astrophic toll on human life wrought by the twinned programs of abolishing religion and implementing atheism.

STATE, PARTY, CONSTITUTION

Now let's take a look at how extreme anticlericalism and atheism were codified into Soviet laws. One caution before we start: a major drawback of trying to understand secularisms through laws and constitutions is that they often don't say what they mean and don't mean what they say. For example, nowhere is it specified that the Soviet Union was an atheist state, but as we shall see, it certainly was.

This constitutional non-compliance occurs in numerous coun-tries, though in the Soviet Union there is an added dimension of imprecision. This would be the (meaningless) distinction between the Communist Party and the state. In *Socialism and Religion*, Lenin famously wrote: "We demand that religion be held a private affair so far as the state is concerned." Lenin then adds a new variable: "But by no means can we consider religion a private affair so far as our Party is concerned."

Lenin is drawing a distinction between state and party. The problem is the distinction is completely fictional. The Communist Party ruled the state and the party was not about to consider reli-gion "a private affair."

Almost immediately after the October 1917 Revolution, a "Decree on Separation of Church and State" was released. The reader might have noticed that its title sounds very much like France's 1905 law which we surveyed in Chapter 6. The very name of the decree substantiates our caution about taking law codes at their word. For while it bills itself as separationist, the truth of the matter is that the USSR *never wanted to separate church from state*. Rather, it set out to ruthlessly control, subordinate, dominate and decimate the Russian Orthodox Church (and soon after, other religious groups).

From the outset, the party constantly meddled in the "internal affairs" of the churches. It hand-selected leaders. It monitored religious personnel and parishioners through formal registration processes. It flooded congregations with informants. It inventoried every possession under every steeple. In Soviet Russia there was anything *but* a wall of separation between church and state.

So while the 1918 Decree sounds separationist, it is more like an extreme, malevolent and homicidal mutation of *laïcité*. The French influence is apparent in Clause 9 which forbids the teaching of religion in public schools, or private schools "where general subjects are taught." In a move aimed to reduce the economic power of the churches, they were prohibited from levying tithes or collections on their members. Naturally, all Church properties were nationalized.

By 1929 a new set of laws mandated that all religious associations of twenty persons or more must register with the state. This Napoleonic flourish resulted in harsh rules such as this one:

> Religious associations are prohibited from ... organizing religious or other meetings specially intended for children, young people or women, biblical or literary meetings, groups, sections, circles, or handicraft meetings, religious instruction, etc., excursions, or children's play-groups, or from opening libraries, reading rooms, sanatoria, or providing medical aid.

By 1936, as the Stalinist purges nearly wiped out the Russian Orthodox Church, a new Constitution was ratified. Its religious legislation adds something new. Article 124 reads

> In order to ensure to citizens freedom of conscience, the church in the U.S.S.R. is separated from the state, and the school from the church. Freedom of religious worship and *freedom of anti-religious propaganda is recognized for all citizens* [emphasis mine].

Once again, these are illusory statements. Though the reference to "freedom of anti-religious propaganda" was all too real and correlates with the Soviet program of "scientific atheism."

As noted above, Stalin changed course strategically in the 1940s. Useful in the war and rebuilding efforts, the church became the "patriotic vanguard." But lest we think that the problem was Lenin and Stalin and not the system itself, we need look no further than First Secretary of the Communist Party Nikita Khrushchev. Despite his reputation as a liberalizer he reignited a vicious crackdown on numerous religious groups between 1959 and 1964.

IS SOVIET (ATHEIST) SECULARISM A SECULARISM?

Now we arrive back to the complex question we posed above: Is Soviet (atheist) secularism a form of political secularism? The USSR usually met the criteria which on paper would qualify it for this designation. Complicating matters was the tendency of the Soviets to enshrine secular principles in their constitutions and law codes, but to violate those principles in their actions. The best I can say is that the USSR conforms to our elementary definition of political secularism, but in a minimalist and upside down sort of way.

In its constitutions it acknowledged the existence of religion and thus superficially recognized that there were *two powers*. By now the reader can grasp that the USSR performed *state supremacy* to perfection (though it might be more accurate to speak of "Party" supremacy). There was little ambiguity as to who was on top. This is political secularism of the lowest common denominator: a state that is distinct from, and superior, to religion(s).

Naturally, the idea of *order* was stressed. Though the rationale was a bit unusual by traditional secular standards. *Order* was deemed necessary because *religion itself*—as opposed to strife between religious groups—was seen as a threat to the Soviet Union's existence.

This is very different from Locke's conception. For him, *order* was necessary because of specific feuds that developed between and among specific religious denominations. But religion itself, as far as Locke was concerned, was not seen as a direct threat to the state. On the contrary, the state wanted it to flourish. It goes without saying that Soviet (Atheist) Secularism is a "religion-negative" framework.

As for the *reason* principle, it is undeniable that the USSR produced scientific and technological advances. To a great extent it tried to guide its public policy on the basis of science and reason. What is peculiar about the Soviets, however, was the attempt to use the *reason* principle to nullify *toleration* and *freedom of conscience*. The regime cracked down on *religion itself* because it contradicted the Party/state's commitment to the *reason* principle in the form of scientific atheism.

While numerous Soviet law codes extolled *freedom of conscience,* how could that exist in a state committed to obliterating religion and replacing it with scientific atheism? (Obviously, the sub-tenet, *freedom of expression* was disregarded as well). The *belief/ acts* distinction was also inoperable since the party was committed to eliminating certain types of beliefs and eliminated certain types of people in pursuit of that goal.

Then there were the components of the secular vision that were never implemented or forcefully suppressed. There was no *equality*. Ironically, in a communist system whose goal was radical equality, the USSR was stratified across numerous dimensions, one being that religious citizens had fewer rights. *Internal constraint*, which could have been granted through a functioning judiciary, was nearly non-existent.

As for *disestablishment/neutrality*, this must be handled carefully. At some points, the state was neutral insofar as it harassed all religions equally (though in others it focused its wrath on particular faiths). In some ways, this conforms to the definition of *neutrality* but not in any manner seen in other political secularisms. This is what I meant by the "upside-down" dimension of Soviet secularism.

To this we should note that the Soviets operationalized a new secular principle: *freedom from religion*. As with all secular principles, the sentiment had existed in vague form for centuries. What the Communist Party did was to elevate *freedom from religion* to an explicit right of the party/state *and* the individual citizen. In fact, they didn't just elevate *freedom from religion*. They were so obsessed with this idea that it essentially pulverized *almost every other secular principle. Freedom from religion*, as we shall see in Chapter 13, is definitely poised to be made a principle of other twenty-first century secular frameworks.

Some charge that it is incorrect to categorize the Soviet framework as a secularism. For it tried to establish a religion—a religion of godlessness (to that, we might add, it deified its leaders in very unsecular ways). Though to the best of my knowledge an explicit avowal of atheism as a state religion was never codified. The closest we might come to that was Article 37 of the 1976 Albanian Constitution, which declared: "The state recognizes no religion and supports and develops atheistic propaganda to engage people in the materialistic scientific worldview."

Is an establishment of "scientific atheism," or in the Albanian case, "the materialistic scientific worldview" equivalent to an establishment of religion? If so, then it is fair to cast doubts on the secular standing of what we have called Soviet (atheist) secularism.

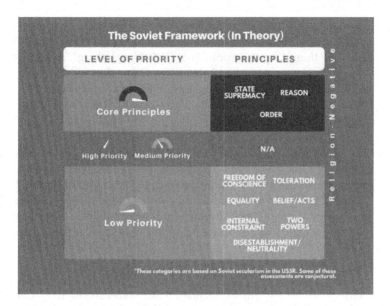

Figure 9.1 The Soviet framework (in theory)

SWERVE 3

The period 1850–1922 in Europe is crucial for the history of global secularisms. It is during that interval when our three swerves occurred.

Ignoring the centuries of thought about political secularism that came before him, Holyoake's ethical Secular*ism* burst upon the scene (swerve 1). It was soon challenged and interrupted by Bradlaugh's atheist intervention (swerve 2). A few decades later a potent mix of atheism and political secularism took hold in Soviet Russia (swerve 3).

How these events are all connected (or not) is still unclear. The only common denominators across all three swerves are anticlericalism and materialism. Much more research needs to be conducted, especially about the Russian and British links.

Yet the result of these sudden swerves was to drown nearly all forthcoming discussions of our subject in total confusion. What is political secularism? Is it a philosophy? An anti-metaphysical movement? A way of regulating relations between government and religion? Some combination of all of these? A French thing? A Russian thing? An American thing? A liberal thing? A socialist thing? A communist thing? Ever since the days of Holyoake, secularism has become an increasingly unruly and multivalent term. Perhaps the reader understands why we started this book with a plea for terms to be defined.

That being said, our job is to make sense of, not succumb to, the confusion. We now have at our disposal a clear inventory of different sorts of political secularism. So far we have encountered four operative secular frameworks: (1) separationism, (2) *laïcité*, (3) accommodationism, and (4) Soviet (atheist) secularism. Let's now turn to other countries that were influenced by these secular models and customized them in their own unique ways.

SUGGESTIONS FOR FURTHER READING

Serious studies of atheist secularism are exceedingly rare. One important exception to that rule is the collected volume Tam T. T. Ngo and Justine B. Quijada (Eds.), *Atheist Secularism and its Discontents: A Comparative Study of Religion and Communism in Eurasia* (New York: Palgrave Macmillan, 2015).

On Lenin embracing the link with French Jacobins see Jay Bergman, *The French Revolutionary Tradition in Russian and Soviet Politics, Political Thought and Culture* (New York: Oxford, 2019); and Robert Mayer, "Lenin and the Jacobin Identity in Russia," *Studies in East European Thought*, 51 (1999), pp. 127–154.

For general studies on religion in the Soviet Union see Catherine Wanner (Ed.), *State Secularism and Lived Religion in Soviet Russia and Ukraine* (New York: Oxford University Press, 2012), which paints a picture of a Communist leadership that was more pragmatic in its response to religion; Bohdan Bociurkiw, "The Formulation of Religious Policy in the Soviet Union," *Journal of Church & State*, 28 (1986), p. 423; John Anderson, "The Council for Religious Affairs and the Shaping of Soviet Religious Policy," *Soviet Studies*, 43, no. 4 (1991), pp. 689–710; Michael Bourdeaux, "The Black Quinquennium: The Russian Orthodox Church 1959–1964," *Religion in Communist Lands*, 9, no. 1 (1981), pp. 18–27; Paul Froese, "Forced

Secularization in Soviet Russia: Why an Atheistic Monopoly Failed," *JSSR*, 43 (2004), pp. 35–50; and William Husband, "Soviet Atheism and Russian Orthodox Strategies of Resistance, 1917–1932," *Journal of Modern History*, 70 (1998), pp. 74–107.

EMBRACE COMPLEXITY!
TURKEY, ETHIOPIA, CHINA

If our first rule for the study of secularism is "*define your terms!*" and our second, "*define other people's terms!*," then our third is "*embrace complexity!*"

Political secularisms are *technically* complex. A lot of variables—cultural, historical, sociological, ideological—need to be taken into consideration as we try to make sense of why a given secular state does what it does (or fails to do what it is supposed to do). Then there is *moral* complexity. Secularisms operate in contexts that make it difficult to simply conclude they are "right" or "wrong." However, this chapter introduces us to much that is "wrong."

We are now going to glance at three countries which have adopted and adapted different secular frameworks. One followed *laïcité* (Turkey). One embraced separationism (Ethiopia). One took up Soviet (Atheist) Secularism (China). Each introduces a new wrinkle, feature, or dilemma. And each ratchets up the complexity around the subject of political secularism.

TURKEY: KEMALIST SECULARISM

In 1923, under the leadership of Mustafa Kemal Atatürk (1881–1938), the Republic of Turkey officially came into being. Within a matter of years, the Ottoman empire, whose founding stretched back to 1299 AD, was disassembled and reconfigured as a modern nation-state and secular republic.

The pre-history of Turkish secularism resembles that of other secularisms we've studied. For starters, there was a long, bitter nineteenth-century struggle with *l'ancien régime*. On the one side,

DOI: 10.4324/9781003140627-12

was a modernizing and westernizing column of reform-minded "Young Turks." Resisting them, fiercely at points, was the ruling Sultanate aligned with the *ulema* (or body of religious scholars and interpreters) of Sunni Islam.

Then there is the spell cast by France. The Turkish model of political secularism is referred to as *laiklik*. Its name indicates its debt to *laïcité*. The secularizing Turks, like the Bolsheviks, were enchanted by Gallic ideas. These included anti-clericalism, the *reason* principle, the drive to modernize, and a preference for nationalism (as opposed to maintaining a sprawling, unruly empire). Naturally, *laïcité* also showed Turkish reformers a system of governance in which religion was not "on top."

Another parallel might be referred to as "rapid combustion." It usually takes political secularisms a very long time to achieve a foothold in politics and law. But once they do, they implement changes quite quickly. Think of how much dynamic transformation there was in France immediately after 1905, Russia after 1917, and the United States after the 1940s.

In Turkey, the window between 1923 and 1937 was equally transformative for *laiklik*. The Turkish Grand National Assembly enacted a series of sweeping reforms. In 1924, the Directorate of Religious Affairs (the *Diyanet*) was established (see below). In 1926, the Swiss, Italian, and German legal codes replaced shariah law. By 1928, Islam was no longer recognized as the official religion of the state. By 1937, Turkey was constitutionally defined as "a democratic, secular, and social state."

Once installed, Kemalists (as followers of the charismatic leader were called) presided over an authoritarian, one-party secular state. The Turkish example gives credence to one of those moral dilemmas mentioned above. Political secularisms tend to neutralize the one source of social organization (i.e., religion) that can effectively resist authoritarianism.

This is true. It is also true that religions themselves can function as the handmaidens of authoritarianism. The perfect political secularism achieves some sort of balance. Which means it must regulate *itself*. Eventually, the Kemalists made gestures towards regulating their own power, but with poor results.

There was just enough *internal constraint* for the Kemalists to endorse a multiple-party system in 1946, and open elections in 1950. *Laiklik* permitted a trickle of democracy. What resulted, though, was a wave of consistent support for leaders who Kemalists, especially those in the military, opposed.

It is a peculiarity of Turkish history that the nation has been periodically convulsed by military interventions. No country has more names for their coups, be they "soft coups," "e-coups," "postmodern coups," "judicial coups," etc. Post-1950, the following cycle kept recurring:

1   parties which the Kemalist establishment disliked gain power in open elections;
2   working within Turkey's secular framework these parties enact policies that may be more popular with Islamists;
3   Kemalist generals intervene, overthrow the elected government; and
4   install secular leaders they prefer.

Coup attempts occurred in 1960, 1971, 1980, 1997, 2002, and (under a non-Kemalist regime) 2016 with different causes and results. So much for *order*.

THE CONSENT OF THE PEOPLE?

An Islamist party, the AK, presently rules Turkey. The moderate and modernizing religious alternative it promised has never materialized. After a hopeful start, the government of Prime Minister, and then president, Tayyip Erdogan devolved rapidly.

The regime displays all the vices that secularists warn about—corruption, kleptocracy, fanaticism, cults of personality, puritanism, goonery, the curtailing of civil rights, women's rights, freedom of expression, etc. Though as much as political secularism would like to shout "*I told you so!*," the truth is that *laiklik* had plenty of its own self-inflicted failures.

Laiklik presents two theoretical issues of interest. The first concerns the *disestablishment/neutrality* principle. It has often been alleged that the secular Turkish state was *never* neutral. The accusation was *not* that *laiklik* was atheist. Nor was it charged with being irreligious or even opposed to religion (a motto of the regime was "laicism does not mean not having a religion").

Instead, critics contended that the Kemalist state endorsed and basically established a non-fundamentalist brand of Sunni Islam.

Thus, the recurring conflict in Turkey was not between atheists and fundamentalists, but rather "two sects of Islam vying for power and competing politically." What Kemalists promoted was "an Islam in their own image." This was a lighter, "protestantized" version of Sunni Islam. Islam became a private affair, a matter of individual conscience. "Islam-lite," some have called it.

Yet the Kemalists endorsed a religion nonetheless. It is not difficult to find evidence for non-neutrality in Kemalist Turkey. One might think of the Directorate of Religious Affairs (*Diyanet*) whose 1924 mandate was "for the dispatch of all cases and concerns for the exalted Islamic faith." It was tasked with the administration of all mosques and schools which teach the Quran. The secular government also created a network of educational institutions, the *Imam Hatip* schools which taught Islamic subjects and trained religious personnel.

In a *laïc* or accommodationist state (but not a separationist one) the government *can* fund or support religions. The key is that this be done with scrupulous neutrality. Religious minorities charged that the Turkish state was not scrupulously neutral. They contended that it endorsed a particular variant of Sunni Islam.

The accusation came from two, mutually antagonistic, sectors of society. First, there were the Alevis, a substantial religious minority. Also suspicious of the state's brand of Islam were conservative Sunnis. Though they viewed Alevis as "heterodox,"—as did the secular state. The Alevis, in turn, viewed the conservative Sunnis *and* the quasi- secular state as patently discriminatory. This tense triangulation indicates that *laiklik* failed to implement the *disestablishment/neutrality* principle.

When the Islamist AK party took over in 2002 it inherited the mighty apparatus of the secular state. This apparatus was battle-tested in its ability to impose a variant of Islam on the populace. The AK proceeded to use it to impose *its* preferred brand of Sunni Islam.

As noted above, once Turkey went to a multi-party system in the mid-twentieth century, the people frequently elected leaders who opposed Kemalist secularism to varying degrees. There, of course, are tens of millions of "secular nationalists" in Turkey (Chapter 13). But politically speaking, they tend not to be a majority.

Present-day Turkey raises a theoretical dilemma. Let's say a majority or plurality of a secular state's citizens don't want it to remain secular. Must the state then remain secular, even *if those elected to lead a country want to make a change*? Put differently, is secularism "untouchable"?

For John Locke, as we saw, secularism *was* untouchable (see Chapter 4). The consent of the people does not permit the magistrate to rule as a religious leader. In other words, secularism trumps the majority, and maybe democracy as well. There is no override, there is no "force quit" button. Secular principles are unalterable; they are the platform, the default operating mode, of a democracy.

But when the platform produces political parties who have the power to upend the platform morally complex questions arise. Is secularism so sacred that it can never be altered or eliminated? And if secularism does not have the consent of the people, on what basis does that sanctity rest?

Turkish political secularism, now nearly a century old, is in the words of one scholar: "confusing and confused." Still, this complex and evolving mode of governance is more flexible, nuanced, and resilient than both opponents *and* supporters make it out to be. It is a system so supple that it could be adapted to the governing needs of militant secular nationalists, centrists *and* conservative religious actors.

Has Turkey invented a new "Islamo-Secularism" that simply needs time to grow and mature? Or, is the country being slowly Islamicized under the AK in a way that will dissolve the secular state?

ETHIOPIA: SUB-SECULARISMS

Comparatively little has been written about African political secularisms. This is unfortunate because more than two dozen countries on this continent have secular constitutions (see Chapter 15). Ethiopia is among them. Its 1995 Constitution is reckoned as "one of Africa's most ambitious."

As usual, we start with an *ancien régime*. The Ethiopian Orthodox Tewahedo Church (EOTC) had been the official religion of the land since the 4th century AD. Emperor Haile Selassie (1892–1975), assumed to be a descendant of King Solomon, was closely aligned with the EOTC. In a society as multi-religious, multilingual, and multiethnic as Ethiopia, that sort of governing status quo was bound to create a catastrophe.

Catastrophe came to a head in the form of a fanatical Marxist group called the Derg. In 1974, the Derg engineered a coup, executed the emperor, and many in his government. They soon unleashed unconscionable violence on the population during the ensuing Red Terror and a civil war. Following the standard script of Soviet secularism, the Derg tried to impose a doctrine of "scientific socialism" on the population.

The revolutionaries quickly stripped the EOTC of its status as an official religion. By nationalizing the land they deprived the church of its lucrative rental incomes. The Derg proceeded to meddle in the EOTC's internal affairs. Some new rights were granted to Islamic communities. This was done not out of grand secular scruples, but as a way of checking the power of the church.

The Derg devoted little thought to secularism. Much more focused on this question was the Ethiopian People's Revolutionary Democratic Front (EPRDF). In 1991, this coalition, dominated by the once Marxist–Leninist Tigray People's Liberation Front (TPLF), overthrew the Derg.

The EPRDF's 1995 constitution has intrigued scholars. This is because of its provisions regarding "ethnic federalism." This system, seen in countries like India and Canada, grants considerable governing authority to federated ethnic units. This makes the work of secular analysis much more difficult. After all, Quebec in Canada, or West Bengal in India, can have their *own* laws regarding their own local government's interaction with religion. What can emerge in an ethnic sub-state is a *sub-secularism* (or a sub-anti-secularism?).

NON-COMPLIANCE

As regards secularism, Ethiopia's 1995 constitution is separationist. The relevant clauses read as follows:

Article 11: Separation of State and Religion

1 State and religion are separate.
2 There shall be no state religion

3a   The state shall not interfere in religious matters
3b   and religion shall not interfere in state affairs.

The formulation is admirably clear. But in the quarter century since the constitution was ratified, only Article 11.2 has been applied in practice. There is no state religion in Ethiopia (though claims of "false neutrality" towards the EOTC do surface). This is a considerable accomplishment. Unfortunately, none of the other provisions have been applied.

State and religion have not been separated (thus violating 11.1). The state has consistently intervened in religious affairs (thus violating 11.3a). Such failure is inevitable. Complete separation, we argued in Chapter 5, *is not possible*. If the majority of citizens are religious—and 98 percent of Ethiopians are—how can the state not "interfere" in their lives?

When the Ethiopian government rejects a land permit from a religious group to build a house of worship—a recurring flashpoint in a country where all land is owned by the state—isn't it interfering in religion in some way? My point is that the government is always enmeshed in religion and vice versa. Separation is a bad metaphor.

It is possible and desirable, however, for a state to exhibit *restraint*. A secular government should *try* as best it can to not interfere in religious affairs. Ethiopian governments have been lacking in this regard.

There are many instances of the state violating Article 11.3a's provision that "The state shall not interfere in religious matters." The most notable centered on the Ethiopian Islamic Affairs Supreme Council (EIASC), or *Majlis*. Established in 1976, this council was denied legal recognition by the Derg. It was recognized by the EPDRF government post-1995. This reminds us that the secular constitution did open up new possibilities and freedoms for religious minorities.

That being said, the EIASC came to be viewed by Muslims as a puppet of the state. Tensions boiled over in 2011 and 2012 when the government deputized a Sufi transnational movement (al-Ahbash) to educate and instruct Ethiopian Muslims in a form of Islam more to the government's liking. Related to this was the closure of the Awaliya institute in 2011 by the EIASC. The shutdown was prompted by concerns over the institute's links to Wahhabi Islam.

It could be argued that the government's actions were warranted in light of the *order* principle. Wahabi movements, funded from Saudi Arabia, have a track record of creating dissent and radicalizing local Muslim populations. I mention this not so much to take sides, as to remind the reader that transnational actors can wreak havoc with rather delicate local religion/government arrangements.

Then again, the state's approach was heavy-handed. Reporting on the Awaliya episode, the US Commission on International Religious Freedom stated that "the arrests, terrorism charges and takeover of EIASC signify a troubling escalation in the government's attempts to control Ethiopia's Muslim community and provide further evidence of a decline in religious freedom in Ethiopia."

The EIASC's meddling highlights the emptiness of the government's separationist rhetoric. That Articles 11.1 and 11.3a do not conform to reality signals a recurring dilemma of secularism. We will refer to this as "constitutional non-compliance," or the inability of a secular state to live in accordance with its own laws.

Constitutional non-compliance might occur because the state is hypocritical. It might occur because the state lacks competence in the ways of governance. It also might occur because some of the population simply will not comply.

This last point is crucial and brings us to Article 11.3b ("Religion shall not interfere in state affairs"). Notice that this law makes a demand on *citizens*. In many countries, religion is one of the sole mechanisms through which disenfranchised citizens gain a public voice. In Africa in particular, religion has been and may be a tool of political protest against corrupt colonial and post-colonial regimes. By removing it from the public sphere, as secularism often does, this potent form of dissent is neutralized. Authoritarian rulers are given free reign.

Though now the aforementioned complexity returns. Political secularisms neutralize religions as a public force, true. But in doing so, they also curtail the possibility of inter-religious violence—not merely a theoretical possibility as the cases of Ethiopia, Nigeria, and Rwanda demonstrate.

Ethiopia is presently experiencing the harsh reality of interethnic and interreligious violence. The unrest of 2021 featured heightened intercommunal, ethnic and land-based violence, with a war in the Tigray region emerging as a major case in point. Years after the dissolution of the EPRDF and the ascension of Prime Minister Abiy Ahmed's Prosperity Party, the country undergoes yet another fraught political transition.

There is much debate about what or whom should be blamed for the current disorder. This conversation is most commonly intertwined with debates about how Ethiopia is governed, and whether it should operate under a unitarist or ethnofederal model. Contemporary thought leaders have gone as far as to suggest that the East African country is in desperate need of a constitutional convention.

As regards secular issues alone, the Constitution's words are clear and reasonable (though on other issues, like ethnic self-determination, the same cannot be said). As we noted in our skinny definition of secularism, one of the tasks of the secular state is to regulate relations *between* religious groups. In this regard, political secularism in Ethiopia has clearly failed. Non-compliance has clearly contributed to that failure.

Complicating this discussion is that other factors of identity, such as ethnicity, are in many ways interlinked with religion. This is to say that religion, as one scholar has noted, is "ancillary" to Ethiopia's political issues, as opposed to "secondary." In many cases, religious tension has been entangled with ethnic tension. The secular articles of the 1995 Constitution could not reduce that tension. Then again, those articles were never really fully implemented in practice.

CHINA: UNCONSCIOUS PROTO-SECULARISM

Chinese religious history is unlike European religious history. The pronounced *two powers* dynamic which developed in Latin Christendom never materialized there. Religious groups in China seldom became a "power" in their own right. There was thus no "binary" and no need for worldly rulers to placate, negotiate with, or combat a menacing Church.

There was, of course, Confucianism—a religion whose adepts essentially ran and staffed numerous regimes from the Han dynasty (202 BC–220 AD) forward. They also provided the overarching philosophical framework for the ruling classes. Yet Confucianism "fits" nicely with political secularism. It advocates a "this-worldly" orientation which minimizes the importance of divinities, the super-natural, and so forth. It also strives for *society-wide* ends. These include order, social harmony, loyalty to the state, etc. These goals line up quite snugly with the secular *reason* and *order* principles we have thus far examined.

Scholars disagree as to whether Confucianism is a religion or an ethical system. For our purposes, we repeat that Confucianism never approximated Christendom's role of becoming an indepen-dent source of authority, a challenger to the throne. The same might be said about Buddhist and Daoist traditions within China.

This means that in China, religions rarely posed a threat to the dominance of the state (possibly because their philosophy was so enmeshed with the state). Nor did these religions serve as a vehicle through which masses mobilized against their rulers. The religions of China rarely needed to be pacified; they were rather naturally decoupled from power.

Arrangements in *pre*-modern China, then, approximate what political secularisms aspire for in the *modern* world. Little theocratic menace; Few interreligious wars; absence of "burning Zeal"; believers who could freely practice their faith; a faith that doesn't contend with worldly authorities; infrequent persecution of minorities on the basis of religion.

If this analysis is correct it means that prior to the twentieth century, China experienced the many benefits of political secular-ism without anyone having put them in place. It practiced a form of unconscious proto-political secularism.

THE PROBLEM

China's unconscious secular status quo came to an end in the twen-tieth century. The story begins with the formation of the Chinese Communist Party (CCP) in 1921. The CCP embraced a Marxist–Leninist approach to religion. We now know (see Chapter 9) that this entails viewing religion as (1) a problem, (2) a symptom of a deeper structural flaw, and (3) inevitably bound to disappear.

Once installed in power in 1949, the CCP under Chairman Mao Zedong set about confronting the religious problem—the problem being the very *existence* of religion. This was more of a theoretical problem than a real one. As we just noted, there was no *ancien régime*. There was no tradition of "reactionary" religious masses.

One wonders if the CCP's confrontation with *all* people of faith was necessary or even worth the fight. Trying to suppress religion, as the USSR learned, almost always backfires. Soviet secularisms often invoke the very outcome they seek to avoid. Today there is a formidable religious resurgence in China.

As with the USSR, China has toggled between different Marxist-inspired solutions to its religion problem. One solution is based on what scholars call "Enlightenment atheism." Here, religion was permitted to exist. The State would simply survey it, squeeze it, pressure it, push it out of schools and public spaces. In such a manner religion would go through its motions, and death throes; eventually it would fade away in accordance with Marxist laws.

Somewhat similar to Kemalist Turkey and its *Diyanet*, the CCP created The State Administration of Religious Affairs (since absorbed in the United Front Work Department). This has mushroomed into a vast state bureaucracy, operating on numerous societal levels. These agencies and their use of "patriotic associations" (see below) relentlessly monitor, interfere and regulate people of faith. Their personnel numbers in the tens of thousands. Their yearly budgets, as best we can tell, amount to hundreds of millions of dollars and likely beyond.

Early on five religions were recognized by the CCP: Buddhism, Daoism, Islam, Protestantism, and Catholicism. The government created "patriotic associations" within each faith. The move was part of a determined and sustained campaign of controlling, monitoring, infiltrating, and co-opting religion.

One rationale for doing this rests on the *order* principle. The CCP is deeply concerned by external enemies. It is thus suspicious of the types of transnational ties that may emerge among people of the same faith. In 1953 Protestant missionaries were banished. Chinese Catholicism, for its part, was uniquely threatening because of its ties to the Vatican in Rome. It goes without saying that transnational Wahabi groups, the likes of which we encountered in Ethiopia and France, would be an impossibility in China.

During the Great Proletarian Cultural Revolution of 1966–1976, China unveiled its second solution to the religion problem. "Militant Atheism," as scholars call it, seeks to liquidate religion. The CCP set out to eliminate the "four olds": old customs, old culture, old habits, and old ideas. Religious institutions were closed, houses of worship were destroyed, as were religious artifacts. Countless human beings were harassed, imprisoned, or murdered.

Religion, as we have seen, has a resilience that confounds Marxist theory. After the death of Chairman Mao in 1976, Deng Xiaoping abandoned the Militant Atheist model, and returned to the Enlightenment version. Perhaps Deng was making a virtue out of necessity. In spite of the Cultural Revolution and its terrors—indeed maybe because of it?—religion was not fading away. The CCP likely realized that its "common goal of building a modernized, powerful socialist state," would fail without the support of the entire population.

New policies were expounded in a 1982 tractate called "The Basic Viewpoint and Policy on the Religious Affairs during the Socialist Period of Our Country." Document 19, as it is known, performs two seemingly contradictory acts at once. It subtly apologizes for, and seeks to end, the disastrous religious policies of the Cultural Revolution. At the same time, it doubles down on the extremist ideology that stimulated the disaster.

Document 19 acknowledges that an error has been made in the treatment of religious citizens. It urges reexamination of "those injustices perpetrated against persons in religious circles and among the mass of religious believers which have not yet been redressed." Casually observing that there are 70,000 fewer houses of worship now than there were at the time of "Liberation" (i.e., the Revolution), the CCP offers to restore them.

Freedom of religious belief is granted (then again, it has been granted in all official CCP documents since 1949). Government non-interference in what are termed "normal" religious activities is promised. Crucially, the document concedes that religion is not about to disappear any time soon. So why not harness the power of patriotic religious citizens in "the common task of building a powerful, modernized Socialist state"?

Let there be no doubt: the CCP knows religion *will* disappear. The day will come when citizens "will no longer have any need for recourse to an illusory world of gods to seek spiritual solace." Wanting to induce that end, the authors remind us of the right to "unremittingly propagate atheism."

Document 19 reiterates that all CCP party members must be atheists: "Unlike the average citizen, the Party member belongs to a Marxist political party, and there can be no doubt at all that s/he must be an atheist and not a theist." John Locke believed that religious people could govern as long as they bracketed their religious beliefs while serving. The CCP, like the USSR, believes that religious people can never govern.

In the aftermath of Tiananmen Square in 1989, Document 19 was replaced in party thought by Document 6. The latter rolled back the CCP's more permissive attitude towards religion. In 2016, President Xi Jinping came to power. His ascendancy coincided with the escalation of crackdowns on religious dissent.

These shifts in party policy demonstrate that the CCP's aggressive brand of secularism is consistently tactical and almost never neutral. On the one hand, Beijing erects concentration camps for Muslim Uyghurs while jailing and exiling followers of the Falun Gong movement (i.e., militant atheism). In the eyes of the CCP, fundamentally *un-Chinese* belief systems with transnational loyalties (like Islam) erode the sacred principle of *state supremacy*.

Simultaneously, however, it allows Confucianism, folk religions, and sinicized variants of Buddhism to flourish (i.e., Enlightenment atheism). This permission is granted because the party now believes that traditional religions are highly effective in pacifying large swaths of the population. The CCP's secular governance fluctuates between brutality and pragmatism.

CONCLUSION

We started this chapter with a plea to embrace complexity. Every political secularism differs from the next. No two are alike. Even one national secularism may change radically across time. Think of the shift from pseudo-separationism, to separationism, to accommodationism in the United States.

As for moral complexity, we have questions, but no easy answers. Question: how does a secular state deal with a vanquished *ancien régime*? The Jacobins, Kemalists, Bolsheviks, and the Derg revolted against conservative Catholics, Sunni Muslims, Orthodox Christians, and the EOTC, respectively. In each case, the old religious authorities were corrupt and unjust. In each case, the desire for "pay back" deformed the incoming secular government and led to human rights abuses. What is the morally correct way for a secular state to reintegrate such bad actors into the body politic?

If such a reintegration occurs, another moral dilemma arises. What is to be done when the vanquished religion comes back—as it inevitably will—and demands to be accorded all of the privileges granted by a secular state? To what, potentially undemocratic, lengths should the latter go to prevent history from repeating itself?

The fear is that ancient orthodoxies (and new transnational movements), will revert to form; they will use the openness of the secular state to tear it down. It's not an unjustified concern, but acting upon that fear always corrodes the integrity of a secular government.

SUGGESTIONS FOR FURTHER READING

There is a truly immense body of literature devoted to the study of Turkish and Ethiopian secularism. Far less is written about China, and this may be related to the fact that there is no word in Chinese that actually approximates "secularism."

On Turkey, Ahmet T. Kuru's *Secularism and State Policies Toward Religion: The United States, France, and Turkey* (Cambridge: Cambridge University Press, 2009) is excellent. An important study of what we call the "false neutrality" principle is Taha Parla and Andrew Davison, "Secularism and Laicism in Turkey," in *Secularisms*, edited by Janet Jakobsen and Ann Pellegrini (Durham, NC: Duke University Press, 2008), pp. 58–75. A fine study of the *Diyanet* is Emir Kaya, *Secularism and State Religion in Modern Turkey* (London: I. B. Tauris, 2018). On the AKP and secularism see the introduction to the special edition by M. Hakan Yavuz and Ahmet Erdi Öztürk, "Turkish Secularism and Islam Under the Reign of Erdoğan," in *Southeast European and Black Sea Studies*, 19 (2019), pp. 1–9.

On Ethiopia, a great deal of literature exists and can usefully be read in light of research on other African political secularisms. Jon Abbink has engaged with the issue of secularism in "Religion and Politics in Africa: The Future of 'The Secular,'" *Africa Spectrum*, 49 (2014), pp. 83–106 (esp. p. 93) and "Religious Freedom and the Political Order: the Ethiopian 'Secular State' and the Containment of Muslim Identity Politics," *Journal of Eastern African Studies*, 8 (2014), pp. 346–365 (esp. p. 347). Also very helpful are Tolera Assefa, "Interrogating Religious Plurality and Separation of State and Religion in Ethiopia," *Eastern Africa Social Science Research Review*, 33 (2017), pp. 39–72 (esp. p. 41); and Berhane Zikarge, "The Scope of Religious Freedom and its Limits under the FDRE Constitution: A Survey of Contemporary Problems and Challenges," LL.M thesis, School of Graduate Studies, Faculty of Law (Addis Ababa: Addis Ababa University, 2009), p. 12. Other scholars who have explored the EOC's role as the empire state's guiding framework include Stephane Ancel, "L'Église Orthodoxe 'Täwahedo' d'Éthiopie et la Révolution: Assurer sa Survie par la Réforme (1974–1991)," *Cahiers d'Études Africaines*, 55 (2015), pp. 687–710 (esp. p. 689); and Terje Østebø, "The Role and Relevance of Religion in Ethiopia's Current Conflicts," *Addis Standard* (November 6, 2019).

The People's Republic of China has attracted less interest in terms of secularism. Three indispensable pieces are Fenggang Yang, *Religion in China: Survival and Revival under Communist Rule* (Oxford: Oxford University Press, 2011); Litao Zhao, "Religious Revival and the Emerging Secularism in China," in *State and Secularism: Perspectives from Asia*, edited by Michael Heng Siam-Heng and Ten Chin Liew (Singapore: World Scientific Publishing Company, 2009), pp. 301–317; and Wang Gungwu, "Secular China," in *Diasporic Chinese Ventures: The Life and Work of Wang Gungwu*, edited by Gregor Benton and Hong Liu (Abingdon: Routledge, 2004).

On Confucianism see Rodney Taylor and Gary Arbuckle, "Confucianism," *The Journal of Asian Studies*, 54, no. 2 (1995), pp. 347–354; and Wei-Ming Tu, "Confucius and Confucianism," *Confucianism and The Family* (1998), pp. 3–36. An analysis of Document 19 can be found in Peter Morrison, "Religious Policy in China and its Implementation in the Light of Document No. 19," *Religion in Communist Lands*, 12, no. 3 (1984), pp. 244–255.

PART III

ANTI-SECULARISM, LIFESTYLE SECULARISMS, AND A CASE STUDY

Prayer was all the recommendation he heard for Nigeria these days. For every crisis, eyes were shut, knees engaged, heads pointed to Mecca, and backs turned to the matter at hand. He did not remember the country being so religious in his childhood. Faith used to be part of the landscape, glimpsed in waxed rosaries and white celestial robes, in wooden prayer beads and the vivid scarves his mother wore when she went to the mosque. None of this obtrusive proselytizing, loud speakers on every corner, blasting calls to prayer, and songs to praise.

—Chibundu Onuzo, *Welcome to Lagos*

DOI: 10.4324/9781003140627-13

ANTI-SECULARISMS OF THE RIGHT
CONSERVATIVE RELIGIOUS ANTI-SECULARISM

To understand secularism, you need to devote some time to understanding *anti*-secularism. There are at least two good reasons for making this effort. The first is that it lets you fully grasp what political secularisms are up against.

Since the nineteenth century, the shape of each national secularism has been formed, deformed, and reformed by the resistance of an anti-secular antagonist. We've seen ample evidence of this in the United States, France, Britain, Turkey, Mexico, and so forth. This is not to say, however, that anti-secularisms are always wrong or reactionary.

In the USSR, the malign secularism of the Communist Party was bravely endured, combated, and ultimately vanquished. Many were the religious groups who dodged or contested the state's "scientific atheism." Perhaps one day—when these stories can be told—we will learn of similar heroisms from China's Muslim Uyghur community.

Every political secularism, beastly or benign, encounters intense opposition. Which brings us to the second reason for exploring anti-secular critique: it sometimes identifies genuine defects, contradictions and areas for improvement.

In this chapter we will focus on anti-secularisms of the right (in the next, we study the left). These are usually promoted by religious movements that can be situated somewhere on a spectrum between deep conservatism and Fundamentalism. Some examples include the

DOI: 10.4324/9781003140627-14

American Christian right, the Hindu nationalist BJP in India (the political affiliate of the Rashtriya Swayamsevak Sangh, or RSS), the Sephardic Shas party in Israel, political Islamists of all stripes, various formations within the Catholic Church, and many others.

No matter how much these traditionalist Christians, Hindus, Muslims, and Jews might disagree with one another—and sometimes violently so—they share similar views about secularism.

THE PUBLIC SPHERE

The first thing to understand about conservative religious anti-secular (CRAS) actors is that they eagerly and passionately participate in politics and political activism. This might seem like it goes without saying. But many CRAS movements once avoided such political engagement.

To use a scholarly term, they used to be "quietist." Quietists may view political activism as a vulgar distraction from holier pursuits. Or, a denomination might become quietist because it is too dangerous to get involved with the powers that be.

In Christianity, the biblical phrase "render unto Caesar" has often been read as a call to quietism. As we saw in Chapter 2, this verse can be interpreted to say that governance should be left to the governing authorities, be they pious or not. Across history, many Christians *chose* to avoid politics and all it entails. Some American Baptist denominations, for example, supported separation of church and state for *theological* reasons. God wanted them at a remove from politics, and politics at a remove from them.

The 1970s marked the decade when CRAS movements in various countries began to abandon quietism, charging headlong into the public sphere. In Iran in 1978–1979, a revolution led by Shiite Muslim fundamentalists ousted the regime of Mohammad Reza Shah. In the United States, White Evangelical Christians emerged from half a century of self-imposed exile. Politics, for these once-quietist Muslim and Christian groups, was now deemed as a legitimate pursuit. God wanted them in politics, fighting on His behalf.

There was a catch though: when these CRAS groups knocked on, or knocked down, the door to government, they found that some type of political secularism was already installed and dwelling within. Since the early 20th century, political secularisms of various sorts had gained (often shaky) footholds in countries like the United States, Mexico, Turkey, Iran, Tunisia, Algeria, Egypt, Syria, Lebanon, India, and so many more.

That these secular governments were not entirely settled or stable is a point that cannot be emphasized enough. The United States is often thought to be among the sturdiest citadels of secularism in the world. Yet separationism only started becoming part of American law in the 1940s (see Chapter 5). Separationist policies (like the prohibition of prayer in public schools) prompted Evangelical Christians to re-enter public life in the 1960s and 1970s. Once there, it took them mere decades to disarm the separationist-secular framework.

The Evangelicals resembled many other global CRAS groups. They engaged in frenzied grass-roots organizing, fundraising, and lobbying. They launched sophisticated mass communications strategies to influence public opinion. They had their members run for various elected positions ranging from federal offices to local school boards. They aligned with existing political parties (first Democrats, then by the late 1970s, Republicans), and periodically made noises about creating their own. And they had, and have, *numbers*. At their height in the early aughts Evangelical Christians were a quarter of the American electorate and voted nearly 80% Republican.

Notice how these behaviors clash with the secular vision of, let's say, Jefferson and Madison. Religious groups, in their opinion, were supposed to accept their "place." And their "place" was in the pews, not in politics. As Jefferson and Madison saw it, citizens of the United States, in public, must reason, act and, especially, *vote* like *United States* citizens, not Congregationalist, Anglican, or Lutheran citizens.

Evangelicals, like other CRAS actors, reject this division and the *beliefs/acts* principle it implies. The demand that they approach politics as citizens first, and servants of God second (or not at all), strikes them as insulting and impossible. How can one turn off, or wall off, one's faith when entering a voting booth? Further, if Evangelicals had the numbers—*which they often did*—why shouldn't their preferred form of governance be implemented?

ANTI-SECULARISTS DEFINE SECULARISM

When groups like the Evangelicals returned to public life in the 1960s and 1970s they were not fixated on something specifically called "secularism." True, they were upset about school prayer—a secular issue through and through. But they were also outraged by the civil rights movement, burgeoning feminism, the sexual revolution, the counterculture, etc. Only later, would the category of "secularism" (somehow) bundle these concerns together. But what was secularism?

In this book, we have aspired—almost obsessively—for clarity and precision when discussing the definition of this word. Unfortunately, this aspiration is not shared by CRAS critics. They rarely define the term. For them, as with George Jacob Holyoake (see Chapter 8), the S-word is associated with a lot of different things. Unlike Holyoake, they associate it with a multitude of sins.

An Australian Evangelical figure reasoned thusly:

> Secularism is Atheism, and by imposing Secularism on the state and saying that everything must have a secular explanation, they're in fact imposing Atheism as a new state religion! ... It's been cleverly used by Marxists, Communists and others involved with Atheistic socio-political global movements to completely gut Christianity.

If there is one series of understandings that binds religious antiseculars together, it is this: (1) secularism is atheism and, as such, it is (2) the *opposite* of religion. If CRAS movements actually believe any of this to be true—and sometimes I suspect that their intellectuals know better—then it accounts for how ferociously they pursue their agenda.

This is because atheism occupies a cursed place in the mindset of many traditionalist faiths. Lack of belief in God is one of the worst individual and collective human attributes imaginable. It is viewed as stupid, immoral, evil, satanic—a danger to the entire social body, if not the species itself.

Few and far between are the religious conservatives that approach atheism with anything approaching curiosity, an open heart, or an urge for dialogue (the most famous example of such open-mindedness being the short glorious, liberalizing Vatican II era. In 1965, the Pastoral Constitution *Gaudium et Spes* acknowledged that the questions that atheism asked were "weighty" and "ought to be examined seriously and more profoundly."). Nor does the specter of non-belief usually inspire a "live and let live" attitude. Fundamentalists cannot easily co-exist with nonbelievers in their midst.

This blurring of atheism and secularism is shared by CRAS movements far and wide. As one scholar of Pakistan observes: "There is no word that evokes so much antipathy in mainstream Pakistani political parlance as does 'secularism'. It is translated as anti-religious rather than a-religious or religiously neutral, as should be its correct connotations." Musa Sulaiman, a Nigerian cleric, sounds similar themes: "All the crises facing the Nigerian state … are the result of the secular system, which demoralized people and accustomed them with materialism."

Little difference is evident in Christian CRAS rhetoric. In 2006, South African pastor Ray McCauley observed that European countries, like Holland and France, were experiencing a precipitous decline in morality. "Once you become a secular state, once you get into a place that is godless," cautioned McCauley, "the country becomes bankrupt."

The Catholic Church, under Pope Benedict XVI, often made similar charges. The pontiff worried that among good American Catholics "the subtle influence of secularism can nevertheless color the way people allow their faith to influence their behavior." That subtle influence leads Catholics to support abortion rights, mistreat the poor, and "promote sexual behavior contrary to Catholic moral teaching." Father Martin Lasarte, a Uruguayan priest who served as a missionary in Africa, complained that "Western secularism … kills the faith."

The equation above (i.e., secularism = atheism = the opposite of religion = the opposite of that which is good) was seen in our Introduction. It has been replicated a thousand times over, on continents far and wide for the past five decades.

SECULAR ELITES

If secularism is atheism and the opposite of religion, then it stands to reason that secular people, or "secularists," are nonbelievers who loathe people of faith. This association is often insinuated in CRAS criticism.

A more sophisticated charge focuses on "secular elites." The phrase has the advantage of being ambiguously broad and sharpening contrasts with the enemy. The elites are affluent, but small in size. The pious are people of modest means who are plentiful in number.

It is a tendency of this elite, they allege, to look down upon religious believers. An American theologian offers the following observation: "One of the characteristics of the secular elite is that they assume that they are the 'brights' who should grasp every opportunity to expand the regulatory state over a benighted citizenry that still clings to 'guns and religion.'"

Secular elites, according to CRAS analysts, tend to cluster around certain types of professional vocations and avoid others. They do not labor with their hands. They do not work in agriculture, nor in "blue-collar" vocations. Rather, secular elites are almost always well educated and wealthy. Upon emerging victorious in India's national election, Prime Minister Modi spoke derisively of the "Khan Market Gang" of Delhi in 2019. This was an allusion to the affluent, English-speaking upper classes in India who do not support the BJP's *Hindutva* brand of politics.

Perched high up in the knowledge economy, secular elites are assumed to be scientists, journalists, and professors. From there, they control public narratives through media manipulation. As a British Islamist website writes: "the denial of a genuine voice to represent Islam is a serious matter, as the people are then denied any information other than what the self-serving secular elite deem to be in their own interests."

They also dominate the arts—where CRAS movements find themselves perpetually incensed by what freedom of expression permits. Be it cinema (e.g., *The Last Temptation of Christ*), or literature (Salman Rushdie's *The Satanic Verses*; Orhan Pamuk's *Snow*), or satire (the *Charlie Hebdo* cartoons), artists use their craft for purposes of blasphemy.

As just noted, CRAS critics contend that secular elites are small in number; a minority who tyrannically impose their beliefs in an apartheid-like manner on the religious majority. As regards the "minority" component of this allegation, the critics are technically correct. This is because very few people, even people who support political secularism, self-identify as "secularists."

People are born and raised as Tamils, Poles, Bangladeshis, Jews, Catholics, Muslims, members of a caste or tribe, male, female, what have you. But they are rarely born and raised as *secularists*, nor are people inclined to self-identify as such. In this book we've learned why that is: secularism refers to state policies that regulate the relation between government and religion(s). It is difficult, if not odd, for a person to adapt that regulatory function as a marker of personal being.

So, yes, self-proclaimed secularists are in the minority. But as we shall see in Chapter 13 this is because political secularism was never meant to be a religion, or a mass movement. It's not a faith, nor an identity, but an approach to governance. It is an approach to governance, I stress, *that people with a religious identity may support*. This, as we are about to see, is something CRAS rhetoric denies.

ON BEHALF OF ALL

CRAS movements often make a subtle, yet clever, rhetorical move, one that completely alters the trajectory of public debates about secularism. They typically frame themselves as defenders of religion, *all* religion. Put differently, they portray their anti-secular activism as *trans-denominational*. By doing that, they negate the existence of *religious* people who disagree with them. The net effect of this move is to create a doubly false binary: religion (by which they mean their religion) versus secularism (which is atheism).

In 1979, the American fundamentalist pastor Jerry Falwell created a political pressure group called the Moral Majority. Closely aligned with the White Evangelicals discussed earlier, Falwell made much of his organization's multi-religious membership, which, in his own words, included "Catholics, Jews, Protestants, Mormons, Fundamentalists." The leader of the Moral Majority also employed a term that has gained prominence in Western anti-secular discourse: "Judeo-Christian" civilization.

The Moral Majority championed an "us" (i.e., religion) versus a "them" (i.e., the secular state, godless liberals, and leftists). The framing, however, is inaccurate—and not only on the secular, "them" side of the equation. Let's take the example of Jewish-Americans, presumably an important pillar of the Judeo-Christian tradition. Falwell situated Jews in the Moral Majority. Yet 70–80 percent of them were voting for Democratic, not Republican, presidential candidates.

Falwell certainly did have some Jews in his ranks. But these were usually Orthodox, and ultra-Orthodox Jews. They were but a sliver of the nation's Jewish population. In fact, Jewish-Americans were overwhelmingly in *favor* of church-state separationism at the time (as religious minorities often are).

Then there was another crack in Falwell's coalition: his own Protestant coreligionists. The fundamentalist Protestantism of the Moral Majority, with its ultra-conservative views on race relations, women, and sexual minorities was fiercely challenged. The challengers were mainline Protestants whose politics were far more liberal. The same conservative/liberal divide is evident in American Catholicism. This is the divide that CRAS rhetoric seeks to obscure.

POWER, NOT METAPHYSICS

An almost universal complaint of CRAS movements is that political secularisms push faith to the sidelines. In a word, the secular state seeks to "privatize" religion. This means more than just saying religion is moved away. It also means that religion is moved away from domains *where it was once central and dominant.*

Such domains include education (e.g., no more prayer in public schools), law (e.g., no more reliance on Islamic or Jewish legal codes), national ceremonies and institutions (e.g., no crucifixes on federal property), and gender (no more strict control of women's bodies and choices). In CRAS circles, the consequences of privatization are seen as nothing short of catastrophic.

Pope Benedict offered a perfect example of this sort of concern when he warned that "any tendency to treat religion as a private matter must be resisted." In 2020 the Ugandan pastor Julius Rwotlonyo described privatization as a danger to the soul:

> There is also a global push for a secular agenda (secularism), that is trying to remove God out of the centre of society. And once God is out of the centre, people become their own masters ... We must resist secularism.

The Egyptian Islamist Abdel Wahab El-Messiri wrote: "far from operating exclusively in a few aspects of public life, [the secular state] has actually ... penetrated to the farthest and deepest concerns of our private lives."

Unlike the accusation of atheism seen above, there is validity to the privatization critique. Political secularisms, even in liberal democracies, *do* regulate how religion functions in classrooms, courts, government ceremonies, and so forth. In some cases—and after *internal constraint* processes are observed—secular states will indeed remove certain practices from public space.

Let's use the example of prayer in American public schools. One can disagree with CRAS activists, but still sympathize with their concerns. They feel it is vitally important for children to pray. This activity is a key component of their formation as moral citizens.

Parents of faith don't see why students should be prohibited from doing that in an educational setting. Let's imagine that the school district in question is overwhelmingly composed of Protestants in general, and Southern Baptists in particular. From the perspective of the aggrieved parents, the prohibition of a daily devotional, lasting a few minutes, seems absurd.

The logic of the secular state, however, is also understandable. It must take into consideration the feelings and rights of *all* students, not just those who are Protestant or Southern Baptist. Religious minorities in these districts, be they Muslims or Mormons, can feel threatened and excluded by prayer rituals.

Likewise, the state must factor in the sensitivities of non-believers. Such children and their parents might find any form of prayer deeply alienating. Finally, and in accordance with the *disestablishment/neutrality* principle, a public school in a secular state cannot favor or endorse one faith over any other. That is precisely what it does when a teacher leads a hymn to this or that God.

Both sides have plausible arguments and heartfelt justifications. Yet if and when the secular state rules against public school prayer, then prayer will be forbidden. With this we get to the crux of the conflict between CRAS movements and political secularism. When both sides have valid arguments (and even sometimes when one side does not) the state *prevails*.

I raise the possibility that what most irritates CRAS critics, is not atheism or irreligion *per se*. Rather, what drives their activism is the principle of *state supremacy*, and the idea that they are the lesser of *two powers*. Hindu nationalists envision a Hindu *rashtra*, a Hindu state. The Sephardic Shas party in Israel, believes that "Religion is an inseparable part of the public sphere and, consequently, state institutions should be subordinated to religious authority." Many types of Islamists hope to re-establish the caliphate where political and religious authority are combined.

Put simply, these groups do not appreciate being subordinate to the state. This dispute is about power, not metaphysics.

ASYMMETRIES

In an address given in 2019 a traditionalist Catholic hammers home many of the CRAS themes we have seen throughout this chapter:

> Over the past 50 years religion has been under increasing attack ... On the one hand, we have seen the steady erosion of our traditional Judeo-Christian moral system and a comprehensive effort to drive it from the public square. On the other hand, we see the growing ascendancy of secularism and the doctrine of moral relativism.

Decades earlier, this same figure had called for the imposition of "God's law" in the United States. The speaker was twice the Attorney General of the United States (under George W. Bush and Donald Trump). William Barr's double ascension to the rank of America's chief law enforcement officer, suggests how far CRAS movements have come since their quietist days.

To use a complicated word, CRAS movements seek to "repristinate" the world. This means they want to return to an earlier time—a "golden age." For Hindu nationalists that period might be "Ancient India"—meaning anything prior to the arrival of the (Muslim) Ottomans and Mughals. For Islamists it might be the era of the Prophet Muhammad and the rightly guided caliphs. For White Evangelical Christians in the United States, it would be the decades and centuries before the anything-goes 1960s. For ultra-Orthodox Jews, perhaps, the days of the Second Temple when Ezra and Nehemiah ran Jerusalem with a firm grip.

Standing in the way of that glorious homecoming is political secularism. It's as if secularism's core principles were built to oppose every aspiration of CRAS movements—which, to a certain degree, they were! The long, complicated history that we have outlined in this book resulted in a series of secular principles of governance. Now, newly re-energized traditionalist religious groups across the globe are committed to overturning them.

We have already seen how these movements reject the *two powers* provision, *state supremacy, disestablishment/neutrality* and *belief/acts* to this we might add the *reason* principle. It places science over scripture, and is thus completely unacceptable to traditionalists.

As for *equality*, that too is unworkable. Fundamentalist groups have their own forms of subordination: "others" are second-class citizens. As a leader in the BJP-affiliated group Vishwa Hindu Parishad, put it "Everyone living in India is a Hindu, including Muslims and Christians. They have to be subservient to Hindus and Hinduism."

In the ongoing, escalating confrontation between CRAS movements and political secularisms there is little common ground. But there is a glaring asymmetry. In liberal democracies, political secularisms must abide by all of the principles we have enumerated when dealing with anti-secular citizens. They must accommodate their critics and respect their rights. The latter, by contrast, have fewer constraints. They can run for office, win elections, appoint sympathetic justices—in short they can (and do) mobilize for the disruption of the secular state or even its eventual collapse.

From the secular perspective, these movements exploit the openness, and procedural fairness that secularism itself made possible. Once religious traditionalists get in the door, so to speak, they will raze the house of secularism and all of its vaunted principles to the ground. In its place they'll erect a temple or mosque or ashram that doubles as the seat of government. That is the evergreen fear of every secular government and citizen.

SUGGESTIONS FOR FURTHER READING

The Pastoral Constitution *Gaudium et Spes* on atheism really is a remarkable document and can be accessed at www.vatican.va/archive/hist_councils/ii_vatican_council/documents/vat-ii_cons_19651207_gaudium-et-spes_en.html.

On fundamentalisms, see Martin E. Marty and R. Scott Appleby (Eds.), *The Fundamentalism Project, Fundamentalisms Observed* (Chicago, IL: University of Chicago Press, 1994); Malise Ruthven, *Fundamentalism: The Search for Meaning* (Oxford: Oxford University Press, 2005); and Rebecca Joyce Frey, *Fundamentalism* (New York: Facts On File, 2007).

ANTI-SECULARISMS OF THE LEFT

Secularism does not lack for people who wish it would disappear! We have just acquainted ourselves with conservative religious anti-secularisms of the right (i.e., CRAS). Coming from a completely different direction, but with an equally negative appraisal, are opponents that emerge from the left.

These critics are almost always scholars. They are clustered in disciplines like anthropology, women's studies, theology, political science, philosophy, and so forth. Schools of thought known as "postmodernism" and "postcolonialism" greatly influence them. As have the writings of the French philosopher Michel Foucault (1926–1984). Foucault himself rarely wrote about secularism. Though one of his most brilliant readers, the anthropologist Talal Asad (1932–), applied Foucault's theories to the study of political secularism.

I will refer to this immense body of research, produced roughly from the 1990s to the present, as POMOFOCO for short. The designation is, admittedly, an oversimplification. It masks the fact that many scholars who work in this tradition are diverse in their methods and theories.

Then again, nearly all POMOFOCO researchers share a deep mistrust of secularisms. In this regard, they closely resemble CRAS critics. As with the latter, they assume secularism is a failed ideological project—and a defunct one as well. So much so, that some refer to the present moment as the "post-secular" era.

The relationship between the far-rightward tilting CRAS movements and the far leftward-leaning POMOFOCO school is hard to pin down. Michel Foucault—the FO in POMOFOCO—

DOI: 10.4324/9781003140627-15

is one of the twentieth century's major intellectuals of the Left and likely the most widely read. For those scholars who are critical of western governments, liberalism, imperialism, militarism, capitalism, Big Science, Big Medicine, the "carceral state," and so forth, Michel Foucault is an icon. His thought would appear to have little in common with that of CRAS activists.

Still, how might we explain this icon's "extraordinary fascination" with the mother of all violent CRAS operations? This would be the Iranian Revolution of 1979, which Foucault witnessed while working as a correspondent for an Italian newspaper. During the events leading to the overthrow of the Shah's regime, he often spoke of Ayatollah Khomeini in a tone of wide-eyed awe. Foucault emphasized the "political spirituality" of the insurgent Islamists. He predicted, accurately, though with little sense of dread, that this type of religious activism would be the wave of the future.

This is relevant because POMOFOCO scholars who train their fire on political secularism conspicuously avoid criticizing CRAS movements of all faiths. Their treatment of Political Islamists is notable in this regard. These scholars will often defend Islamist positions (especially in controversies about women's veiling or art that Islamists find blasphemous). They also engage in a good deal of "whataboutism?" They concede that the violent excesses of some radical Islamists are unfortunate, but what about atrocities committed by Western governments?

On the other hand, POMOFOCO theorists have little sympathy for the patriarchy, homophobia, and sexual puritanism that characterizes Fundamentalist projects. CRAS and POMOFOCO share an adversary: secularism. What else they might share is not entirely clear. Though by the end of this chapter we will better understand *why* they agree on this particular issue.

Whereas CRAS activists target a mass audience, POMOFOCO theorists write exclusively for other scholars. A characteristic of this school is the complexity of its prose. Without an advanced degree in a related field, it is difficult to comprehend their arguments. This probably accounts for why POMOFOCO has rarely penetrated political, policy, or media circles. CRAS activists, by contrast, are very plugged into such networks, which they use to amplify their message far and wide.

DEFINITIONS (ARE POLITICAL)

How you define or don't define secularism is a *political* act with political consequences. We've seen that questions of definition were hugely relevant to the Victorian infidels (Chapter 8). Charles Bradlaugh strongly opposed George Jacob Holyoake's definition of Secular*ism.* The disagreement over what a mere word meant had long-term implications. The dispute cracked open a decades-long rift between centrists and radical atheists in the British freethought movement.

When the CRAS critics we met in the previous chapter define secularism they (intentionally?) blur the line between political secularism and atheism. Their definition is sort of a loop: atheism is secularism and secularism is atheism. In their mass communications, CRAS movements weaponize the confusion around secularism that they themselves perpetuate. For who in a liberal democracy wishes to be subject to a "Soviet-style" regime? What kind of religious believer likes to be told that her religion is being forcibly "privatized," and pushed to the side? And, by godless state bureaucrats, no less?

POMOFOCO scholars add entirely new dimensions to the definitional chaos. Some of them explicitly *refuse* to define the term. This is unusual, especially in the academy, where a very high level of precision is demanded when discussing core concepts. Still, they buck convention and refrain from assigning a fixed meaning to the term. "It is impossible to define secularism," insist two major figures in this school, "rather one must track the diverse ways the insistent claims to being secular are made."

Others, using tools supplied by Foucault, avoid offering a definition by speaking of secularism as a "discourse." They look at the kinds of conversations in which the word "secularism" appears and how power flows from and through these discourses. What effects do these discourses about secularism have? Whose lives do they affect? How do they change relations between citizens and their government?

The following comment, from a scholar of gender, illustrates this well. For her, secularism is "a discursive operation of power whose generative effects need to be examined critically in their historical contexts." "When I refer to secularism," the scholar continues, "it is not an objective definition I have in mind … following Michel Foucault, my approach … analyzes the ways in which the term has been variously deployed and with what effects."

POMOFOCO researchers will not tell us precisely what the term means, if only because it means (and does) so many things. In truth, the POMOFOCO school absolutely *does* have something in mind when it speaks of secularism. And that something is *not* atheism.

POMOFOCO views secularism very much in the sense of "political secularism" that we have been exploring in this book. All of the principles we have identified in previous chapters have been discussed at length and with great sophistication by most POMOFOCO researchers. They are portrayed as elements of the "discourse" of secularism—a discourse whose "effects" have altered history.

WHEN, WHERE, WHAT

In order to reconstruct POMOFOCO's conception of secularism we need to understand *when* and *where* they believe it emerged. Then we will focus on *what* they believe it does. Those three data points, we shall soon learn, are connected in significant ways.

As for *when* and *where* political secularism came on the scene, their answer is: Western modernity. To be more precise, its development is traced to the eighteenth and nineteenth centuries. This is the period of the Enlightenment and its immediate aftermath. "Secularism as a political doctrine," writes Talal Asad, "arose in modern Euro-America."

By situating the origins of political secularism in Christian, Euro-American modernity, POMOFOCO writers can link, or chain, it to a whole range of other contemporaneous concepts. These include (1) colonialism, (2) capitalism, (3) the birth of liberalism and liberal democracies, and (4) the rise of the modern nation-state.

Nowadays, nearly all would view colonialism as an epic human rights disaster (and some might say the same about capitalism). POMOFOCO, however, views all four of these developments with dismay. Here, they draw upon a long tradition in post-Marxist and leftist thought (e.g., critical theory, postmodern thought, critical race theory). For various reasons, these approaches connect the Enlightenment to new forms of political organization and reasoning that induced species-wide catastrophes. The North Atlantic slave trade and the Holocaust are but two consequences.

Now that we are situated in time (i.e., the eighteenth and nineteenth centuries) and space (i.e., Western Europe and the United States), we can engage the question of what political secularism *does*. POMOFOCO scholars implicate it in a project of domestic oppression and Western imperialism. For these theorists, political secularism functions as a weapon in European Christendom's vast arsenal for total, or "hegemonic," domination of other classes, cultures, religions, and peoples. This approach, incidentally, epitomizes the key themes of "postcolonial" thought—the CO in POMOFOCO.

The narrative goes roughly like this: In the eighteenth and nineteenth centuries, and even earlier, new-fangled Western nation-states, flush with a sense of their own power, purpose, and superiority, became obsessed with the idea of *governing*. At home, this led them to subordinate women, minorities, the non-privileged, and others. They also ventured abroad where they ruled and economically exploited the Middle East, Africa, Asia, and the Americas.

What is striking about POMOFOCO is its allegation that political secularism was complicit in this project at every step of the way. Secularism had a mission. It was a "discourse" whose "effect" was not only the subordination of citizens and subjects alike. It also radically remade religion and religious people.

ORDER/ING

Between what both we and POMOFOCO critics call "political secularism," there is common ground. At least in the sense that many of the same concepts are explored and regarded as relevant.

These include *disestablishment/neutrality, freedom of conscience, toleration*, and so forth. In POMOFOCO's telling, however, these concepts are emptied of good intentions and positive effects. Political secularism has no "nice guy/gal" side. All of its lofty and vaunted ideals are placed in the service of an immense and treacherous project of Western domestic and global hegemony.

Let's start with the concept of *state supremacy*. As with CRAS writers, POMOFOCO theorists are alarmed by the secular state's capacity to subordinate those under its jurisdiction. This is textbook Foucault; he devoted much thought to the over-whelming power of western structures of governance.

Modernity, he argued, spawned a new, vastly more efficient and treacherous type of authority. Its reach was so pervasive that it penetrated to "the very grain of the individual, touches his body, intrudes into his gestures, his attitudes, his discourse, his apprenticeship, his daily life." This capacity to alter a human's physical being is known as "embodiment," and we shall return to it momentarily.

Following Foucault, contemporary POMOFOCO theorists assail the state, or, more precisely, the *secular* state. In Asad's words, the secular state "seeks to regulate all aspects of individual life." "No one," he continues, "can avoid encountering its ambitious powers." For another theorist, secularism "is historically and remains today an expression of the state's *sovereign* power."

Hopefully, the reader recognizes that *anti-statism* is a conceptual throughline among all of those opposed to political secularism. These critics would fully concur with our ranking of *state supremacy* and the *two powers* as crucial components of secularism. Though these principles are unsettling to POMOFOCO and CRAS thinkers. The former are uncomfortable with subordination in general. The latter are uncomfortable with subordination of (their) religion.

This also might offer an insight into why disciples of Foucault tend to go easy on fundamentalist movements. The latter are, after all, among the few actors in civil society that have the numbers and the organization to effectively stand up to the state. Both CRAS and POMOFOCO want to overturn the powers that be. But whereas CRAS movements want to *be* the power (and remain as such), POMOFOCO's personnel seem content to critique power.

Order, as we have also shown, is one of the driving obsessions of political secularism. This has not escaped the attention of POMOFOCO writers. They argue that the preservation of order is a pretext—an excuse for the type of relentless domination which is the true aspiration of modern European nation states. That this concern is sometimes justified is demonstrated in our discussions of the British Raj (Chapter 7) and the Soviet Union (Chapter 9).

POMOFOCO critics add a clever, Foucault-inspired, nuance to the *order* principle. In his 1966 work *Les mots et les choses* (translated as *The Order of Things: An Archeology of the Human Sciences*)

Foucault proposed that historical eras were ruled by "*epistemes*." These were somewhat unconscious, ways of perceiving the world shared by an entire civilization. As one scholar put it, an episteme is "a fundamental code governing the way in which people understand, and act in, the world." An episteme teaches us how to classify and categorize what we encounter in our everyday lives.

Modernity's "episteme" was both a cause and effect of a new curiosity among Europeans. Western experts started investigating something called "Man" through the "human sciences." This project, for Foucault, involved a maniacal accounting, categorizing and cataloguing of everything about human existence.

POMOFOCO writers, then, see secular states as not merely trying to (cynically) maintain *order* among religions. In addition, political secularisms engaged in a process of *ordering* religion. They thus force religions and religious people to understand themselves on secularism's terms. Let's delve deeper into this provocative insight.

THE SYLLABUS OF DOMINATION

For POMOFOCO theorists, political secularism had a specific function: re-ordering all the religions under its jurisdiction according to secular specifications. In so doing, it radically changed, or reconfigured, how religious people *thought* about, and behaved within, the world, not to mention their physical posture and bearing.

How precisely secularism accomplished all this is a bit unclear. It was as if secularism was tasked with teaching a master class to an entire civilization. The curriculum tackled questions like what religion is; what religion does; what religion should and should not do; and where it should and should not do it, etc. This new secular discourse taught citizens to divide the world into binaries. We are familiar with some of them by now: civil authority and spiritual authority; beliefs and acts; private and public sphere.

POMOFOCO theorists believe secular states introduced other binaries: rational and irrational; real and imaginary; fact and myth; universal and particular. The modern, European, liberal nation-state depicted itself as logical, fact-based and committed to the wellbeing of all. Religion was the opposite. POMOFOCO scholars are fond of using the term "the secular imaginary." This indicates how little that they believe these secular binaries conform to external reality.

Our metaphor of secularism teaching a master class can only go so far. A "discourse" in Foucault's thought sort of hovers "in the air." It's not a top-down affair. Discourses circulate across society and have multiple effects and encounter all sorts of resistance. Often the people transmitting the discourse don't even know that they are transmitting it, just as the recipients do not know it was received. If this sounds peculiar, then it has to do with complexities of POMOFOCO worldview that we cannot pursue here.

In any case, the effects of this discourse were monumental. "The secular-liberal-project," writes one critic, "is aimed at the moral reconstruction of public and private life." Secularism, according to Talal Asad, was used as a tool to "mediate people's identities, help shape their sensibilities, and guarantee their experiences." Morals. Sensibilities. Identities. Experiences. We are, indeed, getting down to what Foucault called the "grain" of the individual.

POMOFOCO analysis is unlike anything we have seen so far. It ascribes not only physical power to secularism but *psychic* power too. This discourse has the effect of not only colonizing people's land, but their minds as well. Even their bodies—the way they dress, move in space, physically reach out to God—are impacted by secular discourse (i.e., embodiment).

All of which is to say that secular discourse was powerful stuff. The pre-modern religious believer and her religion were subjected to a total makeover. They both became *modern*. Their new identity was crafted by courtesy of secularism's syllabus of total domination.

THE *DISESTABLISHMENT/NEUTRALITY* DOMINO

POMOFOCO theorists, we saw above, concur that secular states subordinate religion in the name of *order*. As for all of the other secular principles we have identified—POMOFOCO analysis drains those concepts of any positive function. If we think of our secular principles as dominoes, then *disestablishment/neutrality* is the first one they tip over. Once the secular state is shown to be biased, as opposed to neutral, then all the other principles fall in line.

Secular states claim that they are impartial, that they are not aligned with any religion. For POMOFOCO that *neutrality* claim is patently false. Every political secularism, they contend, invariably favors and privileges one religion (usually the religion of the majority group in power, which is often Christian). Further, many core secular concepts are built on hidden Protestant foundations which POMOFOCO theorists are eager to excavate.

This "false neutrality" (Chapter 4) approach is often used to destabilize other secular principles. Let's take the *belief/acts distinction*. Separating belief from acts, so goes the critique, is something Protestants can do with ease. Rituals, ceremonies, public rites are far less central to Protestant faiths. But for nearly all other religious traditions, proper religious practice (referred to as "orthopraxy") is as important as what one believes, and maybe even more so.

Secularism, however, forces these religions to perform sacred acts in private. If the state deems the acts a threat to *order*, then they must be abandoned altogether. Beliefs versus acts—it all seems very innocent. But, in truth, secular discourse deploys this quasi-Protestant binary to refashion all non-Protestant religions. Where's the *neutrality* there?

The Danish cartoon controversy provided POMOFOCO theorists the opportunity to demonstrate the *non*-neutrality of the *belief/acts* distinction. The controversy was sparked in 2005 by the publication of 12 images of the Prophet Muhammad in, at first, a right-wing Danish newspaper. These provocative and insulting images were, however, protected by European freedom of speech provisions. The act of visually representing the Prophet is explicitly forbidden in Islamic law. In the aftermath of their appearance, hundreds were killed and countless injured in riots that broke out in numerous countries.

For the anthropologist Saba Mahmood, the episode demonstrated that "Secular liberal principles of freedom of religion and speech are not neutral mechanisms for the negotiation of religious difference." Mahmood observed that in some countries, like Austria, blasphemous materials which offended Christians were in fact prohibited.

This double standard is a clear failure of the *disestablishment/neutrality* protocols. One could counter that the principle itself was sound. The problem was that Austria's application of *neutrality* was inconsistent. POMOFOCO, however, has an issue with the *principle*, not just its application.

Mahmood points out that for Muslims, the prophet Muhammad "is a figure of immanence ... and is therefore not a referential sign that stands apart from an essence that it denotes." Muslims' heart-felt beliefs about the prophet, Mahmood intimates, cannot be separated from (violent?) acts vindicating his honor.

Let's leave aside that the overwhelming majority of Muslims worldwide *did* separate beliefs from acts and did not commit acts of violence. Mahmood's analysis raises a crucial question which John Locke answered to his satisfaction: what would happen if religious believers of all stripes acted on all of their faith-related beliefs?

As for *equality*, if the state is not truly neutral, then how can citizens all be treated the same? Many political secularisms have been charged with discriminating against certain religious groups. Critics of Quebec's secular policies banning "conspicuous religious symbols" charged that it favors Catholicism. The same accusation has recently been made by Muslim citizens of France. If secularisms are never neutral, then they cannot treat citizens equally. Obviously, such a state is incapable of extending true *toleration* to all.

Freedom of conscience is easy to topple once the false neutrality charge is made. Political secularisms, as we saw above, infiltrate people's minds. Can your thought be free, in Luther's sense, when it is downloaded like an app into your mind by the discourses (and educational systems) of the secular state?

As far as POMOFOCO scholars are concerned, Political secularisms are not guided by *reason*. Instead, they are guided by a will to power. All of the drawbacks above invalidate the state's alleged mechanisms of *internal constraint*. How can a secular state, which has clear favorites, be trusted to monitor itself?

PAVING THE WAY

POMOFOCO's intervention is interesting and important. Naturally, it is subject to criticism. POMOFOCO's historical reconstruction of political secularism is problematic. Its scholars locate its birth in eighteenth-century Euro-America. They depict secularism's rise as swift, frictionless, and *very* sudden.

Sudden historical changes and ruptures of this sort were a key theme in Foucault's writing. Our own analysis, however, suggests a good deal of historical continuity. Secularism, we have argued, didn't emerge in a flash. Rather, its different principles developed slowly across time and space.

The Enlightenment was just a "station"—albeit a significant one—in the long, inadvertent, transhistorical journey of political secularism. Modern Euro-America, in our analysis, *inherited* many secular ideas and intuitions from pre-modernity. It did not give birth to them.

These ideas and intuitions, we have demonstrated, encountered intense, even violent, resistance. This is another shortcoming of POMOFOCO's historical reconstruction: the anti-secular religious actors who aggressively opposed secular "discourse" simply disappear from their narrative.

It's as if political secularism ran roughshod over its docile opponents. Our discussions of the "fateful nineteenth century" cast doubts on this claim, as do studies of the frenzied anti-secular, ultramontanism that emerged among conservative Catholics (see Chapters 5, 6, and 8). POMOFOCO's image of political secularism emerging fully formed in the Enlightenment and proceeding to crush anything in its path needs to grapple with the historical record which suggests otherwise.

Even if we accept POMOFOCO's timeline, its theory has a shortcoming that we also encountered among CRAS critics: it does not identify the "secularists." Who invented the "discourse" on secularism? Who put it into place? Where are the secular laws and constitutions from 1750, 1800, 1850, 1900? What are the names of secularism's champions?

POMOFOCO theorists speak of a powerful "discourse" of secularism, yet they rarely identify who its speakers were, where they worked, the actions they took on behalf of secularism, etc. Talal Asad once asked "what might an anthropology of secularism look like?" Yet his proposed anthropology—strangely for an anthropologist—never spoke to secular subjects or even about them. POMOFOCO's conception of secularism lacks secularists.

This may be because political secularism was not really a coherent "project" until the late nineteenth century and only in a few countries. Until then, it was a bundle of stray principles, some of which were advocated by this or that political formation. The truth of the matter is that there is a great degree we do not know about how secularism came into being; POMOFOCO scholars would do well to exhibit less certainty and more curiosity about this subject.

"Secularism," charges a POMOFOCO scholar, "cannot be the solution because it is part of the problem." A zero-sum logic is being applied; if secularism continues to exist, everything else is endangered. Some POMOFOCO analysts, by contrast, claim they simply want to "refashion," not abolish, political secularism. Two proponents put it this way: "Critiques of secularism are an attempt to recognize the vulnerabilities and shortcomings of secularism, so as to contribute to the development of alternative, more inclusive futures."

This is a worthy goal and quite similar to the goal of this book. Yet it often does not square with the uncompromising nature of POMOFOCO critique—a critique which very rarely proposes ways that secularisms can be improved and very often implies that secularisms are so fatally flawed that they must be replaced. But replaced by what? If POMOFOCO theorists have crafted some sort of alternative to political secularism that engenders more inclusive futures, they have yet to share it with their readership.

The secularist's fear is that POMOFOCO's impressive academic critique of political secularism can only help pave the way for the post-secular era which many of these theorists believe we already inhabit. That would be an era of CRAS discourses and Theo States on top.

SUGGESTIONS FOR FURTHER READING

The reader may be wondering about the MO. It stands for "postmodern." Although not discussed much above, the tendency to linger on the Enlightenment and its "heroes of knowledge" working for the greater good is a central component of postmodernism. See for example Jean-François Lyotard, *The Postmodern Condition: A Report on Knowledge* (Minneapolis, MN: University of Minnesota Press, 1993).

For two readable accounts of Foucault's life and work see James Miller, *The Passion of Michel Foucault* (New York: Simon and Schuster, 1993); and Didier Eribon, *Michel Foucault (1926–1984)*

(Paris: Flammarion, 1989). Important is Foucault's essay "Governmentality" in *The Foucault Effect: Studies in Governmentality*, edited by Graham Burchell, Colin Gordon, and Peter Miller (Chicago, IL: University of Chicago Press, 1991), pp. 87–104. On the "episteme" see Mark Bevir, "Foucault, Power, and Institutions," *Political Studies*, 47 (1999), pp. 345–359.

Talal Asad's central work on the subject is *Formations of the Secular: Christianity, Islam, Modernity* (Stanford, CA: Stanford University Press, 2003). An assessment can be found in Sindre Bangstad, "Contesting Secularism/s: Secularism and Islam in the Work of Talal Asad," *Anthropological Theory*, 9 (2009), pp. 188–208.

An overview of the approach discussed in this chapter is Linde Draaisma and Erin Wilson, "Secularism," in *The Routledge Handbook of Religion, Politics and Ideology*, edited by Jeffrey Haynes (Abingdon: Routledge, 2022). Some other workers in this tradition are Hussein Ali Agrama, "Sovereign Power and Secular Indeterminacy: Is Egypt a Secular or Religious State," in *After Secular Law*, edited by Winnifred Sullivan, Robert Yelle, and Mateo Taussig Rubbo (Stanford, CA: Stanford University Press, 2011); William Connolly, *Why I am Not A Secularist* (Minneapolis, MN: University of Minnesota Press, 1999). Connolly is one of many in this school who view secularism as built on a Christian platform. See also Saba Mahmood, "Religious Reason and Secular Affect: An Incommensurable Divide?" *Critical Inquiry*, 35, no. 4 (2009), pp. 836–862; Saba Mahmood, *Politics of Piety: Islamic Revival and the Feminist Subject* (Princeton, NJ: Princeton University Press, 2005); and Elizabeth Shakman Hurd and Linell E. Cady (Eds.), *Comparative Secularisms in a Global Age* (Basingstoke: Palgrave Macmillan, 2010).

On secularism and gender see Joan Wallach Scott, *Sex and Secularism* (Princeton, NJ: Princeton University Press, 2018). A useful collection of articles is Linell Cady and Tracy Fessenden (Eds.), *Religion, the Secular, and the Politics of Difference* (New York: Columbia University Press, 2013).

LIFESTYLE SECULARISMS

Throughout this book we've occasionally alluded to secularism as a category of *identity*. To that end, we've asked: who is "a secularist"? The answers have sprawled in every which direction. That's because there are so many co-existing definitions and conceptions of the S-word.

The chart below summarizes some of the secular identities we've already encountered, plus new ones that we are about to examine.

In what follows we are going to look at four types of "secularists" leading "secular" lives. We shall see that there is sometimes a difference between calling oneself a "secularist" and being *called* a "secularist." When anti- *and* pro-secular groups apply this label to others, they often do so with a specific goal in mind.

THE NEW ATHEISTS

It is very common in the English-speaking world today for atheism to be associated with secularism. In Chapter 8, we visited the moment of that association's genesis. Ever since Charles Bradlaugh's hostile take-over of George Jacob Holyoake's Secular*ism* in the 1870s, there has been some confusion and overlap between the two concepts. But it was during the twenty-first century that the words "atheism" and "secularism" became more entangled than ever before. So much so, that one wonders if these two -isms can ever be disentangled again.

The (final?) knotting of atheism and secularism can be explained by reference to the history, technology, and intellectuals of the new millennium. Historically, the attacks of 9/11 forced many atheist writers to ponder religious extremism with new urgency. Technologically, this was the moment that social media was

DOI: 10.4324/9781003140627-16

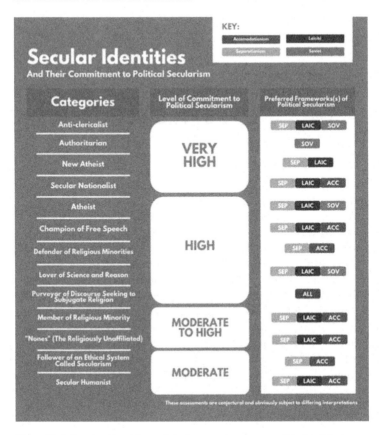

Figure 13.1 Secular identities and their commitment to political secularism

coming into its own. Each passing year of the twenty-first century exponentially magnified the ability of new movements to spread their message, mobilize members, and grow their ranks.

Which brings us to the new class of atheist intellectuals that emerged in the post-9/11 era. These figures were outraged by the violence of militant Islam. They were also stunned by the growing political stature of Christian CRAS movements in the United States and around the world. One important voice was the independent scholar Susan Jacoby. Her 2004 book—notice the subtitle— *Freethinkers: A History of American Secularism* was among a slew of texts that casually drew the association noted above.

Then there were the New Atheists (i.e., Sam Harris, Richard Dawkins, Daniel Dennett, and the late Christopher Hitchens). The so-called "Four Horsemen" published fierce takedowns of religion—and not just the Fundamentalist variants. In the early aughts, they quickly became social media sensations. Their books not only sold millions of physical copies around the world, but energized a growing nonbelief community on the internet.

Two themes emerge in New Atheist interventions: extreme anti-clericalism and a total embrace of science as an alternative to religion. Much of their prose was devoted to proving how senseless, illogical and violent all forms of religion were. Their training in fields like evolutionary biology (Dawkins), neuroscience (Harris), and cognitive science (Dennett) made them worthy ambassadors of the *reason* concept. They believed that all public policy decisions should be based on science, rationality and data.

The New Atheists seldom reflected on political secularism. When they did, they showed themselves to be proponents of strict separation. As Dawkins approvingly observed in *The God Delusion*: "The [American] founders most certainly were secularists who believed in keeping religion out of politics."

New Atheists portrayed their activism as defending aggrieved secular people everywhere. "I think it's us, plus the 82nd Airborne and the 101st," exclaimed Christopher Hitchens, "who are the real fighters for secularism at the moment, the ones who are really fighting the main enemy." Joining the fight were countless other nonbelievers, many with digital platforms and training in STEM disciplines.

The result of this intervention, now twenty years on, is that a good deal of the conversation about *secularism* has been dominated by New Atheist views *and* the anger those views elicited among religious people across the spectrum. One consequence of their back and forth is that the word secularism, which equals atheism in both camps, is increasingly seen as the opposite, or adversary, of religion (see Definitional Set 1 in Chapter 1).

NON-SECULAR ATHEISTS?

There is no Vatican of secularism. No institution exists which retains the power to decide who is, and who is not, a secularist. If an atheist calls himself a secularist, I think there is a moral imperative to respect that self-designation. Media outlets routinely draw this connection as do CRAS activists. Accordingly, the equation that prevails in public discourse is "*all atheists are secularists.*"

Rather than get obsessed by semantics, I wish to note that the New Atheist embrace of secularism raised an interesting theoretical question. Namely, is there such a thing as a *non-*secular atheist? I mention this because extreme atheists sometimes advocate ideas that contradict core principles of political secularism.

This point was particularly obvious in New Atheist discourse. The polemical nature of their intervention led them to make arguments which opposed the very secular principles they claimed to be championing. Sam Harris, for example, argued that beliefs cannot be separated from acts (Here he concurs with CRAS and POMOFOCO critics). "Given the link between belief and action," he wrote in *The End of Faith: Religion, Terror and the Future of Reason*, "it is clear that we can no more tolerate a diversity of religious beliefs."

Toleration was another principle that Harris was eager to deconstruct. He viewed "the very ideal of religious tolerance," as "one of the principal forces driving us towards the abyss." The impression that the New Atheists were deeply intolerant was widespread among their critics. It led many to wonder what they might do if they were "on top."

The sharpest contradiction between New Atheism and political secularism had to do with basic beliefs about religion's legitimacy. Hitchens's catchphrase in his 2007 polemic, *God is Not Great*, was "*religion poisons everything.*" He warned his readers that "people of faith are in their different ways planning your and my destruction." Harris averred that religious moderates were every bit as dangerous as a suicide bomber. Moderate religious faith, he insisted, posed a "threat" to our survival.

Few observers of the New Atheists, pro or con, believe that their true intent was to eliminate religion. Yet their rhetoric, per-formative as it may have been, strongly intimated that goal. This put these champions of secularism in a tense relation with the political secularism they claimed to be defending. The latter, via the *two powers* principle, accords religion a legitimate place within the social body. Political secularism takes the existence of religion as a given. If there were no religion, there would be no need for secularism!

True, there is no Vatican of Secularism. But there are ways for social scientists to define their terms precisely. Given their rejection of so many secular principles, the New Atheists might conceivably be referred to as "*non*-secular atheists."

What must be stressed, is that their position is extreme and unusual among *atheists*. Most non-believers are not bent on the liquidation of religion even in their rhetoric. As we shall see, they request something entirely different from the secular state.

NONES

Two decades after its fiery rollout, New Atheism has lost its momentum. The movement and some of its leaders have been wracked by accusations of sexism and Islamophobia. In a multi-cultural world, the overwhelmingly white and male cast of New Atheism was always a liability and may account an oft-observed drift of some of its members to the alt-right.

Further, the type of strict separation of church and state that New Atheism championed has not fared well. Separationism as a framework has been keeling in the United States since the 1990s. The administration of Donald J. Trump (2017–2021) was the most aggressively anti-secular in modern American history.

Yet in the intervening period a major, and likely independent, development has occurred. It intersects with our interest in secular identity in perplexing ways. For decades, researchers have been charting the growth of an *aggregate* (I'll explain why I use that specific term below) known as "the religiously unaffiliated." In popular parlance, they are referred to as "the Nones." This is because when asked by demographers about their religious preference they respond "none."

The topline numbers regarding the religiously unaffiliated are staggering. Although different surveys report slightly different results, we can say the following with reasonable confidence. In 1990, the Nones were assumed to be 8 percent of the population of the United States. In 2001, the figure jumped to 14 percent. The most recent data from 2018 has them at 31.3 percent of the American people (though demographers using different methodologies have suggested the number could be as much as 8 percentage points lower). One study suggests that their ranks increased by 30 million over the last ten years, bringing the number to 68 million.

But are the Nones "secularists"? Here we run into the problems about politicized definitions articulated above: there is a difference between self-identification on the one side, and partisan and media identification on the other. The New Atheists, for their part, were eager to draft the Nones into their growing secular army. In 2003, Dennett assumed that tens of millions of "secularists," or what he called "Brights," were poised to shift American politics leftwards (This did not come to pass; in 2004 the so-called "values voters," a CRAS movement, propelled George W. Bush to a second term).

Dennett's intuition, namely that the Nones were anti-CRAS voters, was not wrong. Surveys show that they skew towards the Democratic party in the United States (and internationally they show a leftward orientation as well). From support for gay rights, to legalized abortion, to the environment, the unaffiliated are overwhelmingly aligned with the center left and the left.

What Dennett and the New Atheists misunderstood was that the Nones were not an organized political coalition. Rather, they were an *aggregate*, or simply people who share a quality in common and otherwise have little to do with one another. They were not a unified movement with common beliefs, goals, leaders, solidarity, etc. They didn't recognize themselves as part of a group called "the Nones." This is why they couldn't be mobilized for Dennett's "Bright" revolution.

A deeper dive into the data, then and now, revealed something much more difficult to explain. Contrary to what the New Atheists believed, the Nones were not primarily atheists and agnostics (surveys vary rather considerably, but in no survey do the two groups combined comprise a majority of the "religiously unaffiliated"). More than half are deists or theists, or some undefined identity.

The more the data is analyzed, the more complex it becomes. Let's take one of the oft-repeated findings of Nones research: the overrepresentation of Asian-Americans in this category. An impressive 52.1 percent of Chinese Americans are categorized as religiously unaffiliated (and among younger generations even higher: 65.6 percent).

What the data doesn't show is that these Chinese-American "Nones" may simply be adhering to cultural traditions. Their spirituality consists of maintaining "proper relationships," respect for family, and moral rituals (think of our discussion of Confucianism in Chapter 10). These practices don't register as "religious" to Western demographers doing research on people with "no religion." Thus Chinese-Americans, and Asian-Americans more broadly, get shunted into the Nones category. But they'd appear to be more "affiliated" with their own culture than the term "unaffiliated" would suggest.

I draw your attention to this data as a cautionary tale regarding how we speak about secularism. Media stories abound about the growth of the "Nones." It is often stated that they are larger than the largest American religious groups (i.e., Roman Catholics and Evangelicals). But what we've just seen reminds us that most of the religiously unaffiliated are not atheists. More importantly, they are not organized for political action in the manner that CRAS movements are.

What remains to be answered is whether they view *themselves* as secularists living secular lives. Both pro- and anti-secular activists have used the "Nones = secularists" equation to further their goals. All we can say for now, is that the leftward political orientation of the religiously unaffiliated suggests that they will vote like people who support political secularism.

SECULAR NATIONALISM

"Secular nationalism" is a very particular, and not widely studied, type of secular identity. A secular nationalist wants to maintain, or restore, or create a secular state. Her identity is intersectional. She is a proud citizen of a country and convinced that the country must be governed according to secular principles.

France, India, Iran, Israel, and Turkey are some of the countries with significant columns of secular nationalists. All those nations have a large religious majority—of Catholics, Hindus, Shiite Muslims, Jews, and Sunni Muslims, respectively. All, save Israel, have, or once had, a secular government.

It would be inaccurate to say that the majority of secular nationalists in these countries are at war with religion, or that they are atheists. Secular nationalists are often religious themselves. In fact, they often belong to the *same* religion as their opponents. Even if they aren't particularly religious in terms of practice, they usually have no desire to leave the religion they were born into. This isn't to say that religious minorities can't also be secular nationalists. But what makes conflicts involving secular nationalists so unique is that the antagonisms occur *within* the religious majority.

The example of France comes to mind. A secular nationalist in 1905 or 1955 would likely have been born a Catholic. Because of her opposition to the role of the church in the nation's (and her) life, she would have understood herself to be *une française laique*. Her dispute would have been with other Catholics, some of whom were probably in her own extended family. This tends to lend a novelistic quality to conflicts within countries with strong secular-nationalist movements; it's not members of different faiths who are at odds, but co-religionists.

Another example would be the state of Israel. The tense "secular–religious" divide in that country features secularists (*hilonim*) most of whom are Jewish, though not observant, on one side. On the other side are religious-nationalist Zionists (who once played more of a moderating role) and the *haredim*, or ultra-orthodox Jews. The nation's religious minorities, be they Muslim, Druze, Christian, or Bahai, tend to side with the secularists.

In accord with our typology above, the belligerents on both sides of the conflict are overwhelmingly Jewish. A secularist in Tel Aviv often has an ultra-Orthodox cousin in Jerusalem's Mea Sharim neighborhood. An interesting theory to explore is whether these familial connections provide a breaking mechanism on mass internecine violence.

Secular Israelis, or *hilonim*, want the state to be secular. Aware that the Zionist movement, which created the state of Israel, was heavily secular-socialist or secular-liberal, they want to return the country to what they believe it was meant to be. They emphasize the *Israeli* nature of Israel. They place their hopes in the liberal-democratic state.

Their CRAS adversaries, by contrast, emphasize the *Jewish* nature of Israel. Their connection is not to the state, but to the sacred land. Though they increasingly seek to control the state so that they can preserve the sanctity of the land.

The Israeli secular nationalist is adamantly opposed to military exemptions for Yeshiva students; government subsidies for Yeshiva students; orthodox rabbinic control over personal law, involving marriage and divorce. She also advocates for full equality for women and sexual minorities.

Israel is not a secular state. It does not have a constitution, nor a bill of rights. Its way of regulating government–religion relations is largely based on (1) pre-existing laws and customs from the Ottoman era, and (2) one-off "agreements" (like Prime Minister David Ben-Gurion's June 19, 1947 letter to the leaders of the ultra-Orthodox party Agudat Israel) that granted tremendous power to the orthodox rabbinate. The Israeli secular nationalist devotes her political activism to secularizing the state. Her counterpart in Iran or Turkey seeks to *re*-secularize the state.

Secular nationalists, then, are described as secularists by themselves and by their adversaries. They have a high-intensity commitment to political secularism. Referring to them as "secular" seems unproblematic.

SECULAR HUMANISM

Depending on the country, a given secular nationalism might have millions, even tens of millions, of devotees. New Atheism likely possesses a few million followers worldwide. We are now going to look at what is variously called "secular humanism" or sometimes just "humanism." At its peak, between the 1930s to the 1990s, this school of thought attracted, at most, tens of thousands of adherents.

Despite its small size, the movement probably went farther than any other in thinking of secularism as an ethical lifestyle. Two figures stand out in the history of secular humanism, both philosophers. The first was John Dewey (1859–1952), one of the signatories of the 1933 *Humanist Manifesto*. The second was Paul Kurtz (1925–2012) who co-authored *Humanist Manifesto II* (1973) and drafted *A Secular Humanist Declaration* (1980).

These are compelling documents—clearly written, concise and well-conceived. They were composed decades before the internet age which propelled the New Atheists to mass recognition. Maybe that accounts for why the media, politicians, and policy makers largely ignored secular humanism. Only CRAS actors in the 1980s took note of this school (see below).

The intellectual heritage of "secular humanism" is easy to trace. The school basically modifies and updates the ideas of the French Radical Enlightenment and British freethought that we surveyed earlier. If Bradlaugh was the forerunner of the New Atheists, then Holyoake was the "spiritual" father of the secular humanists (see Chapter 8). The latter may be atheists or agnostics or whatever, but their tone was serene, reflective, and fundamentally positive.

Like all of the figures and movements just mentioned, secular humanists advocate a materialist worldview. They are thus deeply suspicious of all religious and supernatural truth claims. It follows that *science* and *reason* were accorded pride of place in their thought. By the 1970s, the school tweaked this intelligently. Secular humanists recognized there was a dark side to technology and science. *Humanist Manifesto II* seeks "to fuse reason with compassion." It continues, and reminds us that "reason must be tempered by humility."

The secular humanists, as with the New Atheists who came later, were overwhelmingly straight, male, and white. For their time, though, they were progressive on sex and gender issues. They supported abortion, birth control and the right of consenting adults to oblige their sexual preferences. Thoughtfully, they worried about humans being "exploited as sexual objects," an allusion to downsides of pornography and sex-work industries.

As early as the 1930s humanists evinced an inclination towards socialism (yet another link to Victorian infidels discussed in Chapter 8). In the 1970s and 1980s they spoke of "universalism," breaking down national boundaries, and a "transnational federal government." By the year 2000 they were calling for "a new planetary humanism." In terms of political secularism, secular humanists are staunchly separationist. For these reasons they chided communist secularisms for being "quasi-religious" and violating the principle of separation.

Like Holyoake, secular humanists did not emphasize politics or political activism. They were educated, reflective individuals who liked to think about what Kurtz called "eupraxsophy." This would be practical wisdom that "draws its basic principles and ethical values from science, ethics, and philosophy." There is a serenity and hopefulness in their rhetoric—the type of qualities that hard politics tends to dissolve.

Which is why it is strange that by the 1980s, this tiny philosophical school of thought found itself in the crosshairs of CRAS outrage. To read the Christian right in this period is to encounter a pervasive fear of "secular humanists." They are cited again and again as a threat to Judeo-Christian civilization. As noted earlier, labelling a group as "secular" is often politically motivated.

It's true that secular humanists defended evolution as part of their respect for science. Though it seems that CRAS activists noticed a stray footnote in a Supreme Court decision (*Torcaso v. Watkins*; 1961) that referred to "secular humanism" as a religion. Some observers believe that making the miniscule secular humanist movement into a monster was a lucrative fundraising ploy.

And so it came to pass, that a tiny, brainy movement became the bane of Christian conservatives for decades. The latter charged that the American government had violated the religion clauses by imposing an establishment of secular humanism on the country by teaching that religion's dogma (i.e., evolution) in public schools.

Secular humanism was basically a philosophy which a small number of people adopted as their own. In retrospect, their concerns about the future were not unfounded: "We are apprehensive that modern civilization," they wrote in 1980 "is threatened by forces antithetical to reason, democracy, and freedom."

FREEDOM FROM RELIGION: A NEW SECULAR PRINCIPLE

Above, we cast doubt on the claim that all *atheists are secularists*. On the basis of what we've just read, it is much more accurate to say that *not all secularists are atheists*.

In previous chapters we've seen that when any given religious group is small and outnumbered within a society it tends to favor political secularism. Religious minority status might be one of the most likely predictors of a self-ascribed secular identity. These are *believers* who take the adjective: secular Muslims in India, secular Jews in the United States, secular Sikhs in Canada, and so forth.

If there is any common denominator that binds all of the groups studied here, from New Atheists, to Nones, to secular nationalists, to secular humanists, to religious minorities, it is this: all seek either freedom *from* religion or freedom *from someone else*'s religion. A

New Atheist in the United States doesn't want his children saying "Under God" in the Pledge of Allegiance at school. A secular-nationalist Israeli woman doesn't want to sit at the back of a public bus in deference to Orthodox Jewish conceptions of modesty.

In the past few decades, this flip side of "religious freedom" has developed into a new core principle of secularism. In the modern multicultural era a liberal democracy must not only defend freedom of religion, but freedom *from* religion. The existence of so many different citizens with so many different secular identities creates significant new challenges for secular states.

SUGGESTIONS FOR FURTHER READING

On the Nones, a readable account of the religiously unaffiliated is offered by a pastor, James White, *The Rise of the Nones: Understanding and Reaching the Religiously Unaffiliated* (Grand Rapids, MI: Baker, 2014). Research about the Nones has positively obsessed religious and non-religious people for reasons having to do with voting blocs and the future of struggling religious denominations.

There are various polls which chart the growth of the Nones. Above, we used a few. These include Barry A. Kosmin, Ariela Keysar with Ryan Cragun, and Juhem Navarro-Rivera, *American Nones: The Profile of the No Religion Population* (Hartford, CT: Institute for the Study of Secularism in Society & Culture, 2009), http://commons.trincoll.edu/aris/publications/2008-2/american-nones-the-profile-of-the-no-religion-population.

For other polls, see Pew Research Forum, "In U.S., Number of Religious 'Nones' has Grown by Nearly Thirty Million Over Past Decade" (October 17, 2019), www.pewforum.org/2019/10/17/in-u-s-decline-of-christianity-continues-at-rapid-pace; Pew Research Center, "The Unaffiliated" (2014), www.pewforum.org/religious-landscape-study/religious-tradition/unaffiliated-religious-nones/#social-and-political-views; and Gregory A. Smith, Anna Schiller, and Haley Nolan, "In US, Decline of Christianity Continues at Rapid Pace." *Pew Research Center* 17 (2019), www.pewforum.org/2019/10/17/in-u-s-decline-of-christianity-continues-at-rapid-pace.

We also factored in some data from Ryan P. Burge, "How Many 'Nones' Are There? Explaining the Discrepancies in Survey Estimates," *Review of Religious Research* (2020), pp. 1–18, https://

link.springer.com/article/10.1007%2Fs13644-020-00400-7;   and Aidan Connaughton, "Religiously Unaffiliated People More Likely Than Those with a Religion to Lean Left, Accept Homosexuality" (2020), www.pewresearch.org/fact-tank/2020/09/28/religiously-unaffiliated-people-more-likely-than-those-with-a-religion-to-lean-left-accept-homosexuality.

The data about Chinese Americans came from Russell Jeung, Brett Esaki, and Alice Liu, "Redefining Religious Nones: Lessons from Chinese and Japanese American Young Adults," *Religions*, 6, no. 3 (2015), pp. 891–911, www.mdpi.com/2077-1444/6/3/891.

On secular nationalism see Uri Ram, "Why Secularism Fails? Secular Nationalism and Religious Revivalism in Israel," *International Journal of Politics, Culture and Society*, 21 (2008), pp. 57–73.

For some studies of religion and government in Israel see the articles by Ilan Greilsammer, "Ben-Gurion's Status Quo and Moving the Frontlines Between *Hilonim* (Secularists) and *Datim* (Religious)," and Denis Charbit, "Israel's *Self-Restrained* Secularism from the 1947 Status Quo Letter to the Present," in *Secularism on the Edge: Rethinking Church-State Relations in the United States, France, and Israel*, edited by Jacques Berlinerblau, Sarah Fainberg, and Aurora Nou (New York: Palgrave Macmillan, 2014).

On secular humanism, Paul Kurtz wrote many works. His *Defense of Secular Humanism* (Amherst, MA: Prometheus Books, 1983) contains many of the manifestos mentioned above.

LGBTQ RIGHTS IN URUGUAY AND SECULARSTAN

With Alexander Lin and Ria Pradhan

Thirteen chapters into our book, we are now familiar with the broad historical outline of political secularism. We have acquainted ourselves with ten secular principles. We have seen how these can be "mixed and matched" and "run through" four distinct "secular frameworks." The tone of these frameworks ranges from "religion-positive" to "religion-negative." The table below places our four frameworks side by side. It shows how each prioritizes (and de-prioritizes) our 10 principles.

Perhaps we could re-title Figure 14.1 "Secularism is complicated and messy." That's because we are about to see that the principles

Political Secularism: Frameworks and Corresponding Emphasis on Principles				
	THE FRAMEWORKS			
The Principles	Accommodationism	Separationism	Laïcité	Soviet Atheism
Equality	CORE	MEDIUM	HIGH	LOW
Two Powers	HIGH	HIGH	CORE	LOW
State Supremacy	HIGH	HIGH	CORE	CORE
Internal Constraint	HIGH	HIGH	MEDIUM	LOW
Freedom of Conscience	CORE	HIGH	HIGH	LOW
Order	HIGH	HIGH	CORE	CORE
Toleration	CORE	HIGH	HIGH	LOW
Beliefs/Acts	LOW	HIGH	CORE	LOW
Disestablishment/Neutrality	HIGH	CORE	MEDIUM	LOW
Reason	LOW	MEDIUM	HIGH	CORE
	RELIGION POSITIVE	RELIGION NEUTRAL	RELIGION NEGATIVE	FREEDOM FROM RELIGION (ZERO)

Figure 14.1 Political secularism: frameworks and corresponding emphasis on principles

DOI: 10.4324/9781003140627-17

and interpretive frameworks of political secularism don't always do what we might expect them to do.

To get this point across we are going to look at the intersection between political secularism and LGBTQ rights. When that intersection is discussed a neat and tidy narrative often emerges. Religion is depicted as *against* LGBTQ rights. Meanwhile, the secular state is assumed to *support* them. But is that actually what happens in reality?

The answer is indeed complicated and messy. We'll start with a case study of a secular state, Uruguay, which supports that narrative. Then, using examples from around the world we'll start to identify exceptions to this rule. In doing so, we will discover some nuances and subtleties about political secularisms which challenge common wisdom. We'll close by imagining how the most ideal, most principled, most constitutionally compliant, and most framework-conforming of secular states would approach the question of LGBTQ rights.

URUGUAY

Uruguay provides an interesting, and unusual, example of how secular states regulate LGBTQ concerns. It is a nation that appears to actually comply with its secular principles. Uruguay's unique history has created unusual church–state dynamics. So unusual that the treatment of LGBTQ communities in Uruguay is among the most progressive in Latin America, if not the world.

The South American nation's framework is closest to Separation. Moreover, its core principle is *disestablishment/neutrality*. Article 5 of its 1918 Constitution declares: "All religious cults are free in Uruguay. The State doesn't endorse any religion."

Uruguay has a high percentage of citizens who are born Catholic (up to 80 percent according to some estimates). Typically, in such societies, be they nineteenth-century France, Spain, Italy, Mexico, etc. a traditionalist church holds strong political sway. On the basis of these data points, this book may have conditioned you to make certain assumptions.

You may be drawing the justifiable conclusion that a muscular Catholic CRAS formation blocks every secular initiative proposed by the secular government. Surprisingly, this is *not* the case in

Uruguay. Presently, the church does not wield the considerable cultural and political power that it does in other Latin American nations.

Various explanations have been proposed for this unusual state of affairs. One takes us back to the fateful nineteenth century. During this period, the religion of Freemasonry was popular in Uruguay. We've already seen examples of religions that may mesh or harmonize with secularism (e.g., Confucianism, American Baptism). Freemasonry, with its skeptical orientation (and long running disagreements with institutions like the Vatican), may be yet another. Its popularity in Uruguay appears to have prevented the Catholic Church from matching the influence it had in, let's say, Mexico.

In terms of the twentieth century, another key variable is education. The teaching of religious dogma in public schools was prohibited in 1909 and more broadly by the 1918 Constitution. Likely as a result of Uruguay's success in keeping the church at bay, control of educational institutions was in the hands of the secular state.

This plausibly accounts for the fact that a very high percentage of Uruguay's population is "religiously unaffiliated" (see Chapter 13). In fact, a 2018 survey showed that more than half the country could be described as such. As noted in our Introduction, both secular states and CRAS actors wish to dominate the public educational sector. The high percentage of Nones in Uruguay demonstrates why each side is so invested in that battle.

That being said, the Uruguayan Catholic Church demonstrates a few anomalous traits. Scholars have noted that, unlike other parts of Latin America, the Church in Uruguay retains weak ties to the military, landowners, and business elites. Too, it does not always align itself with reactionary regimes. In fact during the era of a right-wing military dictatorship (1973–1984) the Uruguayan bishops were critical of the powers that be.

The situation on the ground for LGBTQ Uruguayans today compares favorably to almost any other nation on earth. A few facts confirm this impression. Sex between persons of the same gender has been legal since 1934. Discrimination against LGBTQ persons was outlawed in 2004. Gay adoption was approved in 2009. Same-sex marriage was approved in 2013.

As for trans persons, the progressive nature of Uruguay's commitment to civil rights is again surprising. Its health care system, for example, will subsidize gender confirmation surgery and pay for hormone treatments. Not coincidentally Uruguay was the second Latin American nation after Cuba to decriminalize abortion. This reminds us that the rights of women and sexual minorities are often twinned in disputes between secular states and CRAS movements.

In Uruguay we encounter a secular state that adapts a separationist framework. As Figure 14.1 demonstrates, the core value of such a state is *disestablishment/neutrality*. This government actually complies with this constitutional provision (compare with the non-compliance we saw in the USSR, and Ethiopia in Chapters 9 and 10).

Notice how a small symbolic gesture serves as both a cause and effect of a secular state that abides by its principles. The following quote from the former president of Uruguay, José Mujica, about why he did not attend Pope Francis's inauguration, is instructive in this regard: "Why should I? Uruguay is a lay country. I respect Francis as a person and religious leader, I visited him privately afterward. But I had no official business there."

COMPLEX AND MESSY

Not every state, obviously, is like Uruguay. Not even *secular* states are like secular Uruguay. In order to probe that point, I'll briefly state three ground rules. These will equip us with a more textured portrait of what happens around LGBTQ issues—in fact almost *any* issue involving political secularism.

NOT EVERY RELIGION IS ANTI-LGBTQ

In this book we've focused on a specific type of religious actor (i.e., CRAS) because it often crosses swords with the secular state. But when thinking about political secularism it is essential to recognize that—contrary to the assumptions of New Atheists (Chapter 13)—*not all religious groups are CRAS actors or their enablers.*

All religious groups have LGBTQ members. Further, entire religious denominations may be allies in the struggle for LGBTQ civil rights. In the United States, Reform Judaism and mainline

Protestant denominations like United Church of Christ are gay-affirming. As another example we might think of South Africa, in the post-Apartheid era. In 1994, Bishop Desmond Tutu declared:

> If the church, after the victory over apartheid, is looking for a worthy moral crusade, then this is it: the fight against homophobia and heterosexism. I pray that we will engage in it with the same dedication and fervour which we showed against the injustice of racism.

Thus on a continent where no fewer than 33 countries have sodomy laws prohibiting same-sex relations, it is important to recall that there are dissenting *religious* voices. If you recall our analysis in Chapter 2, we noted that the *equality* principle was born in a religious context. When a cleric like Bishop Tutu invokes this concept, he is interpreting it in accordance with his religious scruples—not in accordance with liberal and secular interpretations of *equality*. Though both arrive at the same conclusions.

We should not then assume that religious groups are always opposed to LGBTQ rights. Nor should it be presumed that traditional CRAS actors, such as Catholicism, are monolithic. Uruguay's neighbor, Argentina, legalized same sex marriage in 2010. There were practicing Catholic lawmakers who voted to support legalization. "A significant number of legislators," writes one scholar, "showed their Catholic identification and voted in favor of same-sex marriage, going against the Vatican's doctrinal principles and instructions." These "dissidents" made explicit reference to their Catholic identity when presenting their arguments against the Church's position.

This last example adds an important nuance. CRAS movements may not be as uniform in their thinking as their leaders allege. This is especially true of Catholicism. Its large international cast of intellectuals features a significant liberal, anti-CRAS wing. In the Argentinian case, those Catholic legislators who voted to legalize same-sex marriage, as with Bishop Tutu, made *theological* arguments. If we think back to the dissent of Marsilius and Ockham (Chapter 2) we recall that political secularism was born of *Christian* thinkers who challenged the authority of the church on the basis of *Christian* doctrine.

Religious diversity complexifies the activism of CRAS movements. As we saw in Chapter 11, they deny the *existence* of other faith-based groups that disagree with them. They do so because they must portray their activism as a struggle of religion—*all* religion—against a godless/secular state. Yet as the Argentinian example indicates, they also must contend with internal dissent as well.

Religious diversity also complexifies the work of the secular state. If you recall our skinny definition of political secularism, it speaks of the state as regulating the relationship *"between religious citizens themselves."* The responsibility of officiating between religious groups (and even an internally divided religious group), as we shall see momentarily, is a true challenge for any secular government.

NOT EVERY SECULAR STATE IS PRO-LGBTQ

If not all religious groups are homophobic, then it follows that not all secular states are *not* homophobic. In the final decades of the twentieth century, when political secularism was in the driver's seat in the United States and India, government treatment of gay people left much to be desired.

For example, in India LGBTQ Muslims face "dual subordination." They have been discriminated against by sharia law *and* by India's Section 377 (a relic of the British colonial era outlawing same-sex relations). Homosexual ties were decriminalized in India in 2018. Despite this, discrimination still runs rampant. India's LGBTQ Muslims (and Hindus) lead secret lives in fear of persecution. This also means that from 1947–2018 the "sovereign, socialist, secular, democratic republic" of India engaged in *de jure* discrimination against its gay citizens.

The Indian case is striking because of the way it contradicts the country's stated secular principles. As Figure 14.1 above indicates, India's Accommodationist framework emphasizes *equality* and *toleration*. Yet its record from 1947 to the present has been unsatisfactory at best in bestowing these amenities upon its LGBTQ citizens.

Then again, one counter-argument might be that *equality* and *toleration* in a secular state only applies to religion. Gandhi said "*sarva dharma samabhava*" ("equal respect for all *religions*," Chapter 7). He did not say "equal respect for all sexual identities." I raise this semantic distinction because it demonstrates the complexity of the issues that we are studying (and because it will invariably be raised by anti-LGBTQ forces in India).

The case of the People's Republic of China also verifies our contention that a secular state is not always a "friend." Homosexuality was decriminalized in 1997. In the intervening quarter of a century, very slow progress has been made towards equal rights for Chinese LGBTQ communities. The secular state's policy nowadays is described by some as "The three nos: no approval, no disapproval, no promotion."

It emerges from this that one cannot always blame religion for the existence of what scholars call "political homophobia." The People's Republic of China is an offshoot of the Soviet (atheist) framework. As Figure 14.1 reminds us, that framework emphasizes *state supremacy*. Insofar as the party *is* the state, and insofar as atheism is required for party membership (See Chapter 10), we can't blame a policy as disappointing as "the three nos" on anything but Soviet (atheist) secularism.

A secular state, then, can have an implicit heteronormative bias, just as it can have an implicit sexist bias. The origins of that bias might indeed be rooted in centuries of religious dogma. Yet, may be traced to non-religious sources as well. Put differently: it isn't always religion's fault.

THE ENIGMA OF TRANSNATIONALISM

A secular state, in theory, pushes theology out of its governance philosophy. With the exception of Soviet frameworks, however, all political secularisms permit religious groups to mobilize in the domain of what is called "civil society."

That's where outside groups enter our consideration. When it comes to LGBTQ issues we should be aware of the added pressures placed on secular states by transnational actors.

It should not come as a surprise that American CRAS movements and NGOs have exported their anti-LGBTQ activism to countries far and wide. In our introduction we mentioned Uganda as one example. Identical forms of anti-LGBTQ transnational activism are witnessed in other African countries.

The Reverend Jackson George Gabriel of the Episcopal Church of South Sudan and Sudan applauds foreign actors who "are telling us to stand firm against homosexuality." These American NGOs are providing more than moral support, pep talks, etc. In addition, they offer considerable financial assistance, legal counsel, and organizational resources to assist various national anti-LGBTQ crusades.

An almost identical situation has long been observed in Latin America. American Evangelicals and Pentecostals have allied with legislators in countries across South America interested in blocking laws that would legalize gay civil unions. This work is done in countries like Peru, Brazil, Costa Rica, Paraguay, Dominican Republic, and Colombia, among others. Interestingly, Uruguay, discussed above, has not developed a burgeoning Evangelical and Pentecostal movement. This might also explain why its laws are so LGBTQ-friendly.

In the face of the aggressive, and highly successful activism of these transnational CRAS movements, there has been a counter-response. In Africa, a group called The Fellowship of Affirming Ministries (TFAM), has come together with the explicit goal of blunting the influence of American white Evangelicals. TFAM has been described as one part of a burgeoning "Pan-African LGBT-affirming Christian movement."

TFAM originated in the United States and is composed of African-American church communities. Interestingly, the group does not seek to ally with political secularists, nor does it deploy traditional secular strategies. Its director of global ministries, Bishop Joseph W. Tolton eschews rights-oriented approaches used by secular LGBTQ activists. Instead of this "secular gospel," he believes successful engagement will "come through the Bible." TFAM's work has taken them to Kenya, Uganda, Rwanda, Zimbabwe, and Côte d'Ivoire.

It would be irresponsible to draw an equivalence between pro- and anti-LGBTQ transnational movements in Africa and Latin America. The latter are infinitely larger, more established and more influential. On the theoretical level, however, a group like TFAM raises an important question. A secular state, according to our skinny definition, must regulate relations *between* religious groups. If different religious groups in civil society disagree strongly about an issue like gay marriage, and if the secular state is supposed to be neutral, how is the government supposed to respond?

SECULARSTAN

As a thought experiment let's imagine LGBTQ rights in the context of an ideal secular state called Secularstan. This new nation is so multi-religious, multi-ethnic, and multicultural that its population seems to have been generated by some algorithm engineered for maximum diversity.

The founders of Secularstan explicitly adopted all ten of our principles in the detailed and precise 2021 constitution. In honor of John Locke, the preamble states that even the "consent of the people" cannot alter "the core secular nature of the Republic." In honor of India, the new state adopted a religion-positive accommodationist framework as the law of the land. It even ranked its secular priorities, explicitly identifying *equality* as its core value.

We noted in Chapter Seven that accommodationism has a bit of a blindspot and liability vis a vis the religiously unaffiliated. Namely, it doesn't seem committed to accommodating them. The ever thoughtful Secularstani constitution is aware of that. It is the first in the world to identify the religiously unaffiliated, or "Nones," as a group eligible to receive state benefits and support equal to, and alongside, every other faith denomination.

There is a CRAS column in Secularstan. These citizens' concerns are identical to those of their co-religionists across the world. In fact, they collaborate with one another in an effort to change laws in the young nation (unlike the People's Republic of China, Secularstan permits foreign missionaries). These religiously conservative Secularstanis repeatedly advocate for laws that deprive LGBTQ people of equal rights, in particular same-sex marriage.

The Pentecostals in Secularstan are opposed to gay marriage. The Reform Jews in Secularstan, by contrast, are in favor. In deference to the fact that different faiths have different views, should the state adopt a position of *disestablishment/neutrality* on LGBTQ issues? How does Secularstan orient its own state policies when its citizens disagree?

We can begin with *state supremacy* and the *two powers* principles. These two provisions, at first, seem to protect LGBTQ rights. If the secular state is "on top," then the subordinate status of a CRAS religious group prevents it from imposing its religious beliefs about sexuality on others.

A few hitches arise though. As we saw above, it is possible that secular state *itself* might possess a heteronormative bias. Let's not presume that the leadership class of Secularstan was immune to that sort of thinking. All of which is to say, the existence of a powerful secular state is never a guarantee of non-homophobic policies.

Disestablishment/neutrality presents a different type of hitch. Today's LGBTQ communities generally want the state to not align its policies with the worldview of conservative religious actors. As we saw above, however, not all religious groups are opposed to LGBTQ rights. This creates an intriguing legal opening for CRAS actors and a dilemma for the secular state.

Consider a state that permits same-sex civil unions, gay people in the military, transgender-friendly bathrooms, etc. From the standpoint of CRAS activists, this state is tacitly engaging in an establishment, or *religious* affirmation of homosexuality and transgender identities. They allege that the government is favoring one type of faith-based approach to sexuality, or what conservatives call the "pro-gay agenda." By linking that so-called agenda to gay-affirming religious groups, the "false neutrality" claim can be made (think of how Evangelicals in America weaponized the Supreme Court's designation of "secular humanism" as a religion; Chapter 13).

Secularstan could avoid the conflict by claiming to be "above the religious fray." It would thus refrain from making any laws on these matters. After all, the state regulates relations *between* religious groups and matters are getting tense between Reform Jews and Pentecostals. The danger here, of course, is that a lot of existing anti-gay discriminatory practices on the ground would continue if no safeguards were in place.

Yet these two hitches would seem to be overruled by the *equality* principle. The logic here is fairly straightforward: all citizens possess fundamentally equal value and rights in the eyes of the state. Full stop. The incidental question of one's sexual preference should in no way impact how the state substantively deals with a citizen's rights. Equality would seem to be political secularisms' "checkmate" to any initiative to deprive LGBTQ persons of full rights under the law.

Still, CRAS activists are masters of system-gaming and exploiting legal loopholes. In the United States they have shrewdly invoked secular principles (the same ones they otherwise reject) as a means of pursuing their agenda.

In a famous case, a county clerk in Kentucky refused to grant marriage licenses to gay couples who were legally entitled to receive them. The clerk, Kim Davis, claimed that her faith prohibited same-sex unions. In her own words: "To issue a marriage license which conflicts with God's definition of marriage, with my name affixed to the certificate, would violate my conscience."

Ms. Davis and her supporters were using a *freedom of conscience* claim *against* an *equality* claim. Pitting secular principles against one another is a common legal tactic of CRAS actors. In the utopian Secularstan, however, the Constitution explicitly prioritizes *equality*. Once the *internal constraint* mechanisms (i.e., the courts) get involved, they issue a ruling: The *equality* principle (intersecting with the *belief/acts* distinction) overrides the claim of *freedom of conscience*.

The Secularstani version of Ms. Davis must grant the license or face the termination of her employment.

NEAT AND SIMPLE SECULARISM

We began this chapter by asking: Is it true that religion nowadays contests LGBTQ rights and the secular state defends them? A scholar of LGBTQ issues answers the question this way:

> One of the most important variables in explaining the expansion of LGBT rights worldwide is the propagation of secularism: the extent to which both the state and citizens are able to adopt positions that are independent of those held by organized religion. Because we know that religious groups are the most vocal and active opponents of LGBT rights, secularism can be an important predictor of whether countries will struggle to adopt strong LGBT rights.

We generally concur, but with two crucial provisos: (1) religious groups are not always opponents of LGBTQ rights; and (2) secular states are not always supporters.

We've also learned that political secularisms need to reach a high bar in order to be perfect. First, they need clear and comprehensive constitutions and law codes (more like France's 1905 Law and less like America's First Amendment). Second, they need to explicitly articulate what their "secular" state believes—as in what its core principles are and how it *prioritizes* them. Finally, they must comply with their own laws. Non-compliance, as we saw in the case of Ethiopia (Chapter 10) has undermined many sound secular constitutions.

If those criteria were met, political secularisms would be a lot less messy and complex.

SUGGESTIONS FOR FURTHER READING

Some articles used above were Javier Corrales, "Understanding the Uneven Spread of LGBT Rights in Latin America and the Caribbean, 1999–2013," *Journal of Research in Gender Studies*, 7, no. 1 (2017), pp. 52–82; Juan Marco Vaggione "Sexual Rights and Religion: Same-sex Marriage and Lawmakers' Catholic Identity in Argentina," *University of Miami Law Review*, 65 (2010), p. 935; Adriaan VanKlinken, "Culture Wars, Race, and Sexuality: A Nascent Pan-African LGBT-Affirming Christian Movement and the Future of Christianity," *Journal of Africana Religions*, 5, no. 2 (2017), pp. 217–238; Siri Gloppen and Lise Rakner, "LGBT Rights in Africa," in *Research Handbook on Gender, Sexuality and the Law*, edited by Chris Ashford and Alexander Maine (Cheltenham: Edward Elgar Publishing, 2020); J. Christopher Soper and Joel S. Fetzer, "Uruguay: Stable Secular Nationalism," in their *Religion and Nationalism in Global Perspective* (Cambridge: Cambridge University Press, 2018). pp, 161–183; and Amy Edmonds, "Moral Authority and Authoritarianism: The Catholic Church and the Military Regime in Uruguay," *Journal of Church and State*, 56, no. 4 (2014), pp. 644–669.

LOVE THE REFEREE?

As far as some are concerned, secularism is nearing the end of its run. Or perhaps it has already expired. A massive body of POMOFOCO scholarship casually refers to the "post-secular." "The historical modus vivendi called secularism is coming apart at the seams," writes one critic.

Predictions of secularism's demise are plausible. We are, after all, half a century into a global conservative religious revival. The national and transnational CRAS movements that assail political secularism are usually immense, organized, staffed by skilled operatives, and exceedingly well-funded. In some cases, they are fully capable of deploying considerable violence.

Secular frameworks in America and India, are being disassembled from within by major political parties. In India, the ruling BJP advances a Hindu nationalist or *hindutva* ideology. Members of the Republican Party in the United States openly speak of the nation's "Anglo-Saxon culture" and their love of "God and country." Secular nationalists and religious minorities in both countries fear the rise of a Theo State.

In addition, an obvious takeaway from the chapters you've read is that political secularisms are highly imperfect. From massive terminological confusion, to "false neutrality," to "constitutional non-compliance," to a yawning gap between words and deeds, to authoritarian one-party states, to very shaky grips on the hearts and minds of the masses—the first century of secular governance leaves much room for improvement.

Yet even if the prediction comes to pass and secularism were to disappear from the earth (and the *Saeculum*) tomorrow, the problem

DOI: 10.4324/9781003140627-18

remains of what its replacement might be. Before confronting that dilemma, let us ask again: *what is secularism?*

DEFINING OUR TERMS

We began with the following "skinny definition": *political secularism refers to legally binding actions of the secular state that seek to regulate the relationship between itself and religious citizens, and between religious citizens themselves.* We then identified ten principles of secularism. We now know three of these must be present for the most basic form of political secularism to exist: (1) *two powers*, (2) *state supremacy*, and (3) *disestablishment/neutrality*.

When one finds a nation with a religion/state binary where the latter is "on top," and constitutionally/legally unaffiliated with religion(s), then one is looking at a political secularism. In this very superficial sense, North Korea and Cuba are yet two more Soviet successor states that check the boxes (even though in practice they don't respect the *disestablishment/neutrality* principle).

But if a secularism is to be livable for its citizens, it must observe and implement some, or ideally all, of the remaining seven core principles we identified. These principles are mixed and matched in what we called the four "secular frameworks." Two of those frameworks, we argued, have serious internal deficiencies. Soviet secularisms seems bound to fail—and create more untold suffering in the process—until they embrace *disestablishment/neutrality*. To survive, they must abandon their quasi-establishment of atheism.

Soviet-style secularisms, such as the one we see in China, also need to truly respect *freedom of conscience, freedom of speech, toleration,* and observe *equality* by not persecuting citizens of faith. An authentic mechanism of *internal constraint*, be it a robust legal system or protections for opposition political parties, would be necessary as well.

A less morally flawed secular framework is separationism. Yet it is based on a metaphor which is problematic. The workings of a government cannot be "walled off" from religion or vice versa. For better or for worse, the two are completely enmeshed. That's because so many citizens are themselves religious. That's also because the history of a country is so tied up with the culture of a given religion or religions. Introductory textbooks sometimes define "secularism" *as* "separation of church and state." I hope this study has convinced you that separationism is just *one* type of political secularism.

As for *laïcité* and accommodationism, the drawbacks we mentioned in Chapters 6 and 7 are not inconsiderable. But let's say that even these two frameworks succumb to the fate that secularism's critics intend. What kind of governance structure would replace them?

ALTERNATIVES

Is secularism, one could ask, even necessary? Admittedly, there are some countries with official state religions that offer citizens all the deliverables that secularism promises. These non-secular nations include England (Church of England) and Denmark (Evangelical Lutheran Church). In the words of one political scientist, these states support a religion, "but the religion is not mandatory and the state does not dominate the official religion's institutions."

Then again, I wouldn't feel comfortable abolishing political secularism on the supposition that all nations will revert to Denmark and Britain's form (or similar examples like Iceland, Finland and Norway). Those countries share three unique ingredients: (1) a government that is itself not preoccupied by religion, and (2) a sizable religious majority, among whom (3) the level of religious belief, church attendance, "burning Zeal," *is quite low.*

An establishment of religion can only provide secularism's benefits when these precise conditions are present. Now, think of countries with religious establishments that lack these features. Iran, Saudi Arabia, Afghanistan, and Pakistan offer worst-case scenarios. Secular principles, such as *disestablishment/neutrality* (and the safety it creates for religious minorities), *equality* (and its respect for the rights of women and sexual minorities), *freedom of conscience,* and *freedom of speech* do not fare well in these countries. The ingredients here are (1) a government that is preoccupied by religion, (2) a sizable religious majority, and (3) extremely high levels of religious belief and passion.

Now let's consider an official religion in a country where the majority/minority ratios are less uneven and the landscape is more diverse. Imagine an establishment of Protestantism in the United States called the Church of America. Such an institution would rapidly create tensions. Disagreements would break out between Evangelical and mainline Protestants over *whose* Protestantism to establish.

Much more explosive would be the opposition of the nation's large Roman Catholic population. Neither would Mormons, not to mention all non-Christian minorities, be comfortable with the Church of America. CRAS actors of all faiths are presently unified in their dislike of political secularism. They might appreciate it much more upon discovering that the religion "on top" (i.e., Church of America) is not their own.

Secularism, then, can't be eliminated because the problems it addresses never go away. Its elimination would present grave dangers for religions not in the majority, women and sexual minorities, the booming international population of Nones, and so many others.

All of which is to say that secularisms likely cannot be replaced. This makes us acknowledge—with a wink and a sigh—John Locke's override clause (see Chapter 4). It doesn't matter whether citizens want political secularism or not; it must exist in some form lest there be complete chaos.

Then again, secularism can and must be *improved*. Most of all it needs *innovation*. We will propose improvements and innovations momentarily.

POLITICAL SECULARISM IN HISTORY: UNKNOWNS

My reconstruction of political secularism's history in this book is fairly original. Even if it is only half correct, it points to many issues about which we know little. If more research is conducted it is entirely possible that the historical framework I advanced will be obsolete in a few decades. Let's review our findings with an eye towards identifying some major areas for future research.

Secularisms, we saw, took a *very* long time to achieve the various shapes and forms that they eventually did. This -ism was not designed at one moment in time. Its "architects" did not usually know one another. A fact that suggests there must be *many* other "architects" besides the handful which we discussed.

Until the nineteenth century, our gaps in knowledge about these figures (who must have lived all over the world) are immense. To give but one example, in the research for this work the name of the poet John Milton (1608–1674) kept surfacing in unexpected ways. Yet studies of the relation between the thought of this huge literary figure and political secularism are few and far between. The investigation of our subject is still in its infancy.

We have also suggested that political secularism is born of trauma. It is an -ism that suffers from PTSD, because it remembers something—something awful—about religion's negative potential. Secularism is built on fear—the fear that faith-based passions can overheat, triggering mass violence. The murder of millions of Hindus, Muslims, and Sikhs at the formation of India and Pakistan in 1947 is just another grim example. It sits aside John Locke's own memories of seventeenth-century Europe.

Are these fears justified? Do the measures that political secularisms enact to tamp down that violence actually work? British colonial secularism—which was a pseudo-secularism—created even more religious unrest. Yet it is undeniable that the United States and France have largely avoided such strife under secular regimes. CRAS actors chide secularism for forbidding seemingly trivial acts like allowing school children to say "under God" in the American Pledge of Allegiance, or the wearing of headscarves in France. Are these prohibitions excessive? Or are they a small price to pay for long lasting religious liberty and peace?

Another of our findings identified the period from 1905 onward as the "rapid combustion" century. Political secularism as a governing principle was first activated in France with the 1905 Law. Then, in 1917, the Bolsheviks radically retooled Jacobin ideas. In the same year, Mexico separated church from state. Between 1923 and 1937, Turkey became a secular republic. The Supreme Court of the United States embraced separationist secularism in the 1940s. India's framework of accommodationism can be traced to its independence and nationhood in 1947.

None of the evidence above leads me to believe that political secularism was operative in the Enlightenment as POMOFOCO scholars contend. Nor was it anywhere near as "hegemonic" in the eighteenth and nineteenth centuries as is alleged. During those periods champions of political secularisms were involved in running battles—many of which they lost—with religious reactionaries.

The "fateful nineteenth" century (see Chapter 8) is fateful not only because of these skirmishes, but because of the "swerve" that led secularism and atheism to lock arms. Given the downstream impact of this coupling on the USSR and the People's Republic of

China, we cannot underestimate the world-historical significance of the swerve.

We know little about how these ideas circulated outward from France, and especially England. The period between, let's say, the Bradlaugh/Holyoake debate in 1870 and the Bolshevik Revolution of 1917 begs for an intellectual history. Such a study would probe how ideas about political secularism diffused across the continent and into the minds of figures as diverse as Lenin and Atatürk.

A final area for future research concerns the Western or "Euro" nature of secularism. We pointed to individual secular principles that developed in pre-modern and Enlightenment Europe. These ideas were later selectively collated into secular frameworks of governance by various Christian nation-states.

Throughout this study, however, we've had reason to complexify such a "pure" European genealogy. Our discussion of ancient India introduced us to emperors who preached religious toleration before John Locke did. Confucian influence in ancient China may have resulted in governing structures that did much of the work of political secularism a thousand years before it existed.

There are other leads to be pursued. One scholar has pointed to the Lebanese Druze prince Fakhr ad-Dīn II al-Ma'an (1585–1635) as a secular person of interest. This ruler may have been a proponent of "premodern proto-secularism." He upheld polices in favor of *toleration*, opposed discrimination and spoke of *equality* between his Muslim and Christian subjects. Another researcher has argued provocatively that Sharia law works best with a neutral state, and that separationist governing arrangements are observable throughout Islamic history.

Its genealogy aside, it is pointless to view contemporary secularism as a monocultural phenomena. As the Table below indicates, upwards of two dozen African countries embrace political secularism, constitutionally at least.

Much more research needs to be conducted on how these secular statutes came to reside in these constitutions. As we saw in the case of Ethiopia (and the United States and the USSR) there is also the issue of non-compliance. As one scholar opines in his study of governments in African nations, separation of church and state exists "only in the area of rhetoric." False neutrality claims have been explicitly made in Tanzania, Ghana, the Democratic

Secularisms and African Constitutions

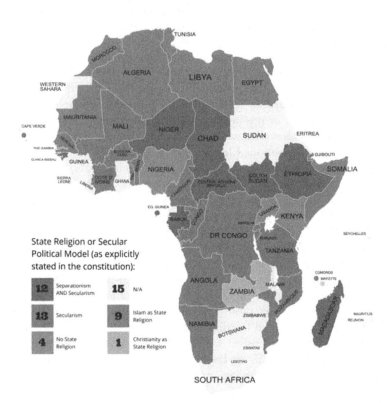

Figure 15.1 Secularisms and African constitutions

Republic of Congo, and Cameroon. The next major area of research in the study of political secularism is Africa.

THE FIFTH FRAMEWORK

Secularism, I observed, was confusing and fascinating. I hope the preceding chapters have made this subject more of the latter and less of the former.

In closing, it must be noted that there has been very little *innovation* in secular theory over the past half century. In fact, there has been almost none. It is hard to think of an individual secular theorist, let alone a think tank, or school of thought that has tried to refresh, update, or improve the secular vision as it lurches into its third millennia. There are few new ideas, even though the implications of a growing Nones population begs us to theorize *freedom from religion* as a new secular principle to be balanced against all the rest. We await a fifth framework.

This lack of energy is partly a consequence of being constantly on the defensive. CRAS movements have applied intense pressure in the political sphere; POMOFOCO in the intellectual sphere. Ultimately, however, the fault lies with secularism. On the national and global levels it has not produced enough leaders and intellectuals to steer it through an era of conservative religious revival. Nor has it ever been able to ameliorate, or even identify, its own flaws.

With that in mind, I would suggest a few innovations. These range from slight tweaks to more substantive overhauls of secular principles. I stress, once again, that not all secularisms are of the Soviet variety, nor are all religions fundamentalist (see Chapter 14). Disagreements between governments, religious citizens, and irreligious citizens are completely normal. There are countless examples of all parties finding ways to resolve these conflicts. The proposals below assume that a "vast middle" exists and common ground can be found.

Many of the issues that need to be urgently rethought are much larger than secularism. For instance, the rise of digital media has made *freedom of expression* infinitely more complicated than it was in the time of the Victorian infidels. In this era of disinformation and conspiracy theories, a new secular analysis of expressive liberties is needed.

We'll leave an issue like that to theorists of democracy, of which secularism is a small but vital component. In terms of secular principles, we propose three innovations, as follows.

TWO POWERS OR THREE?

The *two powers* binary powered conflicts in Medieval and Reformation Christendom—conflicts so unsightly that they eventually created an urgent need for reform. Political secularism was Modernity's way of saying that religion cannot always be left to its own devices.

But the world, obviously, has changed. In light of the remarkable international growth of the religiously unaffiliated (Chapter 13), secular theory must think less of a binary, and more in terms of a *trinary*. It would be composed of a secular state, religious citizens, and the various types of Nones.

Such a recognition would have two immediate effects. First, it would force all parties to pay greater attention to the rights of the non-religious. Their rights tend to get ignored in the constant push and pull between the secular authority and religious groups.

Second, it would help limit those definitional confusions between atheism and secularism that we've been drawing to your attention. The association is problematic, not because there is anything wrong with nonbelief, but because of the intensity of reactions that it stimulates in so many parts of the world.

Practitioners of all sorts of religious faiths find atheism to be immoral and threatening. As puzzling as this attitude is—atheists, after all, are neither more, nor less immoral and threatening than anyone else—this has created a massive "public relations" problem for political secularism. In the Middle East, for example, its association with nonbelief (and colonialism and corrupt authoritarian regimes) has rendered it a non-starter with large sectors of the population. Yet given the religious strife that engulfs the region, a functioning secularism is certainly a plausible governance option.

In North America, similar associations are drawn. In fact, Atheists too now often refer to themselves as "secularists." The intensity of people's dislike or admiration for *atheism* is one reason why debates about *secularism* become so passionate and overheated. Thinking of political secularism in terms of *three powers* (e.g., secular state, religions, and Nones including non-believers) benefits both atheism and secularism. Each can develop and be defined on its own terms.

BEYOND STATE SUPREMACY

Political secularism is a *statist* doctrine; it demands and deploys the full resources of a national government. Students of secularism are thus sometimes ringside observers to a brawl between two of the most formidable vehicles of conflict humans have ever created: the modern nation-state and organized mass religion.

This leads me to point to an imbalance. While political secularisms are statist, CRAS movements are built to operate across borders. In this study we've seen that transnational Catholic, Protestant and Muslim groups can play a destabilizing role in the "internal affairs" of a given nation state. Political secularisms, by contrast, have become locked within the logic of the state.

There are no major secular international movements. Those that do exist are generally small and under-subscribed. This means, among other things, that "secular nationalists" in non-secular countries (e.g., Israel, Jordan, Lebanon, Saudi Arabia, Iran) are completely isolated from one another. Can secular citizens in the non-secular Middle East, from Tel Aviv, to Amman, to Beirut, to Riyadh, to Tehran join in a common cause?

Perhaps the time has come for a "planetary" agenda, the likes of which secular humanism advocated (see Chapter 13). Or at least a regional one. What may be needed is a transnational secular organization, a secular UN, or an Organization of Secular States (OSS). Let it have a "Department of Definitions," staffed with linguists and political scientists; as we've seen again and again, confusion over meanings is terrible for secularism.

NEUTRALITY AND THE REFEREE

POMOFOCO scholars accuse political secularism of false neutrality. Our own analysis corroborates their accusation. This lack of impartiality sows distrust. And distrust, especially in complex multicultural societies, *will* bring about the oft-forecast demise of secularism.

Political secularism would do well to persuade all citizens that it is as impartial as a referee. The metaphor is intriguing. It implies that a secular government cannot favor Protestantism (in the United States), Hinduism (in India), atheism (in the People's Republic of China), and so forth. Then again no one loves, or wants to be, the referee. The role essentially invites abuse. The best umpires are the ones we never notice.

In a way, that sums up the thankless task of secularism. It must try to maintain fairness while not becoming part of the story. It does so while mediating between mutually suspicious believers, and growing ranks of frustrated unbelievers. Its own officiating crew (i.e., the personnel of the state apparatus itself) is drawn from *these very populations*. This makes the achievement of *neutrality* difficult and real separationism almost impossible.

For secularism to work, citizens must accept the legitimacy of a secular state, much in the way that athletes reflexively accept the legitimacy of a referee. Without that acceptance there is no contest. If this metaphor is correct, then political secularism has a new mandate. It must maximize its capacity for, and application of, fairness. Analytically speaking, that is what we've tried to do in this book.

SUGGESTIONS FOR FURTHER READING

On the perception of secularism in the Arab and Muslim world, see Nikki Keddie, "Trajectories of Secularism in the West and the Middle East," *Global Dialogue*, 6 (2004), pp. 23–33. The presecular Druze prince is discussed in Mark Farha, *Lebanon: The Rise and Fall of a Secular State Under Siege* (Cambridge: Cambridge University Press, 2019).

On secularism in Africa see Baffour K. Takyi, "Secular Government in Sub-Saharan Africa," in *The Oxford Handbook of Secularism*, edited by Phil Zuckerman and John Shook (New York: Oxford University Press, 2017), pp. 201–213; and Mohammed A. Bakari, "Religion, Secularism, and Political Discourse in Tanzania: Competing Perspectives by Religious Organizations," *Interdisciplinary Journal of Research on Religion*, 8 (2012), pp. 1–34 (esp. p. 19).

On secularism and Islam, see Abdullahi Ahmed An-Na'im, *Islam and the Secular State: Negotiating the Future of Shari'a* (Cambridge, MA: Harvard University Press, 2008).

GLOSSARY OF KEY TERMS

Accommodationism A secular framework that was operationalized in India after it achieved independence from Britain in 1947. This "religion-positive" approach is based on the assumption that the faith-based activities of a nation's citizens provide innumerable benefits to the nation itself. Religious belief and activity are construed as a social good and hence something whose welfare a secular government should support through various means.

Anti-clericalism Criticism of religion, religious ideas, and religious authorities. Anti-clerical views are not to be confused with atheism (since religions are not one and the same as the divinities they claim to represent) though there sometimes is overlap. Many of the leading anti-clerical thinkers (e.g., Voltaire, Thomas Paine) were *not* non-believers.

Anti-statism An approach which dislikes and distrusts modern nation-states. Political secularism, by contrast, is a deeply statist philosophy. It posits the legal supremacy of the state over all groups and individuals within its jurisdiction. Social actors on both the Left and the Right have passionately held, and often valid, reasons for fearing this type of power, As such, they are often at odds with secularism and its principle of *state supremacy*.

Atheism *"An absence of belief in the existence of a God or Gods"* (Stephen Bullivant, "Defining 'Atheism,'" in *The Oxford Handbook of Atheism*, Eds. Stephen Bullivant and Michael Ruse (Oxford: Oxford University Press, 2013) p. 20 (pp. 11–21). The relation between secularism and atheism is complex and must be considered carefully in spite of popular usages that equate the two. The connection between these -isms first became apparent in Victorian England where Charles Bradlaugh critiqued George Jacob Holyoake's conception of secularism for excluding atheism from its definition. Since then, secularism and atheism—two distinct concepts with distinct intellectual and historical genealogies—have become confused in popular, journalistic and even scholarly discourse.

Belief/acts distinction   A secular principle born of Protestant theologians and political theorists (and thus more congenial to the governance of Protestants than other religious groups). It stipulates that while citizens have a fundamental right to believe anything they wish about God or religion (i.e., *freedom of conscience*), they do not possess a corresponding right to act on those beliefs if those acts contravene the laws of the land.

Binary   Something that involves two things. Political secularism is built on a way of conceptualizing society in binary terms. To wit, there is the spiritual/religious authority on one side, and the temporal/secular authority on the other. In modern parlance this is referred to as "church and state." This *two powers* or "two swords" approach is unique to Christianity which grappled for centuries with the question of the proper relations of subordination and superordination between these two levels.

Conservative religious anti-secular (CRAS)   A term used to describe modern religious movements, many of the fundamentalist variety, which define themselves in opposition to secular states or movements. CRAS actors oppose core secular principles such as *state supremacy, disestablishment/neutrality*, and the *belief/acts distinction*, among others.

Constitutional non-compliance   The tendency of secular constitutions to explicitly articulate laws and amendments which are not adhered to in actual practice. Non-compliance may occur due to intentional or unintentional governmental negligence, and/or the refusal of the governed to comply.

Disestablishment/neutrality   A core secular principle which maintains that the government may not formally enact a union with (i.e., establish) a religion or religions. This is where the corollary of *neutrality* enters the frame, demanding that the government not favor any religion (or, in more recent times, any form of non-religion). *Disestablishment/neutrality* is often seen as a synonym for separation of church and state. Yet a state with no establishment can engage in un-separationist activities like controlling and monitoring religion. This occurs in secular frameworks such as *laïcité*.

Enlightenment The period from the seventeenth to eighteenth centuries in which many pre-existing, albeit amorphous, secular principles were sharpened and rendered more precise, particularly in John Locke's *A Letter Concerning Toleration*. Some scholars see political secularism as a doctrine invented in the Enlightenment, whereas others contend it has evolved across a much longer period of time.

Equality A secular principle which maintains that all citizens are equal in the eyes of the state and thus entitled to equal rights and treatment from the state. Functionally, it means that a state cannot favor or discriminate against any individual on the basis of their religious belief or lack thereof.

False neutrality An oft-made criticism of avowedly secular states and their vaunted *disestablishment/neutrality* principle. The charge maintains that while the state claims to be neutral it actually explicitly or implicitly favors one or more religious groups, or a non-religious group.

"The fateful nineteenth" Our description of the century which witnessed: (1) occasional efforts to actualize secular principles into structures of governance, (2) the rise of anti-liberal and anti-modern movements that would later become anti-secular movements, (3) the rise of Secular*ism* as a distinct worldview encompassing a lifestyle, and (4) the association of political secularism with atheism—an equation which would have a major impact in the twentieth century.

Federalism A term that refers to a system of governance that grants considerable autonomy to ethnic, regional, provincial, or state units within a nation (often these overlap). The units have the right to craft their own laws, maintain their own forms of governance, etc. In terms of political secularism, this potentially creates two levels of rule and thus the possibility of discrepancies between the two levels. For example, a constitutionally secular state may contain within it a province whose laws are anti-secular, or vice versa.

Freedom from religion   What would amount to the eleventh principle of secularism, one that emerges in an age where non-belief and/or religious disaffiliation are much more common and socially acceptable. *Freedom from religion* ensures that citizens do not have to abide by the dictates of any religion. The implications of a citizen's "right" to be free of religion have yet to be thought through.

Freedom of conscience   A secular principle which champions the concept of "psychic sovereignty," or the idea that individuals are free to think of God or religion in any way they see fit. Martin Luther's insistence that "Thought is free" and that heretics should not be coerced is one of the taproots of this idea.

Freedom of speech   A sub-principle of *freedom of conscience* which increasingly gained in significance as technologies of media evolved post-Gutenberg. Controversies about free speech intersected with secularism in 19th-century Britain where numerous freethinkers were imprisoned for violating blasphemy laws. With the evolution of media and then digital media, political secularisms are increasingly immersed in controversies about expressive liberties, especially in the domain of the arts.

Gallicanism   A doctrine of the French King Philippe le Bel stipulating that the French Church was subordinate to the French monarchy. The import of this Medieval conception was to buttress the logic of the *state supremacy* principle which maintained that the earthly rulers (and eventually the state) were "on top."

Great secular chain of being   A term used in this book to suggest that secularisms are all likely related to one another through the exportation and importation of practices and ideas across global time and space. By the same token, the "genome" of secularism is still poorly charted. The evolution of secular principles is not fully understood, nor the countless links between different secular frameworks and national secular projects.

Hierocracy   A term used to describe rule of a society by priests and religious officials. It is the very opposite of political secularism's *state supremacy* principle.

Internal constraint A secular principle which, in its broadest interpretation, maintains that the power of the state is not absolute. It stems from the explicit avowal in the writing of Luther and Locke that there are limits to the power of the prince or magistrate. The constraint is a braking mechanism on governmental power run amuck. Such mechanisms might include free and fair elections, independent judiciary, government oversight boards, protections for unpopular opinions, opposition parties, and so forth.

Laïcité A "religion-neutral" framework of secularism which developed in France starting in the late eighteenth century and was operationalized with the ratification of the 1905 law. Its defining feature is the state's explicit mandate to control the actions of all religious groups under its rule. Laïcité's emphasis on the secular principles of *state supremacy* and *order* is counterbalanced by robust commitments to *toleration, disestablishment/neutrality, freedom of conscience, internal constraint,* and so forth. Given the influence that French thought has had on countries like Turkey and Russia (and given Russia's development of its own, more extreme secular framework which expanded across the globe) it is fair to view laïcité as the most influential secular framework.

Laiklik The form of political secularism that emerged in Turkey and is associated with Mustafa Kemal Atatürk. In practice, *laiklik* greatly overplayed the *order* principle while disregarding others such as *internal constraint, equality,* etc. As for *disestablishment/neutrality,* critics charged that the government actually established a particular, "lite" version of Sunni Islam.

L'ancien régime A term that refers to a recurring tendency of monarchic regimes to unite with a given religion as a means of augmenting the power of both institutions. Such unions typically resulted in deeply conservative forms of political and social governance. Starting in the 19th century and extending into the twentieth century, this form of rule was bitterly and violently contested by liberal and secular national movements in countries such as France, Spain, Italy, Russia, Mexico, Ethiopia, and so forth.

Materialism A philosophical doctrine that can be defined in many ways. For our purposes, it refers to an outlook that rejects supernatural explanations as a means of explaining social phenomena. This materialist outlook characterized the thought of radical French Enlightenment philosophers and soon migrated to England. Materialism, although not necessarily atheistic, contrasted sharply with traditionalist religious dogma. It became a staple of the "Secular*ism*" that developed in Victorian England under George Jacob Holyoake and meshed seamlessly with the *reason* principle.

Non-cognizance   A secular framework that comes to us through scholarly reconstructions of James Madison's writings, albeit one that was never put into practice and therefore exists only as a theoretical possibility. The non-cognizance framework would demand that a government take no note of religion. The implications of such a scheme would likely be dramatic in the United States. Churches would no longer be exempt from paying taxes, there would be no military chaplains, government offices would be open on Christmas, etc.

Nones (religiously unaffiliated)   An aggregate of individuals who are not affiliated with any religious tradition. Although Nones are commonly assumed to be atheists and agnostics, the data shows that these groups are a minority within the Nones category. Claims that the Nones rival other religious denominations in terms of their numbers (which are growing) are misleading. The Nones have yet to achieve "group" status with common goals, beliefs, political views, solidarity, etc. Though once they do, it stands to reason that they will become major players in the ongoing dramas of political secularism.

Order   A secular principle whose centrality to the rise of political secularism is often underappreciated or completely ignored. For many early theorists of secularism, such as Williams and Locke, achieving a state of internal order and religious peace was seen as a structural precondition for religious worship. Only if religious conflict, be it between the state and its religious citizens or citizens themselves, is eliminated can people pursue their faith. Later secular states would disarticulate *order* from this rationale and pursue it for its own sake.

Override clause   A term used in this book to describe a major implication for political secularism of a seemingly minor aside in John Locke's *A Letter Concerning Toleration*. In the latter text,

Locke observes: "It appears not that God has ever given any such Authority to one Man over another, as to compell anyone to his Religion. Nor can any such Power be vested in the Magistrate by the consent of the people." The line calls attention to a paradox of secular rule. Namely, it exists *regardless* of "the consent of the people." The point is intriguing insofar as forms of secular governance are usually disliked by members of religious majorities who may have the numerical superiority to reject secular governance in free elections.

Plenitudo potestatis   A Medieval doctrine of the pope's complete power over any and all rival sources of authority within Latin Christendom. The idea thus accepted the *two powers* framework while negating the principle of *state supremacy*.

Political secularism   Political secularism refers to legally binding actions of the secular state that seek to regulate the relationship between itself and religious citizens, and between religious citizens themselves.

POMOFOCO   An acronym used in this book to describe scholars of secularism who subscribe to postmodern, post-Foucauldian, and postcolonial schools of thought. POMOFOCO researchers, while theoretically and methodologically diverse, are almost always sharply critical of political secularism. They view the latter as a Western ideology in and of itself, one that facilitated forms of domination over religions domestically and —particularly—in regions Europeans had colonized. Political secularism is seen as an insidious technology of Euro-American hegemony. Spawned in the Enlightenment it completely reconfigured and subjugated numerous forms of religious belief and practice in the name of allegedly universal, liberal, and rational values.

Proto-political secularism   A term used in this book to signal that non-Western societies may have been developing their own forms of political secularism before these became operationalized in the West. Proto-political arrangements have been postulated by scholars in India, China, Lebanon, and certain parts of the Islamic world. As with many components of political secularism, more research is required, though if evidence does surface a less Eurocentric, Western, and Christian reading (and critique) of secularism may be warranted.

Pseudo-secularism   A term used in reference to the governing ethos of the British Raj in India. Such forms of rule aim not to deliver peace, *order*, religious freedom, but sustained domination of colonized people. This form of secularism, lacking any organic connection to the "consent of the people," possesses dubious legitimacy and does not share political secularism's commitment to benefitting those it governs.

Quietism   A modality of religious behavior in which a given group consciously decides to forgo involvement in politics. A religious group's quietest stance may be based on a theological interpretation, pragmatism, concerns for safety, or some combination of all.

Radical Enlightenment   A variant of Enlightenment thought which offered a more extreme and aggressive critique of religious and political authority. The materialist and anti-clerical thrusts of the French Radical Enlightenment were to be hugely influential in the development of French, British, and Soviet secularism.

Rapid combustion   A term used in this book to describe the quick implementation of secular laws and governmental practices after the long gestation period of political secularism. It took political secularism centuries to become operational in countries such as the United States, France, Turkey, Russia, India, and so forth, yet once installed political secularisms swiftly enacted sweeping changes. These changes were fiercely resisted and in many cases eventually overturned.

Reason   A secular principle which has evolved greatly from its original statement in the philosophy of John Locke and its elaboration in the works of Thomas Jefferson and James Madison. Originally, the idea of reason as being in perfect harmony with the words of the Bible was maintained. As time progressed, the claim became increasingly untenable and reason was disarticulated from a scriptural basis. In modern secular states the *reason* principle refers to the idea that public policy should be driven by science, data and rationality.

Saeculum   A term used by Augustine to refer to the frame of time prior to the arrival of the Messiah. The pre-eschatological *saeculum* is a sinful and degraded interval, albeit one where all human activities, perforce, must take place. In some interpretations,

Augustine conceded that political authority, lodged in the City of Man, could play a positive role in managing the tumult of creaturely affairs. For secular theory, the concept foreshadows the *two powers* (and two swords) concepts. It also influences Luther's views on the depravity of this unruly *saeculum* (and the importance of a strong prince to keep it all in check). One could say that George Jacob Holyoake secularized the *saeculum* by insisting that we turn our attention exclusively to making this present world a better place through acts of goodwill and the employment of science.

Scientific atheism A Soviet doctrine which magnified the *reason* principle to its most extreme possible point. Science and rationality were not only extolled, but placed in a mutually antagonistic relationship with all forms of religious belief. The program of scientific atheism aimed to ground policy decisions in science and rationality, and simultaneously undertook to convince Soviet citizens of the folly of believing in the divine. The *reason* principle was thus weaponized to neutralize other core secular principles such as *freedom of conscience, toleration,* etc.

Secular frameworks A given nation-state's or social group's way of "mixing and matching," emphasizing and de-emphasizing, our 10 secular principles as a means of establishing a program of secular governance. A framework thus aims to achieve the goals of political secularism, namely, regulating relations (1) between itself and religious citizens, and (2) between religious citizens. The frameworks started to take shape, in fits and starts, in the late 18th and 19th centuries. They were not necessarily consciously crafted. It is only in retrospect that scholars can reconstruct how social actors prioritize, balance and mute secular principles so as to make them into a framework such as accommodationism, *laïcité*, separationism, and Soviet atheism.

Secular humanism The name of a small twentieth-century philosophical school of thought most associated with Paul Kurtz. In its emphasis on science and rationality, secular humanism was deeply indebted to Victorian infidelry. As with George Jacob Holyoake's Secular*ism*, its political program was somewhat muted. The school preferred to focus on how individuals could live ethically in a materialist world.

Secular nationalism   Refers to political actors within a given country who see their identity as bound up with: 1) the nation, and, 2) that nation's commitment to a particular secular framework.

Secular principles   Basic ideas about society and its governance that one finds in various forms of political secularism. The manner in which the principles are "mixed and matched" is essential in giving shape to the framework of secularism that emerges. Most of the principles themselves developed independently of one another across millennia. Each one is worthy of a study in and of itself.

Secularism   One of the most confused and convoluted terms in the global political lexicon. While a few definitions abound and while some insist that the term cannot even be defined, one can identify different sets of prevailing definitions. One set views it as a form of atheism, deeply opposed to the existence of religion. Another views it in the sense of "political secularism" adduced here. Less popular are conceptions of secularism as a "lifestyle" based on a this-worldly orientation and faith in science.

Secularism   A term coined, likely in 1851, by the British Free-thinker George Jacob Holyoake (we add the italics to stress his unique use of the suffix). This "Victorian Infidel" defined the term in numerous and often contradictory ways. Yet he was consistent in stipulating that secularism was a system of ethics which sought the betterment of the present world through scientific means. Holyoake, inexplicably, rarely connected his conception of secularism with the lengthy tradition of speculation on political secularism which preceded him. He also insisted that secularism was distinct from atheism, a clarification which infuriated his Freethinking colleagues.

Separationism   A "religion-neutral" secular framework based on a longstanding metaphor in Christian theology of a "wall" between Church and State. The metaphor was given expression in Thomas Jefferson's "Letter to the Danbury Baptists." Separationism tries to honor the *disestablishment/neutrality* principle by demanding a partition between the government and all religious groups and individuals which it governs. Actual attempts to operationalize the separationist framework were not generally successful in the United States until the mid-twentieth century. A few decades later the courts began to move away from the separationist framework.

Soviet (atheist) secularism   A "religion-negative" secular framework which originated in the Soviet Union and cross-pollinates French *laïcité* with Marxist theory, and Lenin and Stalin's interpretation of this theory. While not explicitly atheist, this framework acted as such. In so doing, it introduced the principle of *freedom from religion* into its imbalanced mix and match of secular principles.

State supremacy   A secular principle which accounts for much of the eternal controversy which surrounds political secularism. It stipulates that the state is "on top," or superordinate to all individuals and groups within a society. Foremost among those groups who are poised to contest this arrangement are religious ones. The principle emerged from centuries of Christian theological speculation about where ultimate power resides in a social body.

Sub-secularism/sub–anti-secularism   A form of secularism or anti-secularism that may arise in federalist nation-states. The point being that a federated unit within the state might legally adopt laws, be they secular or anti-secular, in opposition to the laws of the nation-state itself.

Swerves   A term used in this book to describe sudden and unexpected changes in the history of secularism. One such change occurred when George Jacob Holyoake conceptualized secularism *not* as involving issues of governance, but as an ethical lifestyle grounded in a materialist worldview. The second swerve occurred when Charles Bradlaugh redefined Holyoake's Secular*ism* as atheism (much to Holyoake's dismay). The final and most consequential swerve occurred when Bolsheviks linked atheism to political secularism—a fusion that altered the course of world history.

Toleration   A secular principle which received its most extensive political treatment in John Locke's 1689 *A Letter Concerning Toleration*, though some of its core themes were foreshadowed in the earlier writings of Roger Williams and others. The idea holds that a proper government creates the preconditions in which diverse social actors beholden to different religious beliefs can live in peace with one another and thus worship as they see fit. That Locke specifically identifies *toleration* as a Christian virtue, collides with his support of the *disestablishment/ neutrality* principle. For if the magistrate and his government are not to endorse or establish a religion why predicate the entire ethos of government on the Christian principle of toleration?

Transnational actors Social groups whose field of political activities extends across borders and hence beyond the parameters of individual nation-states. Religions are the transnational actors *par excellence*. The concept is relevant to political secularism insofar as the latter is an idea which is predicated on the idea of bordered, sovereign nation-states. Thus political secularism works within the logic of a bounded territory, whereas transnational religious movements do not. Thus, secular nation-states are often disadvantaged vis a vis transnational actors.

Trinary Political secularism was born of a binary between the domain of the sacred authority and the domain of civil authority. The rise of the Nones as a segment of the population and the emergence of the principle of *freedom from religion* suggests that a third column must be included in coming deliberations about political secularism. This would turn the binary into a trinary. The three levels are: (1) a secular government, (2) a diverse population of religious groups and believers, and (3) a diverse population of nonreligious groups and non-believers.

Two powers A secular principle which is a necessary, but not sufficient, condition for the existence of any political secularism. It conceives of a society as divided between two sources of authority: the religious and the political. That this binary form of ordering a society is uniquely Christian, seems apparent. It was across centuries of arguments about which of the two "swords" was superordinate and which was subordinate that the secular principle of *state supremacy* developed.

INDEX

Italic page numbers indicate illustrations on those pages.

accommodationist framework
(Indian secularism): anti-secular
politics of Modi and BJP party 86;
assistance given to religion 77;
British colonial secularism 77–79,
81; Constitution of India 76, 81,
82–83; drawbacks of 84–85;
education 82–83; hybrid nature
79–80; identity of 79–80; leeway
84–85; multiculturality of India
80; Muslim citizens 81–82, 83,
86; *neutrality* versus *equality* 80–83;
non-religious people 84–85, 174;
positive attitude towards religion
76–77, 85; present, problems of
80; principles of political secularism 82, 85; pseudo-secularism of
the British Raj 77–79; roots in
India past 79–80; in Secularstan
(ideal Secular state) 171; in theory
83; in USA 84
Adityanath, Yogi 2
adversarial nationalisms 69
Africa: pro- and anti-LGBTQ
movements in 173; secularisms in
183–184, *184*
Akbar, Emperor 80
al-Qaradawi, Yusuf 2
American secularism *see* separationist
framework

anti-clericalism 66; defining secularism
2, *3*; Soviet (atheist) secularism
102–104; synergy between anti-
clericalism and atheism 102–105
anti-secularism: definition of secularism 131–133; in the public sphere
130–131; understanding of,
reasons for 129: *see also* left-wing
anti-secularism; right-wing
anti-secularism
Argentina 170, 171
arts, freedom of expression and
10–11
Asad, T. 140, 143, 145, 147, 150
Ashoka, Emperor 80
Asian-Americans 158–159
atheism: Chinese Communist Party
(CCP) 123; defining secularism 2,
3; Enlightenment 122; *laïcité* 66;
New Atheism 155, 156, 157;
non-secular 155–157; Secular*ism,*
Bradlaugh and 89, 95–97; Secular*ism* as atheism 89; Secular*ism* as
not atheism, Holyoake and
94–95; secularism seen as by
Evangelicals 131–133; synergy
between anti-clericalism and
atheism 102–105; three powers,
move towards 186: *see also* Soviet
(atheist) secularism

Augustine 21–22, 29, 40, 52, 93
authoritarianism 113
authorities, obedience to 19–20

Barr, W. 138
beliefs/acts distinction 42–43;
   accommodationist framework
   (Indian secularism) 82; British
   colonial secularism in India 78;
   conservative religious anti-
   secularism and 139; Evangelical
   Christians 131; freedom of
   conscience 90; free exercise clause
   of the First Amendment of the
   US Constitution 56; left-wing
   anti-secularism 148; New Atheist
   discourse 156; Soviet (atheist)
   secularism 108
Benedict XVI, Pope 2, 136
Besant, A. 95–96
binary/ies: introduced by secularism
   146–147; New Testament 18–20;
   terms in secularism discussions *25*;
   trinary, move towards 185–186
Black, H. 60
bodies, control of 9
Bonaparte, N. 68–69, 101
Bradlaugh, C.: atheism, Secular*ism* as
   89; atheism and Secular*ism* 95–97;
   debate with Holyoake on Secular-
   ism 96; definition of secularism 142;
   Soviet (atheist) secularism and 100
British colonial secularism in India 9,
   77–79, 89–90, 145, 171

Catholic Church: in Argentina,
   LGBTQ rights and 170; definition of secularism 133; *laïcité*
   68–69; resistance to political
   secularism in Catholic countries
   52; Uruguay 167, 168
Charlie Hebdo illustrations 10
China: education, secularism and 6;
   gay people, discrimination against
   171–172; political secularism in
   120–124

Chinese-Americans 158–159
Chinese Communist Party (CCP)
   121–122, 123–124
Christianity: Augustinian correction
   20–22; New Testament binary
   18–20; power shift in 4th century
   AD 20–21; principles of political
   secularism and 16; *toleration* and
   40–41
church and state (*two powers*
   principle): Augustinian correction
   20–22; continual scrutiny of 24;
   CRAS movements 139, 145;
   hierocracy 22–24; LGBTQ rights
   174; move to three powers 185–
   186; New Testament binary 18–20;
   Soviet (atheist) secularism 107
City of God 21–22
City of Man 21–22
Civil Constitution of the Clergy of
   1790 67–68
civil peace, *freedom of conscience* and
   34–35
colonial secularism in India 77–79
complexity of political secularism
   112; China 120–124; Ethiopia
   116–120; Kemalist secularism
   (Turkey) 112–116; LGBTQ rights
   and 169–173; moral complexity
   112, 124–125; technical complexity 112
Confucianism 120–121
consent of the people to secularism
   116
conservative religious anti-secularism: asymmetry with political
   secularism 139; atheism, secularism seen as by 131–133; CRAS
   movements 8, 9; definition of
   secularism 131–133, 142; Evangelical Christians in the US 130,
   131; gender and sexuality issues
   and 8, 9; golden age, wish to
   return to 138; left-wing anti-
   secularism and 140–141; Moral
   Majority 135–136; power as basis

of disputes 136–138; principles of political secularism 139; privatization of religion, objections to 136–138; in the public sphere 130–131; quietism 130; secular elites 133–135; secular humanism and 163; Secularstan (ideal secular state) 174, 175–176; state supremacy and 137–138; as trans-denominational, claim of 135–136; transnational actors, anti-LGBTQ 172–173; *two powers* principle 139, 145

constitutional non-compliance 105, 117–120, 169, 177, 178

constitutions: Albanian 108; drawback of 105; Ethiopia 117–118, 119, 120; Fourth and Fifth French Republics 71;India 76, 81–83; Soviet (atheist) secularism 105, 106, 107; United States 55–57; Uruguay 167

Cuba 179

Dalai Lama 1, 2

Dawkins, R. 155

December 9 Law Concerning the Separation of the Churches from the State 70–72

de-Christianizing initiatives: China 122–123; *laïcité* framework (French secularism) 68; Soviet (atheist) secularism 104–105

Declaration of the Rights of Man and Citizen, Article X 67

Deng Xiaoping 123

Dennett, D. 155, 158

Derg, the 117

Dewey, J. 161

discourse, secularism seen as 142–143, 144, 147, 150

disestablishment/neutrality principle 44–45, 46–47; accommodationist framework (Indian secularism) 82; British colonial secularism in India 78; conservative religious anti-

secularism and 139; establishment clause of the First Amendment of the US Constitution 55–56; Kemalist secularism (Turkey) 114–115; left-wing anti-secularism 144, 147–149; prayer in schools 137; Secularstan (ideal secular state) 174–175; separation distinguished from 57–59; separationist framework 61; Soviet (atheist) secularism 108, 179; Uruguay 167, 169

diversity, religious, LGBTQ rights and 169–171

education: accommodationist framework (Indian secularism) 82–83; *laïcité* 70; secularism and 6; Uruguay 168

elites, secular 133–135

el-Messiri, A.W. 136

embodiment 145

Engels, F. 103

Enlightenment atheism (in China) 122

epistemes 146

equality: accommodationist framework (Indian secularism) 82; British colonial secularism in India 78; conservative religious anti-secularism and 139; First Amendment of the US Constitution 57; left-wing anti-secularism 149; as principle of political secularism 16–18, 24; religious diversity 170; Secularstan (ideal secular state) 175–176; Soviet (atheist) secularism 108, 179

establishment clause of the First Amendment of the US Constitution 55–56

establishments of religion 55–56, 77, 90, 175, 180

Ethiopian Islamic Affairs Supreme Council (EIASC) 118–119

Ethiopian Orthodox Tewahedo Church (EPTC) 116, 117

Ethiopian People's Revolutionary Democratic Front (EPRDF) 117
ethnicity, religious tensions and 120
European Union, religious symbolism on euros 7
Evangelical Christians in the US 130, 131

false neutrality (Disestablishment non-Neutrality) 45, 118, 148, 149, 175, 187
Falwell, J. 135–136
fear, political secularism and 182
Fellowship of Affirming Ministries (TFAM) 173
First Amendment of the US Constitution: brevity of religion clauses 54–55, 57, 62; establishment clause 55–56; free exercise clause 56; principles of political secularism 55–57
Foucault, M. 140–141, 145
frameworks of political secularism: China 120–124; defined 53; Ethiopia 116–120; Fifth (proposed) 184–188; Kemalist secularism (Turkey) 112–116: see also accommodationist framework (Indian secularism); laïcité framework (French secularism); separationist framework; Soviet (atheist) secularism
France: burkini ban 9; education, secularism and 6; secular nationalism 160: see also laïcité framework (French secularism)
freedom from religion 108, 163–164, 185
freedom of conscience 176; accommodationist framework (Indian secularism) 82; Declaration of the Rights of Man and Citizen, Article X 67; First Amendment of the US Constitution 57; freedom of speech comparison 90; laïcité 70; left-wing anti-secularism 144, 149; order and 34–35; as principle

of political secularism 32–34, 36; Soviet (atheist) secularism 107, 179
freedom of expression 10–11, 108, 134
freedom of speech 89–90, 93
free exercise clause of the First Amendment of the US Constitution 56
freemasonry 69, 168

Gabriel, J.G. 172–173
Gandhi, Mahatma 81, 82, 84, 171
Gelasius I, Pope 22
gender: conservative religious anti-secular movements (CRAS) 8, 9; men, domination of debates on secularism by 7–8; secularism and issues of 7–9
Genesis 1:27 17, 18
Gramsci, A. 104

Harris, S. 155, 156
hierocracy 22–24
Hitchens, C. 1, 155, 156
Holyoake, G.J.: atheism, Secularism as not 94–95; debate with Bradlaugh on Secularism 96; definition of Secularism 88–89, 142; disconnect with the past 94; freedom of speech 93; French philosophers, link to 91; inconsistent use of 'Secularism' 92–93; Principles of Secularism 92–93; rationalism 93; Soviet (atheist) secularism and 100; on women 93–94
homophobia in secular states 171–172: see also LGBTQ rights
humanism, secular 1, 92, 161–163, 175, 187

identities, secular: commitment to political secularism 154: see also lifestyle secularisms
inalienable human rights 33
India: education, secularism and 6; gay people, discrimination against

171–172: *see also* accommodationist framework (Indian secularism)

internal constraint: British colonial secularism in India 78; Kemalist secularism (Turkey) 113–114; left-wing anti-secularism 149; as principle of political secularism 31–32, 36, 42; privatization of religion, objections to 137; Soviet (atheist) secularism 108, 179

International Court of Justice Statute 17

investiture conflict 22–23

Iranian Revolution 1978–1979 130, 141

Islam: accommodationist framework (Indian secularism) 83, 86; Kemalist secularism (Turkey) 115; *laïcité* framework (French secularism) 72–74; left wing defence of Islamist positions 141

Islamophobia 7, 72, 74, 157

Islamo-Secularism 10, 116

Israel: public spaces 6–7; secular nationalism 45, 69, 130, 137, 159–161, 187

Jacoby, S. 154

Jefferson, T. 46, 53–54, 56, 57, 59, 61, 62

Jesus, obedience to rulers 19

Kemalist secularism (Turkey) 112–116

Kennedy, J.F. 60

Khrushchev, N. 106

Kurtz, P. 161, 162

laïcité framework (French secularism): anti-clericalism 66; Article X, Declaration of the Rights of Man and Citizen 67; atheism 66; balance of principles of secularism 72; Catholic Church 68–69; Civil Constitution of the Clergy of 1790 67–68; Constitutions of the Fourth and Fifth Republic 71; December 9 Law Concerning the Separation of the Churches from the State 70–72, 73–74; de-Christianizing initiatives 68; education 70; exclusion of religion from public sphere 64; *freedom of conscience* 70; intellectual influences 65–66; Islam and radical Islamism 72–74; Kemalist secularism (Turkey) 113; *les philosophes* 66; Macron on 1–2; materialism 66; religious personnel 68; resistance to 69–71; robustness of 72; Soviet (atheist) secularism 101–102, 106; support for 74; in theory 73; two Frances 69–71, 102; USA comparison 64

laiklik see Kemalist secularism (Turkey)

l'ancien régime 52, 66, 67, 71, 101, 112, 116

Lasarte, M. 133

Latin America: Argentina 170, 171; transnational actors, anti-LGBTQ 173; Uruguay 167–169

laws and constitutions, drawback of 105; *see also* constitutions; constitutional non-compliance

left-wing anti-secularism: binaries introduced by secularism 146–147; complexity of prose 141; criticism of 149–151; defence of Islamist positions 141; definition of secularism 142–143; discourse, secularism seen as 142–143, 144, 147, 150; *disestablishment/neutrality* principle 147–149; domination, secularism's syllabus of 146–147; embodiment 145; epistemes 146; functions of political secularism 144; fundamentalist movements and 145; *order* 145–146; origins of secularism 143–144, 149–151; POMOFOCO, meaning of 140;

principles of political secularism 144–145; and right-wing movements 140–141; *state supremacy* 144–145

Lenin, V.I. 99, 100, 102, 103, 105

A Letter Concerning Toleration (Locke) 39–42, 45, 46, 51

LGBTQ rights: Argentina 170; Canadian controversies about 27; as complicated and messy in secular states 167, 169–173; Fellowship of Affirming Ministries (TFAM) 173; gay-affirming religious groups 169–171; homophobic secular states 171–172; religious diversity 169–171; Secularstan (ideal secular state) 174–176; transnational actors 172–173; Uganda 9; Uruguay 167–169, 173

lifestyle secularisms: *freedom from religion* 163–164; New Atheism 155, 156; Nones 157–159; non-secular atheism 155–157; secular humanism 161–163; secular nationalism 159–161

Locke, J. 17, 149; *beliefs/acts* distinction 42, 43; as a Christian 51; override clause 46–48; *reason* 46–48; *toleration* 39–42, 46

Luther, M. 13, 44; criticism of 31; dislike of world and inhabitants 29; *freedom of conscience* 32–33; hatred of the church 30; importance of 28; *internal constraint* 31–32; secular authority as leaders 30; *state supremacy* and 29–30; Sword, the 29

Macron, E. 1–2, 74

Madison, J. 46, 53–54, 55, 57, 59, 61

Mahmood, S. 148, 149

Marsilius of Padua 23–24, 44, 170

Marx, K./Marxism 100, 102–104, 117, 121, 122, 123, 132, 143

materialism 66, 80, 91, 92, 93, 109, 133

McCauley, R. 133

men, domination of debate by 7–8

Mexico: civil war 52; education, secularism and 6

Militant Atheism 122–123

Mill, J.S. 90

Milton, J. 17, 181–182

minority rights: *disestablishment/neutrality* principle 45: *see also* LGBTQ rights

moral complexity 112, 124–125

Moral Majority 135–136

Muslim citizens: accommodationist framework (Indian secularism) 81–82, 83, 86; *laïcité* framework (French secularism) 72–74: *see also* Islam

nationalism, secular 159–161

natural law 33

neutrality principle 44–45, 46–47; accommodationist framework (Indian secularism) 82; British colonial secularism in India 78; conservative religious anti-secularism and 139; establishment clause of the First Amendment of the US Constitution 55–56; Kemalist secularism (Turkey) 114–115; left-wing anti-secularism 144, 147–149; prayer in schools 137; referee, political secularism as 187–188; Secularstan (ideal secular state) 174–175; separation distinguished from 57–59; separationist framework 61; Soviet (atheist) secularism 108, 179; Uruguay 167, 169

New Atheism 155, 156, 157

New Testament binary 18–20

Nigeria 133

Nones 157–159, 164, 168, 174, 181, 185, 186

non-secular atheism 155–157

North Korea 179

Ockham, William of 23

Onuzo, C. 127

order: accommodationist framework (Indian secularism) 82; British colonial secularism in India 78, 79; Chinese political secularism 122; Confucianism 121; Declaration of the Rights of Man and Citizen, Article X 67; Ethiopia 119; *freedom of conscience* and 34–35; free exercise clause of the First Amendment of the US Constitution 56; Kemalist secularism (Turkey) 114; left-wing anti-secularism 145–146; as principle of political secularism 33–35; Soviet (atheist) secularism 107

override clause 46–48, 116

Padmavaat (film), protests regarding 10

Pakistan 10, 45, 81, 82, 133, 180, 182

Pamuk, O. 11, 49

papal supremacy 23–24

Parishad, V.H. 139

1 Peter 2 19–20

Philippe le Bel 23, 65

Pius IX, Pope 52, 53

planetary agenda 187

plenitudo potestatis 23–24

political secularism: asymmetry with conservative religious anti-secularism 139; Bradlaugh and Holyoake 96; China 120–124; commitment to of secular identities *154*; complexity of 112; defined 5–6, 7, 10, 179–180; early resistance to 51–53; essence of 24–25; Ethiopia 116–120; frameworks of *3*; future research in history of 181–184; Kemalist secularism (Turkey) 112–116; New Atheism, contradictions with 156; as referee 187–188; as separation of church and state 2: *see also* left-wing anti-secularism; LGBTQ rights; principles of political secularism; separationist framework; Soviet (atheist) secularism

POMOFOCO scholars, anti-secularism of: binaries introduced by secularism 146–147; complexity of prose 141; criticism of 149–151; defence of Islamist positions 141; definition of secularism 142–143; discourse, secularism seen as 142–143, 144, 147, 150; *disestablishment/neutrality* principle 147–149; domination, secularism's syllabus of 146–147; embodiment 145; epistemes 146; functions of political secularism 144; fundamentalist movements and 145; meaning of abbreviation 140; *order* 145–146; origins of secularism 143–144, 149–151; principles of political secularism 144–145; *state supremacy* 144–145

power as basis of disputes 136–138

principles of political secularism: accommodationist framework (Indian secularism) 82, 85; balance of in *laïcité* (French secularism) 72; *beliefs/acts* distinction 42–43; Christianity and 16; conservative religious anti-secularism 139; development of 15–16, *37; disestablishment/neutrality* 44–45, 46–47; *equality* 16–18, 24; First Amendment of the US Constitution 55–57; frameworks' emphasis on *166; freedom from religion* 108; *freedom of conscience* 32–34, 36; *freedom of speech* 89–90; *internal constraint* 31–32, 36, 42; left-wing anti-secularism 144–145, 147–149; *order* 33–35; override clause 46–48; overview of *35; reason* 46–48; religion and 16; Secularstan (ideal secular state) 174–175; Soviet (atheist) secularism 107–108, 179; *state supremacy* 28–30; toleration 40–42; *two powers* 18–24

Principles of Secularism (Holyoake) 92–93

privatization of religion 136–138
public spaces 6–7

quietism 130

rationalism 93
reason: Confucianism 121; First
    Amendment of the US Constitu-
    tion 57; left-wing anti-secularism
    149; New Atheists 155; as princi-
    ple of political secularism 46–48;
    secular humanism 162; Soviet
    (atheist) secularism 107
referee, political secularism as
    187–188
religious conflicts: Locke and 39–40;
    trauma, political secularism and
    182
religious minorities: *disestablishment/
    neutrality* principle 45; rights of,
    secularism and 9–10
religious symbolism, contentiousness
    of 7
religious thinkers: opposition to
    papal supremacy 23–24; overview
    of principles of political secularism
    35: see also Locke, J.; Luther, M.;
    St. Augustine; Williams, R.
resistance to political secularism:
    Catholic countries 52; early
    51–53; France 69–71; USA
    61–62: *see also* anti-secularism
right-wing anti-secularism: asym-
    metry with political secularism
    139; atheism, secularism seen as
    by 131–133; definition of secu-
    larism 131–133, 142; golden age,
    wish to return to 138; left-wing
    anti-secularism and 140–141;
    Moral Majority 135–136; power
    as basis of disputes 136–138;
    principles of political secularism
    139; privatization of religion,
    objections to 136–138; secular
    elites 133–135; secular humanism
    and 163; Secularstan (ideal secular

state) 174, 175–176; *state
    supremacy* and 137–138; as
    trans-denominational, claim of
    135–136; transnational actors,
    anti-LGBTQ 172–173; *two powers*
    principle 139, 145
Romans 13 19
rulers, obedience to 19–20
Rushdie, S. 10–11
Rwotlonyo, J. 136

Saeculum 21, 22, 29, 42, 93, 178
same sex relationships *see* LGBTQ
    rights
scientific atheism 104–105
secular elites 133–135
secular humanism 161–163
secular identities: commitment to
    political secularism *154: see also*
    lifestyle secularisms
secularism: Africa *184*; anti-secular-
    ists' definition of 131–133; binary
    terms in secularism discussions *25*;
    confusion about meaning 85,
    109–110; consent of the people to
    116; defining 1–4, *3, 4,* 5–6;
    demise, predictions of 178–179; as
    doctrine of the state 28; elimina-
    tion of, problems with 180–181;
    freedom of expression 10–11; future
    research in history of 181–184;
    gender, issues of 7–9; increase in
    use of term 1; innovation in 185;
    laws and constitutions, drawback
    of 105; men, domination of
    debate by 7–8; overview of
    development 4–5; religious
    minorities, rights of 9–10; sexu-
    ality, issues of 7–9; state institu-
    tions, spaces and symbols 6–7; as
    untouchable 116: *see also* political
    secularism; principles of political
    secularism; Secularism (Holyoake);
    Soviet (atheist) secularism
Secularism (Holyoake): atheism, Bra-
    dlaugh and 95–97; class and 92; as

confused with secularism 97; defined 88; disconnect with the past 94; French philosophers, link to 91; inconsistent use of term 92–93; number of British freethinkers 92; Soviet (atheist) secularism and 100

secular nationalism 159–161

Secularstan (ideal secular state) 174–176

secular states: clashes with religious laws 27–28; homophobic 171–172: *see also state supremacy*

self-identification as secularist 134–135

separationist framework 157; abandonment of in 1980s 60; anti-religion 59; disestablishment distinguished from separation 57–59; *disestablishment/neutrality* principle 61; early attempts 53–54; Ethiopia, non-separation in 117–120; First Amendment of the US Constitution 54–57; *laïcité* comparison 64–65; problematic metaphor of 179–180; resistance to 59, 61–62; secular humanism 162; in theory 61; true separation, difficulties with 59; Uruguay 169; wall image 57, 58; as wobbly and unstable 61–62: *see also* political secularism

September 11 terrorist attacks 153–154

sexuality: conservative religious anti-secular movements (CRAS) 8, 9; secularism and issues of 7–9: *see also* LGBTQ rights

Snow (Pamuk) (novel) 11, 49

South America: Argentina 170, 171; transnational actors, anti-LGBTQ 173; Uruguay 167–169

Soviet (atheist) secularism 122; anti-clericalism 102–104; anti-religious program 101; British freethinkers and 100; church/state separation 105–106; communist thought and 102–105; connections with other political secularisms 100–102; as consequential development 99; constitution 105, 106, 107; de-Christianization initiatives 104–105; Decree on Separation of Church and State 105–106; defining secularism 4, *4*; distinctiveness 102–105; as form of political secularism 107–108; French connections 101–102, 106; laws 105–106; October 1917 revolution 99; principles of political secularism 107–108, 179; resistance to 129; scientific atheism 104–105; state/party as meaningless distinction 105; *state supremacy* 107; synergy between anti-clericalism and atheism 102–105; in theory *109*

St. Augustine 21–22, 29, 93

Stalin, J. 100, 102, 106

state and church (*two powers* principle): Augustinian correction 20–22; continual scrutiny of 24; CRAS movements 139, 145; hierocracy 22–24; LGBTQ rights 174; move to three powers 185–186; New Testament binary 18–20; principle of political secularism 18–24; Soviet (atheist) secularism 107

state institutions, spaces and symbols, secularism and 6–7

states, all citizens as subordinate to 28

state supremacy: conservative religious anti-secularism and 137–138, 139; early resistance to 51–53; *freedom of conscience* under 32–33; internal constraints on 31–32, 36; left-wing anti-secularism 144–145; LGBTQ rights 174; as principle of political secularism 28–30; Secularstan (ideal secular state) 174–175; Soviet (atheist) secularism 107: see also *laïcité* framework (French secularism)

Sulaiman, M. 133
Sword, the 29
Syllabus of Errors 53
symbolism: contentiousness of religious 7; state institutions, spaces and symbols, secularism and 6–7

technical complexity of secularism 112
9/11 terrorist attacks 153–154
three powers 185–186
toleration: accommodationist framework (Indian secularism) 82; British colonial secularism in India 78; First Amendment of the US Constitution 57; left-wing anti-secularism 144; New Atheist discourse 156; as principle of political secularism 40–42, 46; Soviet (atheist) secularism 107, 179
Tolton, J.W. 173
transnational actors 9, 72, 118, 119, 122, 124, 125, 162, 172–173, 178, 187
transnational secular organizations 187
trans people in Uruguay 169
trauma, political secularism and 182
trinary (three powers) 185–186
Turkey (Kemalist secularism) 112–116
Tutu, D. 170
two powers principle: Augustinian correction 20–22; continual scrutiny of 24; CRAS movements 139, 145; hierocracy 22–24; LGBTQ rights 174; move to three powers 185–186; New Testament binary 18–20; Soviet (atheist) secularism 107
two swords 22–23

Uganda 172; LGBTQ communities, civil rights of 9
ultramontanism 69; resistance to political secularism 52
unaffiliation, religious 84–85, 157–159, 168, 174
United Nations Charter 17
United States: accommodationist framework 84; Asian-Americans 158–159; Declaration of Independence 17; education, secularism and 6; Evangelical Christians 130, 131; *laïcité* comparison 64–65; Moral Majority 135–136; National Reform Association 53; prayer in schools 137; religious symbolism, contentiousness of 7; White House Office of Faith-Based and Community Initiatives (OFBCI) 84: *see also* separationist framework
Uruguay 167–169, 173

violence between religious groups in Ethiopia 119–120

wall image 57, 58
William of Ockham 23, 170
Williams, R. 29, 33–34, 44, 47, 56
women, Holyoake on 93–94

Xi Jinping 124

Printed in the United States
by Baker & Taylor Publisher Services